The AI Product Playbook

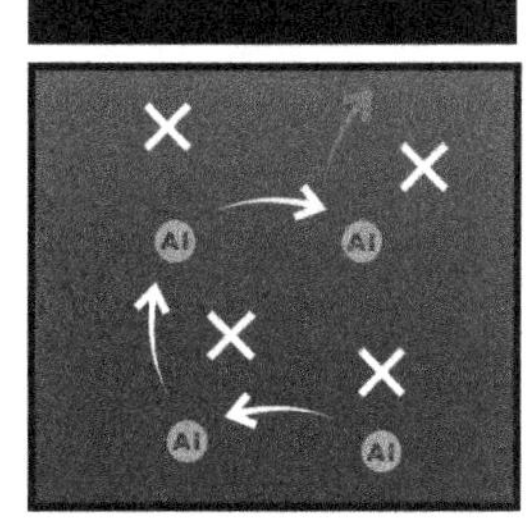

The AI Product Playbook

Strategies, Skills, and Frameworks for the AI-Driven Product Manager

Dr. Marily Nika
Diego Granados

WILEY

About the Authors

Dr. Marily Nika is an award-winning GenAI product leader at Google and one of the world's foremost AI educators, with over 13 years of experience building AI products at Google and Meta. She holds a PhD in machine learning and is an author, TED AI speaker, Harvard Business School fellow and co-founder of the AI Product Hub that offers AI product management courses at `aiproduct.com`.

Originally from Mexico and now based in Seattle, **Diego Granados** is an AI Product Manager at Google Cloud, where he focuses on building the products and tools that empower AI developers and data scientists. With a unique background that combines an MBA from Duke University's Fuqua School of Business and an MS in Computer Science with a focus in AI from Georgia Tech, Diego has built his career on bridging the gap between business strategy and deep technical execution. He believes this combination is a PM's superpower in the age of AI, allowing for better communication, strategy, and a true understanding of the entire data science lifecycle.

Acknowledgments

I would like to thank my husband, Ray, for his encouragement throughout my journey as an author and educator. His belief in me and this project made the long hours truly purposeful.

I am also grateful to the mentors, peers, and colleagues in the AI product management communities who inspired and challenged me to think deeply and critically. Your conversations, feedback, and insights helped shape the direction of this book.

Finally, to our readers, current students and alumni of the AI Product Hub—thank you for your curiosity, your passion for building meaningful AI products, and your commitment to learning.

—Marily

To my wife, Daniela. While my name is on the cover, her support is on every page. She is the reason I've gotten so far in my career, and her partnership is what created the space for me to pursue the work that made this book possible. For her constant belief in me, I am eternally grateful.

—Diego

Contents at a Glance

Contents

Introduction

This playbook is the culmination of our combined experience working at the forefront of AI innovation at companies like Google and Microsoft, and from teaching and mentoring thousands of Product Managers. Over the years, we've seen brilliant technical teams build powerful AI models, only to see the resulting products fail to connect with users. We've also seen product leaders struggle to navigate the hype, intimidated by the jargon and uncertain how to bridge the gap between a business problem and a technical AI solution.

This new landscape demands a new kind of product manager. This playbook was born from our passion to define and support that evolution. It is built on the belief that the most successful PMs will be those who can blend timeless product craft with a modern understanding of AI, enabling them to guide their teams and products through the most significant technological shift of our generation.

This book is your hands-on guide to developing that blend of skills. It's designed for the non-technical professional, cutting through the hype to focus on actionable frameworks and real-world application. To help you navigate this journey, we have structured the book into three parts:

- **Part I: Foundational AI/ML Concepts** will build your core literacy. We will demystify the essential concepts of AI and Machine Learning, from how models are trained and evaluated to the different types of ML and the end-to-end data science lifecycle.

- **Part II: AI PM Specializations** will help you find your place. We will deep-dive into the three key PM personas—AI Experiences, AI Builder, and AI-Enhanced—so you can understand your strengths and chart a clear career path.

- **Part III: Connecting the Dots Between AI/ML Knowledge and PM Craft** will show you how to put it all into practice. You'll learn frameworks for identifying AI opportunities, calculating ROI, navigating ethical challenges, and deploying real-world AI solutions.

This playbook is your roadmap. Let's get started.

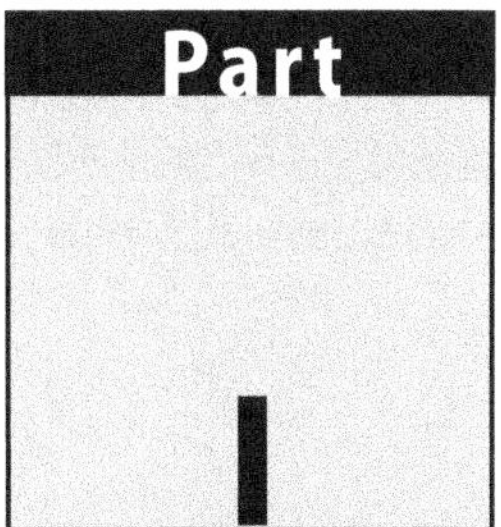

Foundational AI/ML Concepts

Before diving into the unique AI Product Manager roles in the next section, it's essential to first build a strong foundation in the concepts that power modern product experiences. This part of the book is designed to demystify the core of AI and Machine Learning from a Product Manager's perspective. Our goal isn't to turn you into a data scientist, but to equip you with the essential knowledge to collaborate effectively, evaluate feasibility, and lead with confidence in the AI era.

In Part I, you will learn to:

- Distinguish between AI, ML, and Deep Learning, and understand why those differences matter to your product strategy.

- Recognize the four primary types of machine learning—supervised, unsupervised, reinforcement, and generative—with real product examples to ground the theory.

- Grasp the fundamentals of how models are trained, validated, and tested, including critical concepts like overfitting, bias, and the role of Human-in-the-Loop (HITL).

- Visualize the end-to-end Data Science Lifecycle, understanding the PM's role at each stage.

By the end of Part I, you won't just recognize technical terminology—you'll understand how to apply it to your product work and be ready to bridge the gap between technical complexity and user value.

Artificial Intelligence and Machine Learning: What Every Product Manager Needs to Know

Stepping into the world of AI product management can feel like learning a new language. You may find yourself in meetings where the conversation suddenly shifts to "training the model," "feature vectors," and "precision versus recall." This technical jargon can be intimidating and can create a barrier between you and your technical counterparts, making it difficult to contribute meaningfully or ask the right strategic questions.

This chapter is designed to break down that barrier. Our goal is to provide you with a solid, PM-focused foundation in the core concepts of Artificial Intelligence and Machine Learning. We will demystify the terminology and explain the fundamental principles in a clear, accessible way, using real-world analogies and product examples.

This isn't about learning to code algorithms; it's about learning to "speak the language" of AI so you can lead your products and teams with confidence. In this chapter, we will clarify the very important difference between AI and ML, explore the major types of Machine Learning, see how models actually learn from data, and walk through the data science lifecycle from a PM's perspective.

AI vs. ML

The terms "Artificial Intelligence" (AI) and "Machine Learning" (ML) are often used interchangeably, but for a Product Manager, understanding their distinction is very important. Think of AI as the broad goal of creating intelligent systems, while ML is a specific and powerful method used to achieve that intelligence.

AI aims to simulate human intelligence in machines to perform tasks like problem-solving, understanding language, and making decisions. Historically, this often involved programming explicit rules. For example, an early chess-playing computer was a form of AI, but it didn't learn; it simply followed a massive set of pre-programmed instructions for every possible move.

Machine Learning (ML), in contrast, is a subset of AI where systems learn directly from data. Instead of being explicitly programmed for every scenario, ML algorithms identify patterns to make predictions and improve their performance over time. This is the key difference. Within ML, Deep Learning (DL) is a specialized branch that employs multi-layered neural networks to automatically learn highly complex patterns from vast amounts of data. Figure 1-1 illustrates the relationship between these concepts.

NOTE Think of teaching a dog a trick. You don't program the dog's muscles; you show examples, give rewards, and the dog *learns*. ML is similar.

Why This Matters to a PM

Understanding this distinction is not just academic; it directly impacts your day-to-day role as an AI Product Manager in several critical ways:

- **Feasibility:** Knowing whether a problem is best solved with rule-based AI or data-driven ML helps you assess technical feasibility.

- **Resource Allocation:** ML requires data—often lots of it. Understanding this helps you plan resources (data collection, labeling, engineering time).

- **Iteration Cycles:** ML models learn and improve over time. This impacts your product roadmap and release planning.

- **User Expectations:** ML-powered features can be less predictable than rule-based systems. This requires careful management of user expectations.

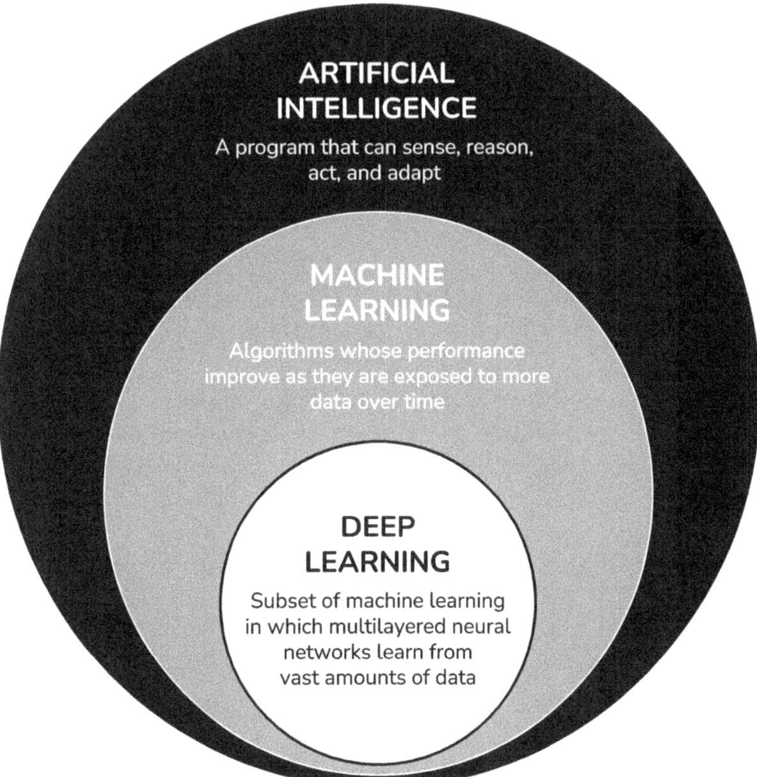

Figure 1-1: The relationship between Artificial Intelligence (AI), Machine Learning (ML), and Deep Learning (DL). ML is a subfield of AI, and DL is a specialized subfield within ML.

Key Differences Between AI and ML

To summarize these core distinctions, the following table provides a clear, side-by-side comparison.

FEATURE	ARTIFICIAL INTELLIGENCE (AI)	MACHINE LEARNING (ML)
Scope	Broad: Machines simulating human intelligence.	Specific: A way to achieve AI by learning from data.
Method	Can be rule-based, logic-based, or learning-based.	Relies on algorithms that learn patterns and make predictions from data.
Learning	Not always required.	Essential; systems improve with experience (data).
Example (Product)	Smart thermostat with a pre-set schedule.	Recommendation engine that learns your viewing preferences and recommends new shows to watch.
PM Implication	Simpler to implement, less adaptable.	More powerful, requires data and iteration.

This distinction is key: a PM guiding a simple, rule-based AI feature will have very different planning and resource conversations than one guiding a feature powered by ML. The following examples further illustrate this difference:

- **AI (Not ML):** A customer service chatbot that uses predefined scripts to answer FAQs. It's "intelligent" in a limited way, but it doesn't learn.

- **ML:** A spam filter that learns to identify spam emails based on patterns in the text and sender information. It gets better over time as it sees more data.

- **AI *Powered by* ML:** Self-driving cars. They use ML extensively (to process sensor data, understand the environment) to achieve the broader AI goal of autonomous navigation.

- **AI *Powered by* ML (Generative AI):** Models like DALL-E 2 (image generation) or ChatGPT (text generation). They've learned from vast datasets to create new content.

Common Misconceptions for PMs: Myths vs. Reality

As you begin your AI PM journey, it's important to dispel some common myths. Navigating these misconceptions early will save you time, help you set realistic expectations, and allow you to collaborate more effectively with your technical teams.

MYTH	REALITY
"AI is a magic black box that just works."	AI is applied mathematics and statistics running on data. Its success depends entirely on the quality of the data, the chosen algorithm, and the clarity of the problem definition—all areas where a Product Manager has significant influence.
"We need a massive, perfect dataset before we can start."	While more high-quality data is better, many impactful AI projects start with smaller, well-curated datasets to build a baseline model (an "AI MVP"). The process is iterative; the model and data can be improved over time.
"AI will replace the need for user research."	AI amplifies the need for user research. AI can tell you what users are doing, but it can't tell you why. Qualitative user research is essential for understanding the context behind the data and ensuring you're solving the right problem.
"Launching an AI feature is a one-and-done project."	An AI model is a living system. Its performance can degrade over time as real-world data changes (a concept called "model drift"). AI features require ongoing monitoring, maintenance, and retraining, which must be planned for in your roadmap.

Internalizing these realities is a key step in shifting from a traditional software mindset to an AI-first product mindset.

Your Glossary as a PM

To help you speak the language of AI confidently, the following table breaks down the core AI/ML terms you'll need in your toolkit. We'll go beyond simple definitions and provide context to help you truly grasp the concepts:

TERM	DEFINITION	IN SIMPLE TERMS	EXAMPLE
Artificial Intelligence (AI)	The broad field of computer science focused on creating machines capable of intelligent behavior.	Making computers "smart" enough to do things that normally require human intelligence, like problem-solving, learning, and decision-making.	A chatbot that understands customer questions and provides helpful answers, or an image recognition system that can identify objects in a photo.
Machine Learning (ML)	A subset of AI that focuses on enabling machines to learn from data without being explicitly programmed.	Teaching computers to learn from examples, so they can make predictions or decisions on their own, without us having to tell them exactly what to do every time.	Predicting which customers are likely to churn, or recommending products based on a user's past purchases.
Deep Learning (DL)	A subfield of ML that uses artificial neural networks with multiple layers (hence "deep") to analyze complex data.	A more advanced type of Machine Learning that's particularly good at handling very complex patterns, like those found in images or language.	Facial recognition in photos, real-time language translation tools.
Algorithm	A set of rules or instructions that a computer follows to solve a problem.	A recipe that tells the computer what to do step-by-step to achieve a specific goal.	Sorting search results from most relevant to least, or recommending movies based on your viewing history.

TERM	DEFINITION	IN SIMPLE TERMS	EXAMPLE
Model	A representation of a real-world process or system, created by training an algorithm on data.	The "brain" that the computer builds after learning from examples. It's what makes the predictions.	A model that predicts the weather, or recognizes spam emails.
Training Data	The data used to teach a Machine Learning model.	The examples that the computer learns from. It's like a textbook for the AI.	A collection of customer emails, each labeled as "spam" or "not spam."
Inference	The process of using a trained model to make predictions or decisions on new, unseen data.	When the "brain" (the trained model) is used to make a prediction on new information it hasn't seen before.	Using the trained email spam model to classify a new incoming email as "spam" or "not spam."
Features	The measurable properties or characteristics of data used as input to a Machine Learning model.	The "ingredients" that the computer uses to make a prediction.	The sender's email address, the subject line, and the body content of an email.
Labels	The correct outcomes or categories associated with data, used for supervised learning (a type of ML).	The "answers" that the computer learns from during training.	"Spam" or "not spam" designations assigned to each training email.

Continues

(continued)

TERM	DEFINITION	IN SIMPLE TERMS	EXAMPLE
Neural Network	A computational model inspired by the structure of the human brain, with interconnected nodes.	A complex network of "neurons" that work together to learn patterns. It's like a simplified digital brain.	Used in deep learning for tasks like image recognition and natural language processing.
Dataset	A collection of data used for training or evaluating a Machine Learning model.	A collection of examples that the computer learns from or tests its knowledge on.	A dataset of customer reviews, each labeled with a sentiment score (positive, negative, neutral).
Natural Language Processing (NLP)	A field of AI that enables computers to understand, interpret, and generate human language.	Making computers understand and "speak" human language, bridging the gap between us and machines.	Chatbots, language translation tools, and sentiment analysis of text.
Generative AI	A type of AI that can create new content, such as text, images, or music.	AI that can create new things, acting like an artist, writer, or composer.	Models that generate realistic images, write articles, or compose original music.
Prompt Engineering	The process of designing and refining prompts to elicit desired outputs from Generative AI models.	Carefully writing the instructions that tell the AI what to create, like giving a detailed brief to an artist.	Crafting a precise prompt to generate a specific type of image or a well-structured article on a given topic.

Grounding the Concepts: Real-World AI in Action

Understanding the distinction between different AI approaches is best done by examining real-world products. The following case studies illustrate how AI and ML are used to solve specific problems and highlight the very important role of the Product Manager in scoping, defining, and guiding these initiatives. Notice how in each case, the starting point was a deep understanding of a user or business problem.

Case Study 1 (Successful ML): Spotify's "Discover Weekly"

- **The User Problem:** With a library of over 100 million songs, users often face the "paradox of choice." They want to discover new music they'll love but don't know where to start, often falling back on listening to the same songs repeatedly.

- **The AI Solution:** Instead of simple rules ("Listeners who like Artist X also like Artist Y"), Spotify uses a sophisticated form of Machine Learning called collaborative filtering. The system analyzes your unique listening history—what you play, skip, add to playlists, and repeat—and compares it to the habits of millions of other users. It then identifies users with similar "taste profiles" and recommends songs that they are playing but that you haven't heard yet, delivered in a personalized playlist each week.

- **The PM Takeaway:** The PM's core job wasn't to invent the algorithm. It was to deeply understand the user problem ("music discovery is hard and time-consuming") and champion a data-driven, highly personalized solution. Their focus was on the *experience*—the weekly surprise, the delight of finding a new favorite artist—which drove massive user engagement and retention.

Case Study 2 (Managing Risk & Cost of Error): Zillow's "Zestimate" and "Zillow Offers"

- **The User Problem:** Homeowners and buyers want a quick, easy way to understand the potential market value of a home without hiring an appraiser.

- **The AI Solution ("Zestimate"):** Zillow built a Machine Learning regression model that learns from vast amounts of data—home characteristics, recent sales in the area, market trends—to predict a home's value. As a product feature for *providing information*, the "Zestimate" has been incredibly successful and has become a household name.

- **The PM Takeaway and Challenge ("Zillow Offers"):** The challenge arose when the company tried to use these same predictions for a different, high-stakes application: automatically buying thousands of homes with the intent to flip them for a profit. Small model prediction errors, which are acceptable for an informational "Zestimate," became financially catastrophic when multiplied across thousands of high-value transactions, ultimately leading to the shutdown of the Zillow Offers business and hundreds of millions in losses. This illustrates a very important lesson for AI PMs: you must deeply understand not just the model's accuracy, but the business risk and the cost of being wrong, and scope the feature's application accordingly.

Case Study 3 (Balancing Supply and Demand): Uber's "Surge" Pricing

- **The Business Problem:** In times of high demand (e.g., after a concert, during a rainstorm), there are more riders requesting trips than available drivers. This leads to long wait times and a poor user experience.

- **The AI Solution:** Uber's dynamic pricing algorithm uses ML to predict rider demand and driver supply in real-time, based on factors like time of day, weather, local events, and historical data. When demand outstrips supply, the system automatically increases prices ("surge pricing"). This has a dual effect: it incentivizes more drivers to get on the road and reduces demand from price-sensitive riders, helping the market find equilibrium faster.

- **The PM Takeaway:** This is a classic example of using AI for real-time optimization. The PM's challenge is not just technical but also psychological: managing a user experience that can sometimes feel negative (higher prices) while communicating that it's necessary to ensure the service remains reliable (i.e., you can actually get a car). It requires balancing marketplace health with individual user perception.

Case Study 4 (Content Moderation at Scale): Meta's Proactive Detection

- **The Business Problem:** How can platforms like Facebook and Instagram possibly review billions of daily posts to remove harmful content (like hate speech, graphic violence, and bullying) before it spreads widely? Manual human moderation is too slow to handle this volume.

- **The AI Solution:** Meta uses a multi-layered AI system. First, simple models proactively flag known violating content. More advanced AI systems, including deep learning models and now even Large Language Models (LLMs), are trained to understand context and detect new and evolving types of harmful content, often removing it before any user reports it. These AI systems prioritize the most severe content and send borderline or highly nuanced cases to human review teams.

- **The PM Takeaway:** This showcases AI's power in solving massive operational safety challenges. The PM's work involves constantly managing the critical trade-off between *false negatives* (missing harmful content) and *false positives* (incorrectly removing legitimate content, which can be perceived as censorship). They must focus on defining clear policies, establishing transparent reporting, creating appeal processes for users, and working with data science to improve the accuracy and fairness of these high-stakes systems.

Case Study 5 (Driving Core User Outcomes): Duolingo's AI-Powered Learning

- **The User Problem:** Learning a new language is difficult, and motivation wanes when the material is too hard, too easy, or not relevant to the learner's goals. A one-size-fits-all curriculum doesn't work.

- **The AI Solution:** Duolingo uses a suite of AI models (internally called "Birdbrain") to personalize the learning experience. The system predicts the probability that a user will get an exercise right or wrong, and then custom-tailors lessons to keep the user in the "Goldilocks zone"—not too hard, not too easy. It also uses Generative AI (GPT-4) to create features like "Roleplay" and "Explain my Answer," allowing users to practice real-world conversations and get personalized feedback.

- **The PM Takeaway:** This demonstrates how multiple AI features can work together to drive a core business metric (user retention) by improving a core user outcome (effective learning). The PM's job is to identify every opportunity in the learning journey where

AI can create a more personalized, engaging, and effective experience, and then prioritize and integrate these features into a cohesive product.

The AI PM's Guiding Principles

As you move forward, keep these five guiding principles in mind. They are the foundation of effective and responsible AI product management. Think of them as your core tenets—the "first principles" you should return to when navigating the complexity of building with AI.

Start with the Problem, Not the Technology   This is the most important principle in all of product management, and it becomes even more critical with AI. The allure of sophisticated technology like Large Language Models or advanced prediction algorithms can create a "solution in search of a problem" scenario. As a Product Manager, your role is to be the anchor, constantly pulling the conversation back to the fundamental user need or business problem. Before asking "How can we use AI?", you must rigorously ask "What is the most valuable problem to solve, and is AI truly the most effective way to solve it?"

Often, a simpler, non-AI solution might be faster to implement, more reliable, and better for the user experience. Your responsibility is to champion the best solution, not necessarily the most technically complex one.

Key Question for PMs: "What is the core user problem we are trying to solve, and what evidence do we have that AI is a uniquely effective way to solve it compared to simpler, non-AI alternatives?"

Data Is the Foundation of Your Product   In traditional software development, the core logic is written in code. In Machine Learning, the core logic is *learned from data*. This is a fundamental shift. The quality, quantity, relevance, and ethical sourcing of your data will directly determine the performance ceiling of your AI product. You can have the most brilliant algorithm in the world, but with poor data, you will have a poor product. The phrase "garbage in, garbage out" is the law of the land.

As a PM, you must become deeply involved in your product's data strategy. This means understanding where your data comes from, advocating for data quality, questioning potential biases within datasets, and ensuring you have the legal and ethical rights to use it. Data is no longer just a byproduct; it is the foundational raw material of your feature.

Key Question for PMs: "Do we have access to a high-quality, representative, and ethically-sourced dataset that can effectively train a model to solve our defined problem?"

Embrace Probability, Not Determinism   Traditional software is deterministic: if you click a button, the same, predictable action happens every time. AI models, however, are probabilistic. They don't provide absolute certainties; they provide predictions with a certain level of confidence. A model doesn't say "This is spam"; it says "There is a 98 percent probability that this is spam."

This shift requires you to design products that gracefully handle uncertainty. What happens when the model is wrong? How do you communicate the model's confidence to the user in an understandable way? What are the fallback mechanisms when the AI's confidence is low? Thinking probabilistically means planning for errors and designing a user experience that builds trust despite the inherent uncertainty.

Key Question for PMs: "How will our product behave when the AI's prediction is wrong, and how will we design a user experience that manages that uncertainty and maintains user trust?"

Prioritize Trust and Responsibility from Day One   Ethical considerations like fairness, bias, privacy, and transparency are not features to be added at the end of a development cycle. They are core, nonnegotiable requirements that must be integrated from the very beginning of the ideation process. Waiting to "check for bias" just before launch is too late; by then, it may be deeply embedded in your data and model architecture.

Your role as a PM is to be the primary advocate for the user and for society within the development process. You must champion ethical reviews, ask hard questions about potential for bias and misuse, and ensure that user privacy is protected by design. Building user trust is a prerequisite for any successful AI product.

Key Question for PMs: "What are the potential ethical risks and unintended consequences of this AI system, and how will we proactively design our product and processes to mitigate them from the start?"

Think in Lifecycles, Not Projects   Launching a traditional software feature is often seen as the finish line of a project. Launching an AI model is just the starting line of its lifecycle. Unlike a button that, once coded, works the same way forever, a model's performance can degrade over time as the real-world data it encounters "drifts" away from the data it was trained on.

This means you must plan for a continuous lifecycle of monitoring, evaluating, maintaining, and retraining your model. This "MLOps" mindset must be reflected in your product roadmap, your resource planning, and your team's ongoing responsibilities. The work isn't done at launch; it's just beginning.

Key Question for PMs: "What is our long-term plan for monitoring, maintaining, and retraining this model after it launches to ensure its performance and relevance over time?"

Chapter Summary and Key Takeaways

You now have a foundational understanding of the AI landscape and the mindset required to lead within it. In this chapter, you learned to distinguish between the broad goal of Artificial Intelligence and the powerful, data-driven method of Machine Learning. We demystified common misconceptions, moving beyond the idea of AI as "magic" to understand it as a practical discipline. By exploring real-world case studies like Spotify's personalization and Zillow's predictive challenges, you've seen how these concepts translate into product successes and strategic lessons. Most importantly, this chapter equipped you with a set of guiding principles that will serve as your strategic compass for every AI project you undertake.

Key Takeaways

- You always start with the user problem first, evaluating if AI is the most effective solution, not just the most exciting one.

- You recognize that data is the foundational raw material for modern AI products, and its quality directly impacts your feature's success.

- You think in terms of probability, not just deterministic rules, and plan for the uncertainty inherent in AI predictions.

- You treat ethical considerations like fairness and trust as core requirements, not as afterthoughts.

- You view AI products as living systems that require a continuous lifecycle of monitoring and maintenance.

Onward: Peeking Under the Hood

With this foundational landscape in place, you are now ready to peek "under the hood." The next chapter will explore the fundamental process of how Machine Learning models actually learn from data.

How Machine Learning Models Learn: A Peek Under the Hood

You don't need to be a data scientist to manage AI products, but understanding the *basics* of how ML models learn is essential. This knowledge empowers you to collaborate effectively with your technical team, make informed product decisions, and set realistic expectations. We'll use a simple, relatable example: classifying fruits.

Imagine teaching a child to identify fruits. You show them Apples, Bananas, and Oranges, pointing out their differences. ML models learn similarly: they analyze examples and identify patterns.

"Features" are the specific characteristics the model uses to make predictions. Think of them as the *descriptive attributes* of your data. The example shown in Figure 2-1 uses the following features:

- **Color:** (Represented numerically: 1 = Red, 2 = Yellow, 3 = Orange)

- **Shape:** (Represented numerically: 1 = Round, 2 = Elongated)

Choosing the *right* features is key to building successful ML models. As a PM, you'll collaborate with your data science team to identify features that are:

- **Relevant:** They should have a strong connection to the outcome you're trying to predict.

- **Available:** You need to be able to collect and use this data.

- **Understandable:** Features should be relatively easy to interpret (even if the model itself is complex).

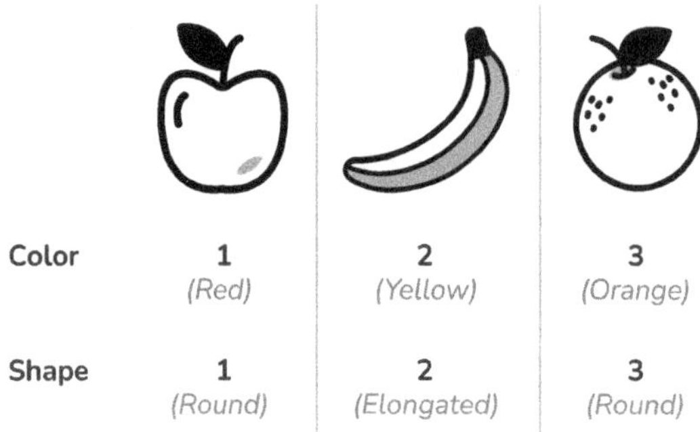

Figure 2-1: An illustration of fruits and features Color and Shape

The Learning Process: Training, Validation, and Testing

To build a model that doesn't just memorize but truly learns, data scientists use a critical three-phase process. They start by splitting their full dataset into distinct parts, as illustrated in Figure 2-2. The largest part is the *training set*, used to teach the model patterns. A smaller *validation set* is used *during* development to tune the model's settings (called hyperparameters), acting like a practice quiz to prevent *overfitting*. Finally, the model's real-world performance is judged against a *testing set*—data it has never seen before—which serves as its final exam.

1. **Training:** The model is fed a large dataset (the *training data*) and identifies patterns between the features and the correct outcome (e.g., which fruit it is). This is like showing the child many examples of each fruit.

2. **Validation:** *During* training, a separate portion of the data (the *validation data*) is used to tune the model's settings (called *hyperparameters*). This is like giving the child practice quizzes and adjusting your teaching based on their performance, and it helps prevent overfitting.

3. **Testing**: *After* training, the model is evaluated on a completely new dataset (the *testing data*) that it hasn't seen before. This is like giving the child a final exam with new fruits to identify and it measures how well the model generalizes to unseen data.

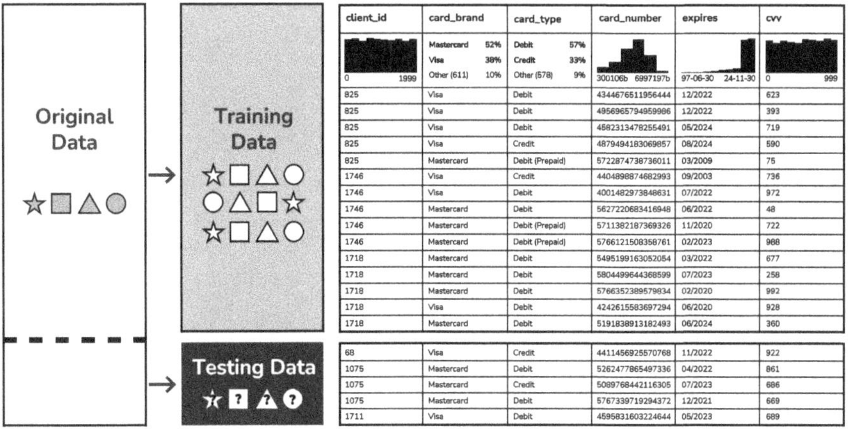

client_id	card_brand	card_type	card_number	expires	cvv
	Mastercard 52%	Debit 57%			
	Visa 38%	Credit 33%			
0 1999	Other (611) 10%	Other (578) 9%	300106b 6997197b	97-06-30 24-11-30	0 999
825	Visa	Debit	4344676511956444	12/2022	623
825	Visa	Debit	4956965794959986	12/2022	393
825	Visa	Debit	4582313478255491	05/2024	719
825	Visa	Credit	4879494183069857	08/2024	590
825	Mastercard	Debit (Prepaid)	5722874738736011	03/2009	75
1746	Visa	Credit	4404898874682993	09/2003	736
1746	Visa	Debit	4001482973848631	07/2022	972
1746	Mastercard	Debit	5627220683416948	06/2022	48
1746	Mastercard	Debit (Prepaid)	5711382187369326	11/2020	722
1746	Mastercard	Debit (Prepaid)	5766121508358761	02/2023	988
1718	Mastercard	Debit	5495199163052054	03/2022	677
1718	Mastercard	Debit	5804499644368599	07/2023	258
1718	Mastercard	Debit	5766352389579834	02/2020	992
1718	Visa	Debit	4242615583697294	06/2020	928
1718	Mastercard	Debit	5191838913182493	06/2024	360
68	Visa	Credit	4411456925570768	11/2022	922
1075	Mastercard	Debit	5262477865497336	04/2022	861
1075	Mastercard	Credit	5089768442116305	07/2023	686
1075	Mastercard	Debit	5767339719294372	12/2021	669
1711	Visa	Debit	4595831603224644	05/2023	689

Figure 2-2: A visual example of splitting a dataset into training and testing sets—an essential step in supervised learning for evaluating model performance. (*Source*: Kaggle).

This learning process has important implications for Product Managers:

- **Data Requirements:** Understanding the need for training, validation, and testing data helps you plan for data collection and labeling efforts.

- **Model Performance:** You'll understand why a model that performs well on training data might not perform well in the real world (overfitting).

- **Iteration:** The validation and testing phases are very important for iterating and improving the model—a key part of the product development lifecycle.

Let's use the simplified dataset shown in Figure 2-3 to illustrate how a Machine Learning model learns from data and makes predictions—an idea we'll explore next using the k-Nearest Neighbors algorithm.

We'll use the first six rows as our *training data* and the last three rows as our *testing data*. Notice we have examples of all three fruits types.

Now, let's look at *how* a model uses this data to actually make predictions. We'll explore a simple algorithm called k-Nearest Neighbors (k-NN) to illustrate the core concepts.

Fruit	Color (1=Red, 2=Yellow, 3=Orange)	Shape (1=Round, 2=Elongated)
Apple 1	1	1
Apple 2	1	1
Apple 3	1	1
Banana 1	2	2
Banana 2	2	2
Banana 3	2	2
Orange 1	3	1
Orange 2	3	1
Orange 3	3	1

Rows Apple 1 through Banana 3 are marked as the **Training Set**; rows Orange 1 through Orange 3 are marked as the **Testing Set**.

Figure 2-3: A simplified training and testing dataset of fruits, represented by color and shape features, used to illustrate how ML models make predictions

How Models Learn: An Example with k-Nearest Neighbors (k-NN)

ML models use different algorithms—sets of rules—to find patterns in data. One simple example is *k-Nearest Neighbors (k-NN)*. Figure 2-4 shows how k-NN can visually separate data points into different groups based on feature similarity. Think of it like this:

Imagine you have a map showing the locations of different fruits based on their color and shape. To classify a *new* fruit, k-NN says: "Look at the 'k' closest fruits on the map. The most common type among those neighbors is likely the type of the new fruit."

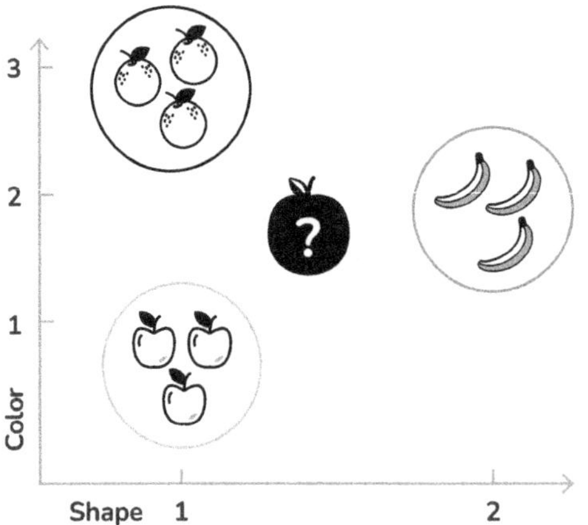

Figure 2-4: K-NN can help separate data into segments.

Let's walk through an example. Recall our training data (only Apples and Bananas):

FRUIT	COLOR (1=RED, 2=YELLOW, 3=ORANGE)	SHAPE (1=ROUND, 2=ELONGATED)
Apple 1	1	1
Apple 2	1	1
Apple 3	1	1
Banana 1	2	2
Banana 2	2	2
Banana 3	2	2

Now, let's introduce a new fruit from our testing data: an Orange (Color = 3, Shape = 1). Remember that our training data contained no Oranges.

FRUIT	COLOR (1=RED, 2=YELLOW, 3=ORANGE)	SHAPE (1=ROUND, 2=ELONGATED)
Orange 1	3	1

Applying k-NN (with k=1):

We'll start with k=1, meaning we look at only the *single* nearest neighbor. The k-NN algorithm calculates the "distance" between our new Orange and every fruit in the training data. While there are different ways to calculate distance, we'll use a simple one:

$$\text{Distance} = |\text{Difference in Color}| + |\text{Difference in Shape}|$$

Let's calculate the distances:

- **Distance to Apple 1 (1, 1):** $|3 - 1| + |1 - 1| = 2$
- **Distance to Apple 1 (1,1):** $|\text{Orange Color} - \text{Apple Color}| + |\text{Orange Shape} - \text{Apple Shape}|$
- **Distance to Apple 2 (1, 1):** $|3 - 1| + |1 - 1| = 2$

- **Distance to Apple 3 (1, 1):** $|3 - 1| + |1 - 1| = 2$
- **Distance to Banana 1 (2, 2):** $|3 - 2| + |1 - 2| = 2$
- **Distance to Banana 2 (2, 2):** $|3 - 2| + |1 - 2| = 2$
- **Distance to Banana 3 (2, 2):** $|3 - 2| + |1 - 2| = 2$

The problem: all the distances are the same! With k=1, the model could randomly choose Apple or Banana. Figure 2-5 illustrates this ambiguity, showing that the Orange lies equidistant from both Apples and Bananas, making classification uncertain when k=1. It *cannot* correctly predict Orange because it has never seen an Orange before.

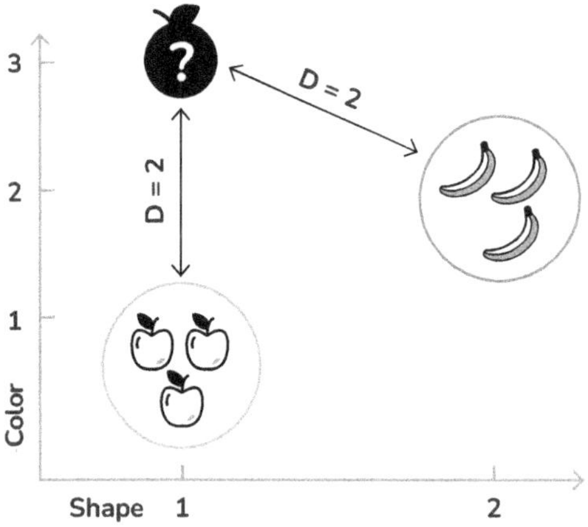

Figure 2-5: When using k=1 in k-NN, all distances from the new fruit (an Orange) to existing training points are equal, making the classification ambiguous.

What if we increase "k" to find more neighbors? Let's try k=3. In this case, the model looks for the three closest data points. Since all training points have a distance of 2, the model would likely select three neighbors at random, for instance, two Apples and one Banana. Based on this "vote," it would incorrectly classify the new fruit as an Apple. This outcome, where the model is forced to make a "best guess" from known categories, is visualized in Figure 2-6.

This highlights a key point about Machine Learning: a model's predictions are only as good as the data it's trained on. If the training data doesn't contain representative examples of a particular category (like Oranges in our case), the model will have difficulty recognizing it and will likely make an incorrect prediction.

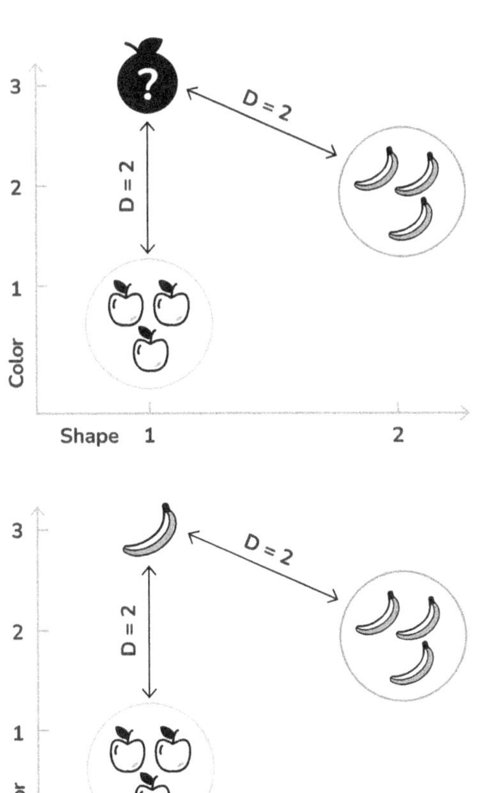

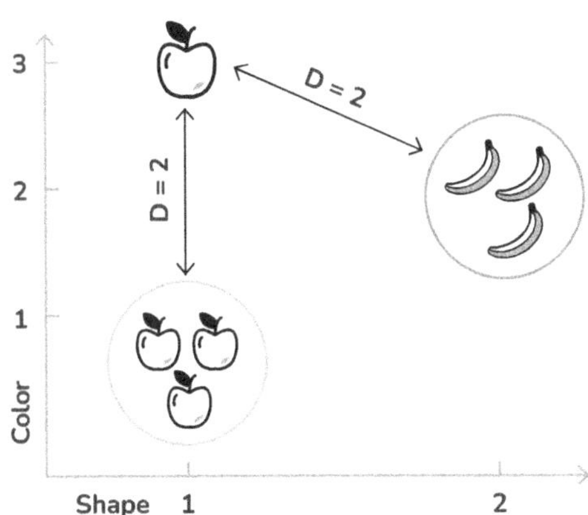

Figure 2-6: An illustration of the k-NN algorithm with k=3. Even with more neighbors, the new fruit (Orange) is incorrectly classified because its nearest neighbors in the training data are a mix of Apples and Bananas, highlighting the model's dependence on representative training data.

Another Example: Testing an Unknown Fruit

Let's try a different test fruit:

FRUIT	COLOR (1=RED, 2=YELLOW, 3=ORANGE)	SHAPE (1=ROUND, 2=ELONGATED)
Unknown	2	1

- **With k=1:** Just like in the previous example, the nearest neighbor is again either an Apple (1,2) or a Banana (2, 2). So, the prediction can be either of them. Figure 2-7 illustrates this misclassification by showing how k=3 can still fail when the correct fruit category is missing from the training data.

- **With k=3:** We look at the *three* nearest neighbors. They might be:

  - Banana (2, 2)

  - Banana (2, 2)

  - Apple (1, 1)

Since the distance is the same, if the majority (2 out of 3) are Bananas, the prediction is likely Banana.

This prediction is very strange because the unknown fruit (color = yellow and shape = round) is predicted to be a Banana even though it's supposed to be elongated! Figure 2-7 visualizes this behavior by showing how the model, lacking examples of Yellow and round fruit in the training data, misclassifies the unknown fruit based on its nearest neighbors.

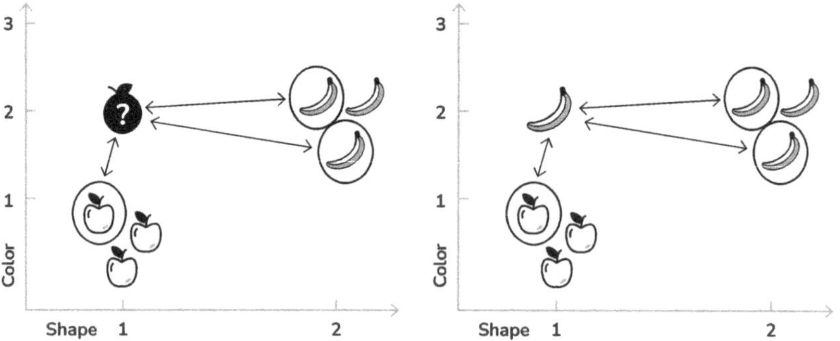

Figure 2-7: The effect of using k=3 in k-NN classification. The new fruit is misclassified because the nearest neighbors only include Apples and Bananas—highlighting the need for diverse and representative training data.

Note that the value of "k" influences the model's behavior:

- **Small k (e.g., k=1):** More sensitive to noise and outliers in the data. Can lead to overfitting (performing well on training data but poorly on new data).

- **Large k:** Smoother decision boundaries, less sensitive to noise. Can lead to underfitting (failing to capture important patterns).

As a PM, you won't typically choose "k" directly, but you should understand that it's a *tunable parameter* that impacts model performance and discuss it with your data science team.

We've seen how k-NN works and the critical importance of data. Now, let's examine how we *measure* a model's performance using metrics like accuracy, precision, and recall.

Evaluating Model Performance

After training, we need to *evaluate* our model's performance. Think of this as the model's "report card." We use various *metrics* to measure how well it performs on the *testing data* (data it hasn't seen before). As a PM, understanding these metrics is critical for:

- **Assessing Product Viability:** Is the model good enough to solve the user problem?

- **Making Trade-Offs:** Different metrics highlight different aspects of performance. You'll need to prioritize based on your product goals.

- **Communicating with Data Science:** You'll need to discuss these metrics intelligently with your technical team.

Since our fruit example is a *classification* problem (predicting a category), we'll focus on classification metrics.

The Confusion Matrix: A Foundation for Understanding

Before diving into specific metrics, let's introduce the *confusion matrix*. This table summarizes the performance of a classification model by showing the counts of:

- **True Positives (TP):** Correctly predicted positive cases (e.g., the model predicted "Apple," and it *was* an Apple).

- **True Negatives (TN):** Correctly predicted negative cases (e.g., the model predicted "Not Apple," and it *wasn't* an Apple).

- **False Positives (FP):** Incorrectly predicted positive cases (e.g., the model predicted "Apple," but it was an Orange—a *Type I error*).

- **False Negatives (FN):** Incorrectly predicted negative cases (e.g., the model predicted "Not Apple," but it *was* an Apple—a *Type II error*).

Here's an example of a confusion matrix if we asked our model to predict whether a new fruit is an apple or not.

	PREDICTED APPLE	PREDICTED NOT APPLE
Actual Apple	TP = 8	FN = 2
Actual Not Apple	FP = 3	TN = 7

This matrix tells us that:

- The model correctly predicted "Apple" eight times (TP).

- The model incorrectly predicted "Not Apple" when it *was* an Apple two times (FN).

- The model incorrectly predicted "Apple" when it *wasn't* an Apple three times (FP).

- The model correctly predicted "Not Apple" seven times (TN).

Key Classification Metrics (and Their PM Implications)

Now, let's define the key metrics, using the confusion matrix concepts:

- **Accuracy:** The overall percentage of correct predictions.

$$Accuracy = (TP + TN) / (TP + TN + FP + FN)$$

  - Example (from the matrix above): (8 + 7) / (8 + 7 + 3 + 2) = 0.75 or 75 percent.

  - **PM Implication:** A good starting point, but can be misleading if the classes are imbalanced (e.g., if you have many more Apples than Oranges in your dataset).

- **Precision:** Out of all the times the model predicted "positive" (e.g., "Apple"), what percentage were *actually* positive?

$$\text{Precision} = TP / (TP + FP)$$

  - Example (from the matrix above): 8 / (8 + 3) = 0.73 or 73 percent.

  - **PM Implication:** Important when the cost of a *false positive* is high. For example, in a spam filter, you want high precision (you don't want to send important emails to the spam folder).

- **Recall:** Out of all the *actual* positive cases (e.g., all the actual Apples), what percentage did the model correctly identify?

$$\text{Recall} = TP / (TP + FN)$$

Figure 2-8 provides a visual summary of how precision and recall relate to true positives, false positives, and false negatives in a classification setting.

  - Example (from the matrix above): 8 / (8 + 2) = 0.80 or 80 percent.

  - **PM Implication:** Important when the cost of a *false negative* is high. For example, in medical diagnosis, you want high recall (you don't want to miss any cases of a disease).

The Precision-Recall Trade-Off

Often, there's a trade-off between precision and recall. Increasing one might decrease the other. As a PM, you need to decide which is more important for your specific product and user needs.

- **Example:** Search Engine:

  - **High Precision:** The search results are highly relevant, but some relevant results might be missed.

  - **High Recall:** All relevant results are shown, but there might be some irrelevant ones too.

- **Example:** Fraud Detection:

  - **High Recall:** It is critical to catch *all* the fraudulent cases, even if the system calls a few legit cases as fraudulent.

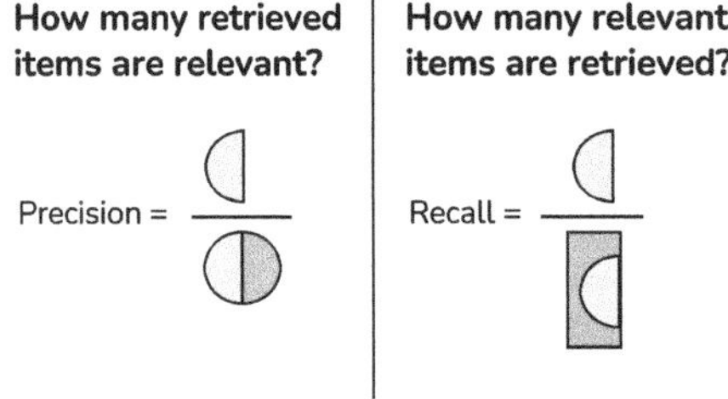

Figure 2-8: A visual representation of precision and recall, showing how true positives intersect with false positives and false negatives in classification tasks. (*Source:* Creative Commons)

Choosing the Right Metric

The *best* metric depends on your product's goals. Ask yourself:

- What are the consequences of false positives?
- What are the consequences of false negatives?
- Is it more important to be precise or to have high recall?

Understanding these metrics is fundamental, but models aren't perfect. Let's explore two common problems: overfitting and underfitting.

Overfitting and Underfitting: Striking the Right Balance for Real-World Performance

Even with good metrics, a model can still have problems. Two common issues are *overfitting* and *underfitting*. Finding the right balance between these is critical for building a model that performs well in the real world, not just on your training data. Figure 2-9 illustrates how, without a balance between bias and variance, your model can have issues of overfitting, underfitting, or even be a completely sub-optimal model.

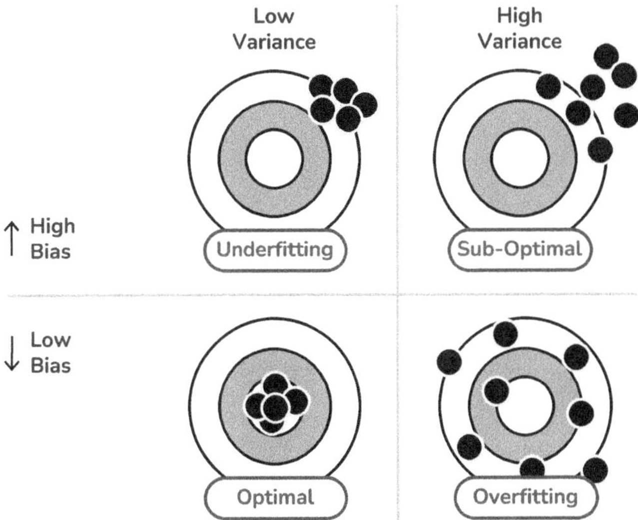

Figure 2-9: Visual comparison of underfitting, overfitting, and ideal model performance in Machine Learning. It shows how model complexity impacts the ability to generalize from data.

Overfitting: Memorizing Instead of Learning

An *overfit* model is like a student who memorizes the answers to practice questions without understanding the underlying concepts. It performs exceptionally well on the *training data* (the practice questions) but poorly on the *testing data* (the real exam).

- **What it Looks Like:** High accuracy on training data, low accuracy on testing data.

- **Why it Happens:** The model is too complex. It has learned the noise and specific details of the training data, rather than the general patterns.

- **PM Implication:** Your product will perform poorly in the real world, even if initial tests look promising. Users will encounter scenarios the model hasn't seen before, leading to errors and frustration.

Underfitting: Missing the Forest for the Trees

An *underfit* model is like a student who hasn't studied enough and can't answer even basic questions. It performs poorly on *both* the training and testing data.

- **What it Looks Like:** Low accuracy on both training and testing data.

- **Why it Happens:** The model is too simple. It hasn't captured the underlying patterns in the data.

- **PM Implication:** Your product won't be effective at solving the user problem, as the model is too simplistic to make useful predictions.

Visual Analogy: Fitting a Curve

Imagine you're trying to fit a curve to a set of data points. Figure 2-10 illustrates this concept by comparing underfitting, overfitting, and a well-generalized model through simple curve-fitting examples.

- **Underfitting:** A straight line that doesn't capture the curve's shape.

- **Overfitting:** A highly complex, wiggly line that passes perfectly through every training point but doesn't generalize well to new points.

- **Just right:** A smooth curve that captures the general trend of the data without being overly sensitive to individual points.

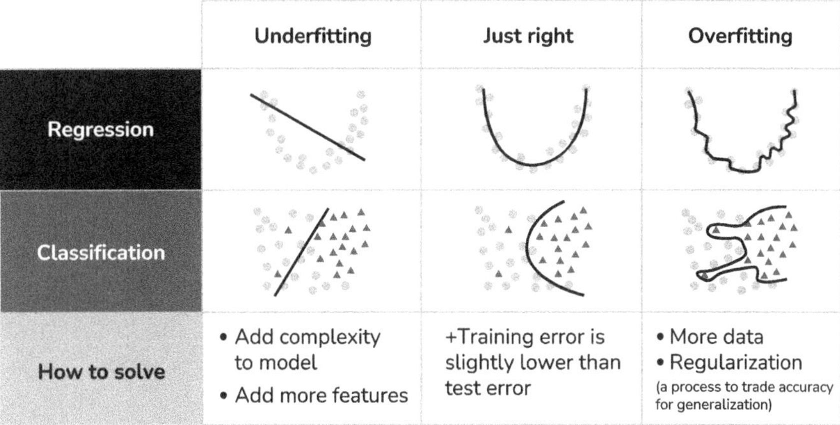

Figure 2-10: A visual comparison of underfitting, overfitting, and an ideal ("just right") model for both regression and classification tasks. This illustrates the fundamental challenge of finding the right level of model complexity to ensure good generalization.

Finding the Sweet Spot: Generalization

The goal is *generalization*: building a model that performs well on *new, unseen data*. This requires finding the right balance between complexity and simplicity.

Data Scientists have many techniques, such as *regularization* (penalizing overly complex models) and *cross-validation* (using different subsets of data for training and testing), and choosing the right model.

In our k-NN fruit previous example:

- **Small k (e.g., k=1):** More prone to *overfitting*. The model is overly sensitive to individual training examples.

- **Large k:** More prone to *underfitting*. The model becomes too general and might ignore important distinctions between fruit types. Figure 2-10 illustrates how varying the value of k in k-NN impacts model behavior—from overfitting at low values to underfitting at high values.

The PM's Role

As a PM, you don't need to implement these techniques, but you should:

- **Understand the Concepts:** Know what overfitting and underfitting are and their implications.

- **Ask the Right Questions:** Inquire about how your data science team is addressing these issues. For instance: "How are we ensuring the model generalizes well to new data?" "What techniques are we using to prevent overfitting?" "Are we using cross-validation?"

- **Monitor Performance:** Track performance on both training and testing data to detect potential overfitting or underfitting.

- **Prioritize Data:** Work to prioritize the acquisition of more, and more varied, data.

Now that you understand how models learn, are evaluated, and potential problems, let's explore the concept of "Human-in-the-Loop" and why it's critical for building robust and responsible AI systems

Human-in-the-Loop: Blending AI Power with Human Expertise

While we often envision AI as fully automated, the reality is that *human expertise remains critical* in many AI applications. This is where *Human-in-the-Loop (HITL)* comes in. HITL is not about replacing AI; it's about strategically integrating human judgment and oversight into the AI system to improve accuracy, handle ambiguity, mitigate bias, and build trust. Think of it as a *partnership* between humans and machines, leveraging the strengths of both.

What Is Human-in-the-Loop?

As illustrated in Figure 2-11, HITL is a design pattern where humans are actively involved in *various stages* of the AI lifecycle, including:

- **Data Labeling:** Providing accurate labels for training data (essential for supervised learning).

- **Model Validation:** Reviewing and correcting the model's predictions or generated outputs.

- **Decision-Making:** Making final decisions in cases where the model is uncertain or the stakes are high.

- **Providing Feedback:** Giving feedback to improve the model's performance and address biases.

- **Edge Cases:** Dealing with situations that are not covered in the training data.

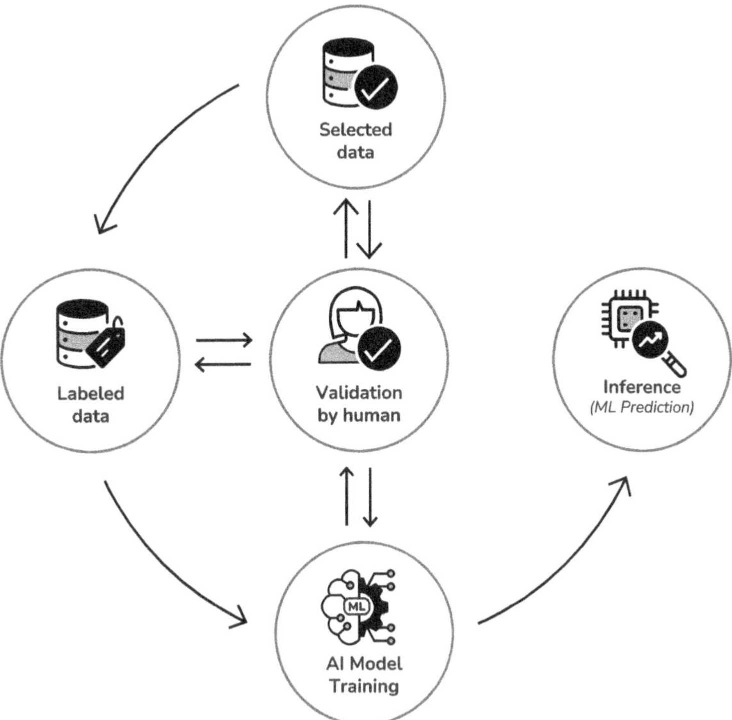

Figure 2-11: Human-in-the-loop. A design pattern where humans are actively involved in various stages of the AI lifecycle.

Why HITL Is Essential for Product Managers (and Their Products)

HITL isn't just a technical consideration; it's a *product strategy* decision. Here's why it's critical for PMs:

- **Improved Accuracy and Reliability:** Humans can often catch errors or nuances that AI models miss, especially in complex or subjective domains.

- **Handling Ambiguity and Edge Cases:** AI models can struggle with ambiguous input or situations outside their training data. Humans can provide the context and judgment needed to handle these cases.

- **Mitigating Bias and Ensuring Fairness:** As we discussed extensively, AI models can perpetuate biases. Human review can help identify and correct biased outputs, ensuring fairer outcomes. This is a *direct application* of the ethical considerations we covered earlier.

- **Building User Trust:** Knowing that a human is "in the loop" can increase user trust, particularly for high-stakes applications.

- **Adapting to Change:** Humans can help the AI system adapt to changing data patterns or user needs, providing feedback and guidance for model retraining.

- **Complex Tasks:** For situations that are difficult for current AI models.

The following table shows real-world examples of how HITL is applied across different AI product scenarios, highlighting the AI's task, the human's role, and the resulting product benefits.

SCENARIO	AI TASK	HITL ROLE	PM BENEFIT
Content Moderation (Social Media)	Identifying and flagging inappropriate content.	AI flags potentially harmful posts; human moderators review flagged content and make final decisions.	Reduces risk of wrongly censoring content (false positives) or allowing harmful content (false negatives). Improves community safety.
Medical Diagnosis Assistance	Analyzing medical images (X-rays, MRIs).	AI highlights potential anomalies; doctors make the final diagnosis.	Improves diagnostic accuracy and efficiency while ensuring human oversight for critical decisions.
Customer Support Chatbot	Answering customer questions.	AI handles routine inquiries; complex or sensitive questions are escalated to human agents.	Provides fast responses for common issues while ensuring human support is available when needed. Improves customer satisfaction.
Financial Fraud Detection	Identifying suspicious transactions.	AI flags potentially fraudulent transactions; fraud analysts investigate and take action.	Reduces financial losses while minimizing inconvenience to legitimate customers.

SCENARIO	AI TASK	HITL ROLE	PM BENEFIT
Hiring (Resume Screening)	Ranking candidates based on resumes.	AI scores resumes; recruiters review top candidates and make hiring decisions. This is a high-risk area for bias; HITL is critical.	Reduces time spent screening resumes while mitigating the risk of biased hiring decisions.
Product Recommendation	Suggesting products or content.	AI generates personalized recommendations; editors or curators review and refine recommendations, especially for high-value or sensitive items.	Provides the personalization and scale, while applying human curation and editorial judgment, ensuring high quality.
Autonomous Driving	Making real time driving decisions.	AI is in charge of driving. In edge cases, a remote human operator can be in charge.	Reduces risks and improves safety.

This table shows that HITL is a versatile strategy. Successfully implementing it in your product, however, requires thoughtful planning.

How to Implement HITL (PM Considerations)

Successfully implementing HITL in your product requires thoughtful planning and cross-functional collaboration. Below are key considerations for Product Managers to ensure HITL systems are practical, effective, and scalable.

1. **Identify Critical Decision Points:** Determine *where* in your AI workflow human intervention is most valuable and feasible. This depends on the risk level, the complexity of the task, and the model's confidence levels.

2. **Design Clear Workflows:** Create clear and efficient workflows for how humans will interact with the AI system. This includes defining roles and responsibilities, providing clear guidelines, and designing user interfaces that facilitate human review and input.

3. **Provide Training and Support:** Train human reviewers on how to effectively interact with the AI system and how to identify and address potential biases or errors.

4. **Measure and Optimize:** Track the performance of both the AI model *and* the human-in-the-loop system. Identify areas for improvement and optimize the workflow over time. Key metrics might include:

   - **Agreement Rate:** How often do humans and the AI agree?

   - **Intervention Rate:** How often do humans need to intervene?

   - **Time to Resolution:** How long does it take to resolve cases with HITL?

   - **User Satisfaction:** How satisfied are users with the outcomes?

5. **Iterate:** HITL is not a static system. It should be designed to handle changes.

HITL is a powerful approach for building more reliable, responsible, and effective AI-powered products. It recognizes that AI is not a replacement for human judgment, but rather a tool that can be enhanced by human expertise. As a Product Manager, you play a key role in designing and implementing HITL systems that leverage the strengths of both humans and machines. By doing so, you will be able to provide better and more reliable products.

Chapter Summary and Key Takeaways

You have now taken a detailed look "under the hood" at how Machine Learning models function. This chapter walked you through the core mechanics of model development, starting with how raw data is transformed into meaningful features for a model to learn from. You've seen the critical importance of splitting data for training, validation, and testing, a fundamental practice to avoid the common pitfall of overfitting. We unpacked the confusion matrix to show that evaluating a model is far more nuanced than a single accuracy score, forcing you to consider the trade-offs between metrics like precision and recall. Finally, you learned that when models reach their limits, incorporating a Human-in-the-Loop is a powerful strategy, not a sign of failure.

Key Takeaways

- Your evaluation of a model must go beyond simple accuracy; you now focus on the critical trade-offs between different metrics like precision and recall to make smart product decisions based on the cost of specific errors.

- You understand that the goal is generalization; a model that can't perform well on new, unseen data is not ready for your product.

- You see HITL not as a weakness, but as a strategic tool to improve accuracy, handle ambiguity, and build user trust.

- You recognize there is no single "ML" solution; the different types of Machine Learning (supervised, unsupervised, etc.) are a toolkit, and you must choose the right tool for the job.

Onward: Understanding the Broader Process

Now that you've covered the core mechanics of a model, you can place these concepts within the broader, end-to-end workflow. The next chapter will detail the Data Science Life Cycle, showing how these steps fit into the bigger picture.

The Big Picture: AI, ML, and You

In the previous chapters, we explored the mechanics of Machine Learning and the foundational concepts that every AI Product Manager should understand. Now, we zoom out to understand how these elements connect to the bigger picture: what AI really means in a product context, how Machine Learning fits into the broader AI landscape, and how you—as a PM—can use this understanding to drive strategy and innovation.

This chapter focuses on strategic fluency: recognizing the different types of AI, understanding when to apply Machine Learning, and appreciating how the technical choices made by your team affect the product's capabilities, risks, and user value.

Understanding the Relationship Between AI, ML, and Product Goals

It's helpful to visualize the relationship between artificial intelligence, Machine Learning, and your product strategy.

AI is the goal; ML is a means   Think of AI as the overarching ambition: to create products that exhibit intelligent behavior, ultimately solving user problems in a smarter, more efficient way. Machine Learning is one of the most powerful techniques we currently have to achieve that. It's not the *only* way, but it's often the most adaptable and scalable.

Example: Let's say your product is a music streaming service. Your *AI goal* might be to "provide personalized music recommendations that delight each user and keep them engaged." *Machine Learning* is a powerful *means* to achieve this. You could use ML algorithms to analyze a user's listening history, their likes/dislikes, and even the listening habits of users with similar tastes to predict which songs and artists they'll enjoy. This is a much more sophisticated approach than simply offering pre-set playlists (which would be a rule-based system, and technically AI, but not *ML*). Another means could be a knowledge-based AI system, that understands music using ontologies, but maintaining that knowledge base is often hard and costly.

Not All AI is ML, But ML is Always AI   You can have AI systems within your product that don't rely on learning from data. However, any feature that uses Machine Learning is, by definition, leveraging AI. This includes Deep Learning, a powerful subfield of ML that uses structures called Neural Networks to learn from vast amounts of data.

The relationship between these concepts is often visualized as a series of nested and overlapping fields, as shown in Figure 3-1.

Example (Non-ML AI): Consider a simple "smart" email filter in your product that automatically moves emails containing specific keywords (like "unsubscribe" or "invoice") to specific folders. This is a rule-based system. You, as the PM (or your team), define the rules: IF email contains "unsubscribe," THEN move to the "Promotions" folder. This is AI because it's automating a task that usually requires human intelligence, but it's *not* learning. It won't get better at filtering unless you manually update the rules.

Example (ML-Based AI): Now, imagine a *spam* filter that learns from user behavior. When a user marks an email as spam, the system learns from that action and improves its ability to identify and filter similar spam emails in the future. This is ML (and therefore AI) because it's learning and adapting without explicit programming.

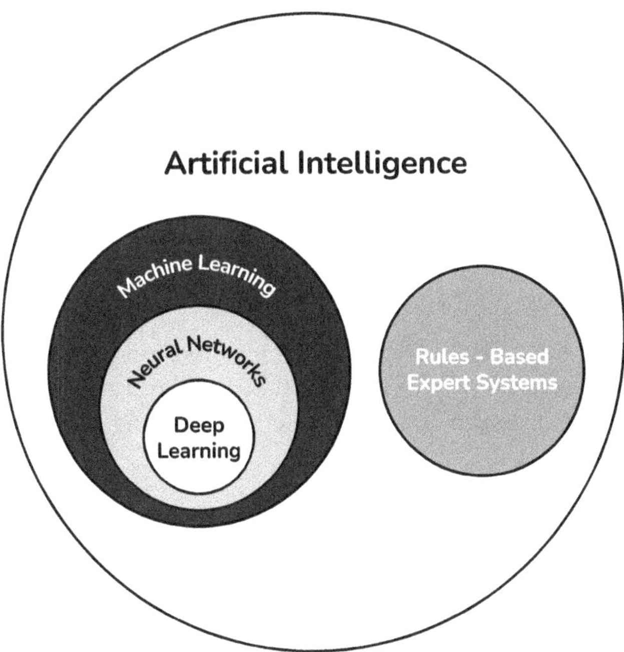

Figure 3-1: A visual representation of the AI landscape. Both Machine Learning and Rule-Based Expert Systems are subsets of the broader field of Artificial Intelligence. Within Machine Learning, Neural Networks are a key technique, and Deep Learning is a specialized subfield of Neural Networks.

ML enables adaptability: The Dynamic Product Advantage   This is where Machine Learning truly shines in product management. Unlike static, rule-based systems, ML models can adapt to changing data patterns and improve their performance over time. This is critical because user behavior, market trends, and competitive landscapes are constantly evolving.

Example: Think about a ride-sharing app. Initially, the app might estimate arrival times based on simple rules (distance, average speed limits). However, with ML, the app can learn from *real-world data*—traffic patterns, driver behavior, time of day, even weather conditions—to provide increasingly accurate arrival time predictions. As more data is collected, the model gets better and better, providing a superior user experience. This adaptability is a key competitive advantage.

Understanding Method Choices: A PM's Strategic Advantage   Your role isn't to code the algorithms, but to understand the strategic implications of different AI approaches.

This allows for productive conversations with your engineering team and informed product roadmap decisions. The key is to match the tool to the task.

When you need a system to follow a strict set of predefined rules, a rule-based AI approach might be perfectly sufficient, and it could be simpler and faster to implement.

Example: A customer support chatbot that provides answers to frequently asked questions (FAQs) based on keyword matching.

When you need a system to learn from data and make predictions, Machine Learning is likely the way to go. You'll be able to discuss the type of data needed, the potential accuracy, and the ongoing maintenance with your team.

Example: A fraud detection system for an e-commerce platform where an ML model learns to identify patterns indicative of fraud from historical data.

When dealing with incredibly complex patterns, like those found in images or natural language, Deep Learning, with its powerful Neural Networks, might be necessary.

Example: A social media platform that automatically tags people in photos, which requires a deep understanding of facial features.

By learning these core AI/ML terms, you're not just learning vocabulary; you're building a foundation for strategic thinking. You'll be able to collaborate more effectively with your technical teams, evaluate the feasibility of AI-driven features with greater confidence, and ultimately, make more informed product decisions that lead to successful outcomes. You'll be able to ask questions like, "What kind of training data will we need for this model?" or "Is deep learning really necessary for this feature, or could we achieve similar results with a simpler approach?" This level of understanding is what separates a good Product Manager from a *great* one in the age of AI.

Types of Machine Learning: Understanding the Spectrum of Learning

We've established that Machine Learning is a powerful tool. But to understand its place, it's helpful to look at the entire landscape of Artificial Intelligence, from the products we build today to the ambitious goals of the future. This spectrum of AI capability is often broken down into three main levels:

- **Traditional or Narrow AI (ANI):** This is the AI we have today. It's designed to perform a specific, "narrow" task—like playing chess, recommending music, or generating text. Every AI product you've ever used, including the most advanced Generative AI, falls into this category.

- **Artificial General Intelligence (AGI):** This is the next frontier. AGI refers to a hypothetical AI with the ability to understand, learn, and apply its intelligence to solve any problem a human can. It would possess consciousness, self-awareness, and adaptable problem-solving skills.

- **Artificial Superintelligence (ASI):** This is a theoretical form of AI that would surpass human intelligence and cognitive ability in virtually every domain.

Figure 3-2 illustrates this entire spectrum, from the powerful tools of today to the theoretical possibilities of tomorrow.

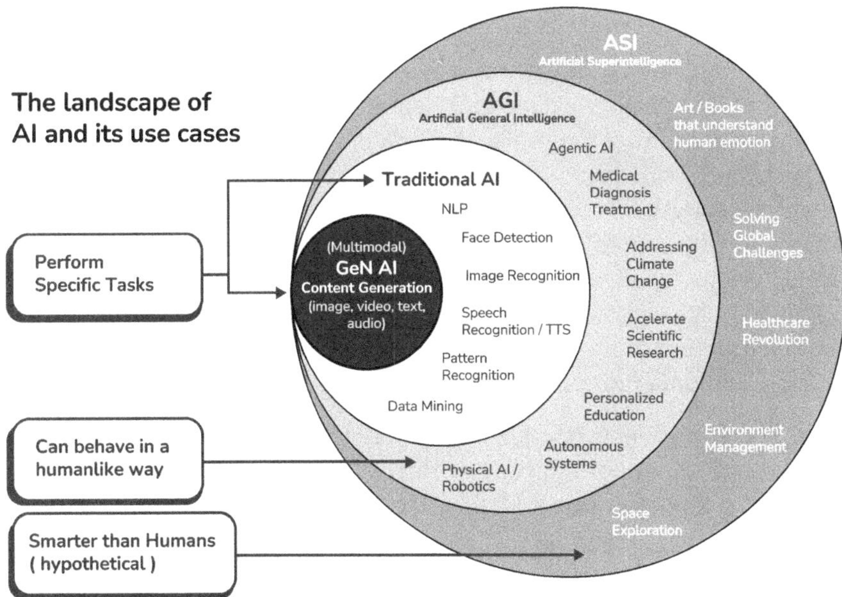

Figure 3-2: The spectrum of AI capabilities. All of today's systems, including Traditional AI and the more recent Generative AI, are forms of Artificial Narrow Intelligence (ANI). Artificial General Intelligence (AGI) and Artificial Superintelligence (ASI) remain future, theoretical goals.

As a Product Manager, while it's exciting to think about AGI and ASI, your focus will be firmly rooted in the first category. The key takeaway is that to build today's powerful Narrow AI products, we use a "toolkit" of different Machine Learning approaches.

Think of it like cooking: there's not just one way to cook; you have baking, grilling, and frying—each technique best suited for different outcomes. Similarly, the Machine Learning toolkit contains a range of approaches. In this section, we'll explore the four major techniques you're most likely to encounter:

- **Supervised Learning:** Learning from labeled examples.

- **Unsupervised Learning:** Discovering hidden patterns in data.

- **Reinforcement Learning:** Learning through trial and error.

- **Generative AI:** Creating new content.

Let's start with the most common and, often, the most intuitive type: supervised learning.

Supervised Learning: Guiding the Model with Labeled Examples

Imagine you're onboarding a new customer support agent. You wouldn't just throw them into the deep end, would you? Instead, you'd provide them with a training manual and a stack of past support tickets, each clearly labeled with the type of issue: "Technical Issue," "Billing Question," "Feature Request," etc. The agent would study these examples, learning to associate the content of the ticket with the correct category. Over time, they'd become proficient at classifying new, unseen tickets.

This is precisely the essence of *supervised learning*. We're providing the Machine Learning model with a "teacher" in the form of a *labeled dataset*. Each data point in this dataset has two parts:

- **The Input Features:** The characteristics or attributes of the data. In our customer support example, this could be the text of the ticket, the customer's history, the product they're using, etc.

- **The Output Label:** The correct answer or category. In our example, this would be "Technical Issue," "Billing Question," or "Feature Request."

This process, where an ML model learns from labeled inputs to classify them into distinct categories, is illustrated in Figure 3-3.

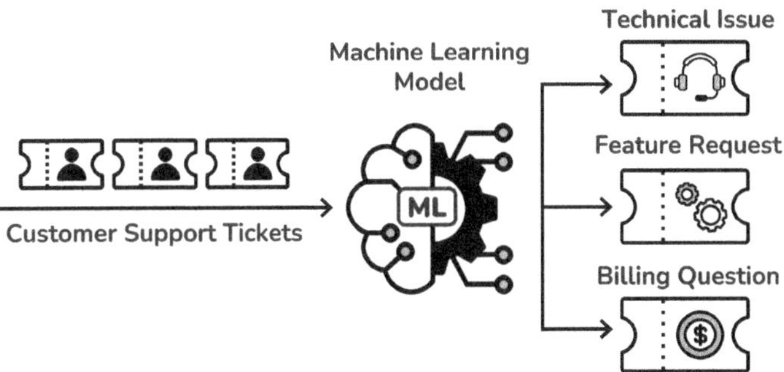

Figure 3-3: A conceptual diagram of a supervised learning classification model. The ML model is trained on labeled customer support tickets to learn how to automatically sort new, incoming tickets into predefined categories like "Technical Issues," "Feature Requests," and "Billing Questions."

The model's job is to learn the relationship between the input features and the output label. It's like learning to connect the dots. The better the model understands this relationship, the more accurately it can predict the correct label for *new, unseen* data.

Supervised learning is the workhorse behind many of the AI-powered products you use every day. It's the foundation for:

- **Predicting Customer Churn:** Identifying which customers are at risk of leaving your service, based on their past behavior, demographics, and interactions with your product.

- **Fraud Detection:** Flagging suspicious transactions in real-time, based on patterns learned from past fraudulent activities.

- **Image Classification:** Identifying objects within images, such as tagging photos on social media or enabling self-driving cars to "see" the road.

- **Personalized Recommendations:** Suggesting products, movies, or articles a user might enjoy, based on their past preferences and the preferences of similar users.

- **Sales Forecasting:** Predicting future sales based on historical data, seasonality, marketing campaigns, and other relevant factors. A model might learn that sales spike during holiday seasons or after specific promotional events.

- **Medical Diagnosis Assistance:** Assisting doctors to make faster and more accurate diagnoses, based on a dataset of patients records, labeled with the corresponding diagnosis.

Think of a spam filter in your email inbox (see Figure 3-4). It's a supervised learning model that has been trained on millions of emails, each labeled as "spam" or "not spam." The model learns to identify the characteristics of spam emails (certain keywords, sender addresses, etc.) and uses that knowledge to classify new emails.

The power of supervised learning lies in its ability to automate decision-making and make predictions based on data. As a Product Manager, understanding this allows you to identify opportunities to leverage labeled data to improve your product and solve user problems.

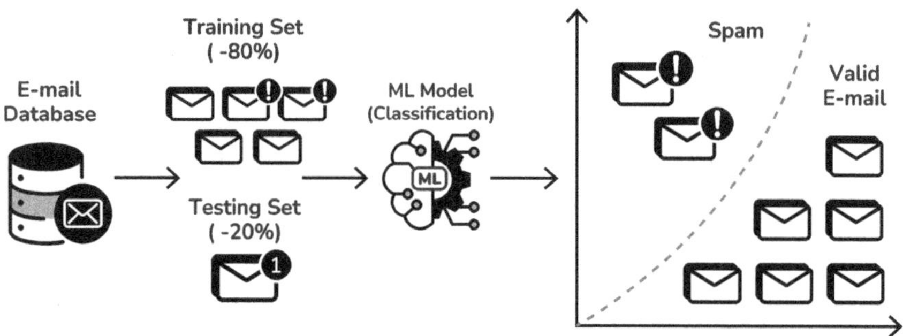

Figure 3-4: Email spam classification.

Technical Deep Dive: How Supervised Learning Models Learn from Labeled Data

Let's go a bit deeper under the hood and explore how supervised learning models actually "learn." The core objective is to find a mathematical function—think of it as a formula—that best approximates the relationship between the *input features* (like the text of a customer support ticket) and the *output labels* ("Technical Issue," "Billing Question," etc.). The model is trying to find the best formula to predict the correct label given the input features.

This "finding the best formula" is achieved through algorithms that minimize the difference between the model's predictions and the *actual* labels in the training data. Remember our customer support agent analogy? Imagine the agent making initial guesses about how to categorize tickets. They'll get some right and some wrong. The "learning" process involves analyzing those mistakes, figuring out *why* they were wrong, and adjusting their internal understanding to make better guesses next time. A supervised learning model does something similar, but in a mathematical way.

Here's a simplified, step-by-step breakdown of the process:

1. **Data Preparation: Setting Up the "Classroom"**

   The labeled dataset is like the textbook and practice exams for our model. We split this dataset into two critical parts. Figure 3-5 visually depicts this split between training and testing data.

   - **Training Set:** This is the primary "study material" the model uses to learn. It's the largest portion of the data.

   - **Testing Set:** This is a "final exam" held back to evaluate how well the model has *generalized* its learning. It contains data the model *hasn't* seen during training. This is critical to ensure the model isn't just memorizing the training data (more on that later).

   Example: For our customer support ticket classification, we might have 10,000 labeled tickets. We might use 8,000 for training and hold back 2,000 for testing.

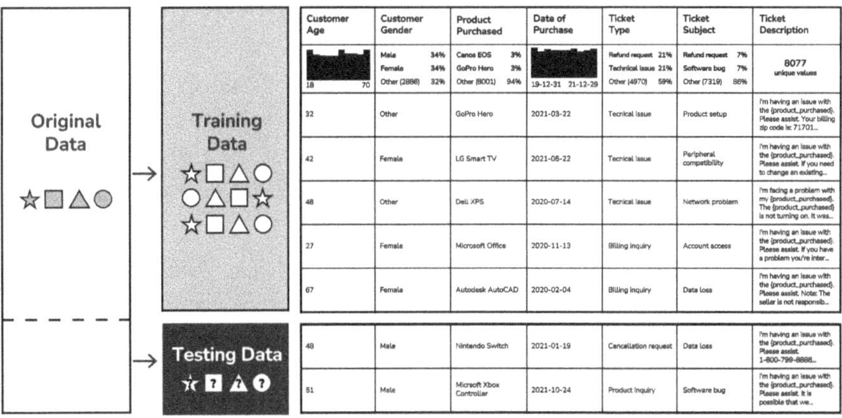

Customer Age	Customer Gender	Product Purchased	Date of Purchase	Ticket Type	Ticket Subject	Ticket Description
18 70	Male 34% Female 34% Other (2886) 32%	Canos EOS 3% GoPro Hero 3% Other (8001) 94%	19-12-31 21-12-29	Refund request 21% Technical issue 21% Other (4970) 59%	Refund request 7% Software bug 7% Other (7319) 86%	8077 unique values
32	Other	GoPro Hero	2021-03-22	Tecnical Issue	Product setup	I'm having an issue with the {product_purchased}. Please assist. Your billing zip code is: 71701...
42	Female	LG Smart TV	2021-05-22	Tecnical Issue	Peripheral compatibility	I'm having an issue with the {product_purchased}. Please assist. If you need to change an existing...
48	Other	Dell XPS	2020-07-14	Tecnical Issue	Network problem	I'm facing a problem with my {product_purchased}. The {product_purchased} is not turning on. It was...
27	Female	Microsoft Office	2020-11-13	Billing inquiry	Account access	I'm having an issue with the {product_purchased}. Please assist. If you have a problem you're inter...
67	Female	Autodesk AutoCAD	2020-02-04	Billing inquiry	Data loss	I'm having an issue with the {product_purchased}. Please assist. Note: The seller is not responsib...
48	Male	Nintendo Switch	2021-01-19	Cancellation request	Data loss	I'm having an issue with the {product_purchased}. Please assist. 1-800-799-8888...
51	Male	Micrsoft Xbox Controller	2021-10-24	Product Inquiry	Software bug	I'm having an issue with the {product_purchased}. Please assist. It is possible that we...

Figure 3-5: An illustration of how a labeled dataset is split into a larger training set for the model to learn from and a smaller testing set to evaluate its performance on unseen data. (*Source*: Kaggle).

2. **Model Selection: Choosing the Right "Learning Style"**
   Just like different students learn best through different methods (visual, auditory, kinesthetic), different Machine Learning algorithms are better suited for different types of data and tasks.

The choice of algorithm depends on whether we're predicting a continuous value (like a customer's lifetime value) or a categorical value (like our ticket types).

Common Algorithms (And When a PM Might Encounter Them):

- **Linear Regression:** Used for predicting *continuous* values. *Think*: predicting the price of a house based on its size, location, and number of bedrooms. Or, predicting how much a customer will spend in the next year.

- **Logistic Regression:** Used for predicting *categorical* values (i.e., which category something belongs to). *Think*: predicting whether a customer will click on an ad (yes/no) or whether a transaction is fraudulent (fraudulent/not fraudulent). Our customer support ticket classification is a good example.

- **Decision Trees:** These create a tree-like structure of decisions to classify data. *Think*: a flowchart that helps determine if a loan application should be approved. They are often easy to interpret. Figure 3-6 shows how a decision tree model branches through a series of feature-based questions to arrive at a prediction.

- **Neural Networks (Including Deep Learning):** These are more complex models, inspired by the human brain, that can learn very intricate patterns. *Think*: image recognition, natural language processing, and other tasks involving complex, unstructured data.

- **Random Forests:** These combine multiple decision trees to improve accuracy and reduce overfitting. *Think*: making a decision by asking a group of experts instead of relying on just one. Used for tasks like customer churn prediction and fraud detection.

- **Gradient Boosting:** A powerful technique that builds models sequentially, with each new model correcting errors made by the previous ones. Often used in winning Kaggle competitions and real-world applications like credit scoring or personalized recommendations.

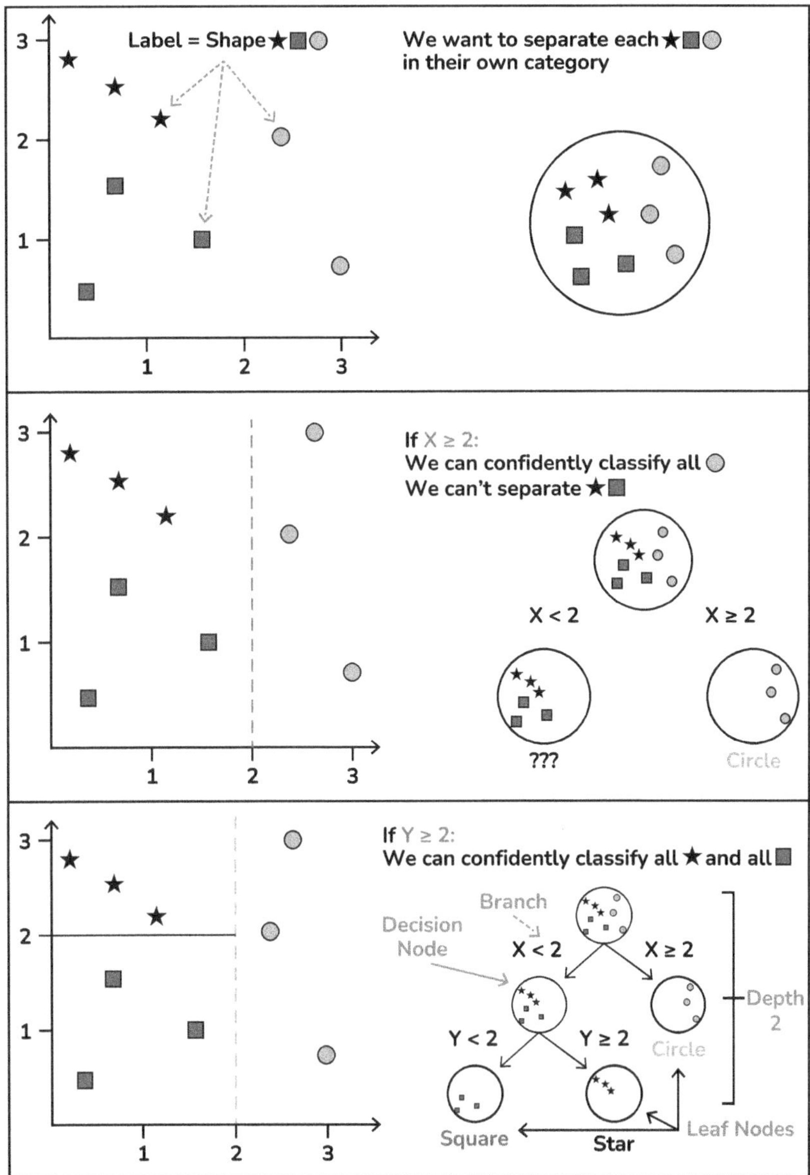

Figure 3-6: An example of how decision trees can solve Machine Learning problems.

3. Model Training: The "Learning" Process

The model training process involves several key components that work together to help the algorithm learn from labeled data and improve its predictions over time.

This is where the magic happens. The algorithm is fed the training data and iteratively adjusts its internal parameters (the "dials and knobs" of the model) to minimize the error between its predictions and the actual labels.

- **Loss Function:** This is a mathematical function that quantifies how "wrong" the model's predictions are. It's like a score-keeper that tells the model how well it's doing. Different algorithms use different loss functions.

- **Optimization Algorithm:** This is the process the model uses to adjust its internal parameters to *minimize* the loss function. Think of it as the model's strategy for studying and improving its performance. A common optimization algorithm is *gradient descent*, which is like rolling a ball downhill to find the lowest point (the minimum loss). A key setting for gradient descent is the learning rate, which you can think of as the size of the steps the model takes as it tries to minimize error. The choice of learning rate has a significant impact on training efficiency, as illustrated in Figure 3-7. If the rate is too low, the model learns very slowly; if it's too high, it can overshoot the optimal point and fail to find the best solution.

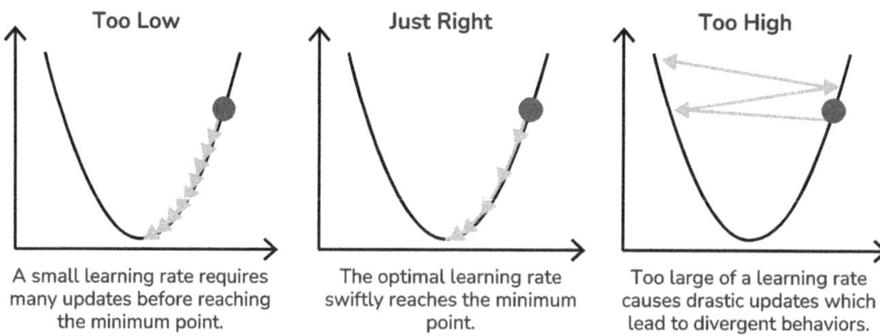

Figure 3-7: An illustration of gradient descent and the impact of the learning rate. The goal is to find the "Just right" learning rate that allows the model to find the point of minimum error efficiently, without taking too many small steps ("Too low") or over-shooting the target ("Too high").

Example: In our customer support ticket scenario, the model might initially predict that a ticket containing the word "password" is a "Billing Question." If the correct label is "Technical Issue," the loss function would indicate an error. The optimization algorithm would then slightly adjust the model's parameters so that it's *more* likely to classify similar tickets as "Technical Issue" in the future.

4. **Model Evaluation: The "Final Exam"**

   Once the model has been trained, we need to see how well it performs on unseen data. This is where the testing set comes in. Understanding the key evaluation metrics is very important for you as a PM to interpret the model's "final exam" score and decide if it's ready for the real world.

   The relationship between how we measure "correct" vs. "incorrect" predictions is best understood using the *confusion matrix*, which gives us the raw counts for every outcome (True Positives, False Positives, False Negatives, and True Negatives). From those counts, we derive more insightful metrics.

   The table below breaks down the most important metrics for a classification problem.

METRIC	KEY QUESTION IT ANSWERS	PM IMPLICATION AND WHEN TO PRIORITIZE
Accuracy	"Overall, what percentage of predictions did the model get right?"	A good high-level summary, but it can be misleading if your data is imbalanced (e.g., 99% of transactions are not fraud).
Precision	"Of all the times the model predicted 'positive,' how often was it correct?"	Prioritize this when the cost of a **False Positive** is high. You want to avoid bothering users or creating unnecessary work (e.g., flagging a legitimate email as spam).
Recall	"Of all the actual 'positive' cases, how many did the model find?"	Prioritize this when the cost of a **False Negative** is high. You want to avoid missing important events (e.g., failing to detect a fraudulent transaction or a medical disease).
F1-Score	"What is the balanced score between Precision and Recall?"	Use this when both False Positives and False Negatives have significant costs, and you need a single metric that represents the balance between them.

As table shows, there is often a trade-off between Precision and Recall. A high-precision spam filter might miss some spam, but it rarely bothers you with false alarms. A high-recall fraud detection system will catch almost every fraudulent case but might occasionally flag a legitimate purchase. As a PM, you must decide which trade-off is more acceptable for your users and business goals.

5. **Model Deployment: Putting the Model to Work**

   Once the model meets the desired performance criteria on the testing set, it can be deployed to make predictions on new, real-world data. This is where the model starts providing value to your product.

Critical Considerations for Product Managers

Understanding the mechanics of supervised learning is important, but knowing where projects can go wrong is essential for a Product Manager. These aren't just technical problems for the data science team to solve; they are fundamental product risks that can impact your timeline, budget, and the user experience. By keeping the following critical considerations on your radar, you can ask smarter questions, anticipate roadblocks, and guide your team more effectively.

- **Data Quality and Quantity:** The effectiveness of supervised learning hinges on the quality and quantity of the training data. A diverse, representative, and accurately labeled dataset is *essential* for building a robust and accurate model. Garbage in, garbage out!

- **Labeled Data Challenges:** Obtaining labeled data can be a significant bottleneck. It often requires human expertise and manual effort, which can be time-consuming and expensive. Consider strategies like active learning (where the model helps identify the most informative data points to label) or leveraging existing data sources.

- **Overfitting:** This is a critical pitfall. Overfitting occurs when the model memorizes the training data *too well*, including its noise and idiosyncrasies, rather than learning the underlying generalizable patterns. An overfit model performs well on the training data but poorly on the testing data (and in the real world). Techniques like *regularization* and *cross-validation* are used to combat overfitting.

- **Underfitting:** This occurs when a model is too simple to capture the complexity present in the data.

- **Bias:** If the training data reflects existing biases (e.g., underrepresentation of certain demographics), the model will likely inherit and amplify those biases, leading to unfair or discriminatory outcomes. This is a critical ethical consideration.

Unsupervised Learning: Discovering Hidden Patterns in Your Data

Let's shift gears from the structured world of supervised learning to a more exploratory approach: *Unsupervised Learning*. Think of it like this: instead of training a customer support agent with labeled tickets (supervised learning), you're now giving a market researcher a massive dataset of customer purchase histories *without* any predefined categories. You're asking them to find interesting patterns, groupings, or insights—*without* telling them what to look for. This is the essence of unsupervised learning.

In unsupervised learning, we're dealing with *unlabeled data*. There are no "right answers" provided to the model. Instead, the model's task is to explore the data and uncover hidden structures, relationships, and patterns *on its own*. It's like sifting through raw data to find the hidden gems.

Why is this valuable? Because often, we *don't know* what patterns exist in our data. We might have a hunch, but unsupervised learning can reveal surprising insights that we would never have discovered otherwise. It's a powerful tool for:

- **Customer Segmentation:** Dividing your customer base into distinct groups based on their behavior, demographics, or other characteristics. This allows for more targeted marketing campaigns and personalized product experiences. For example, an unsupervised learning model might reveal a group of "high-value, early-adopter" customers that you weren't even aware of.

- **Anomaly Detection:** Identifying unusual data points that deviate significantly from the norm. This is critical for fraud detection, network intrusion detection, and identifying manufacturing defects. Imagine spotting a single unusual transaction pattern among millions of legitimate ones.

- **Recommendation Systems (In Some Cases):** While many recommendation systems use supervised learning, some approaches leverage unsupervised learning to find similarities between items or users. For example, grouping similar products together based on their descriptions or features.

- **Data Compression and Dimensionality Reduction:** Simplifying complex datasets by reducing the number of variables while preserving important information. This can make data visualization and analysis easier.

- **Topic Extraction:** Identifying the main topics or themes present in a collection of text documents. For example, analyzing customer reviews to understand the most common complaints or praise.

Imagine you have a massive dataset of website activity—page views, clicks, time spent on each page, etc. You *don't* have labels telling you what each user was trying to achieve. An unsupervised learning algorithm could be used to:

- **Group Users with Similar Browsing Patterns:** This might reveal segments like "researchers" (who spend a lot of time on in-depth content), "casual browsers" (who skim through many pages quickly), and "potential buyers" (who focus on product pages and pricing information).

- **Identify Unusual User Behavior:** This could flag potentially fraudulent activity or identify users who are having trouble navigating your website.

Figure 3-8 illustrates the process of using an unsupervised model to discover distinct user groups and identify outliers from raw data.

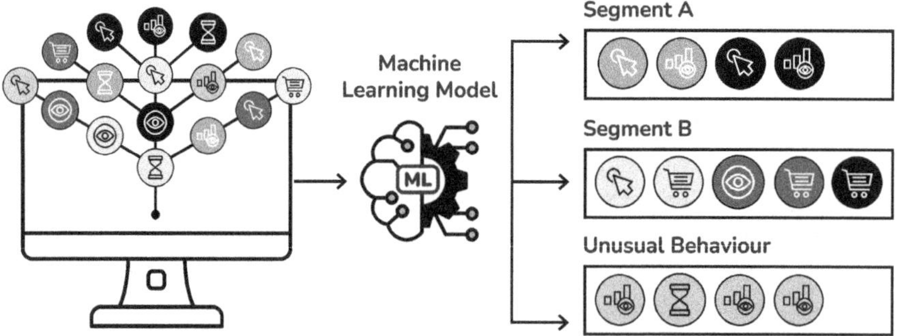

Figure 3-8: An example of unsupervised learning in action. An ML model processes various unlabeled user activity data points (clicks, page views, time spent) to automatically discover distinct user segments and identify anomalous or unusual behavior.

Unsupervised learning is like having a data detective on your team, uncovering hidden clues and revealing unexpected insights that can drive better product decisions and improve user experiences. It allows us to explore data, to ask open questions, and let the data speak, to a certain extent.

Technical Deep Dive: How Unsupervised Learning Models Discover Patterns

Let's delve into the mechanics of how unsupervised learning models uncover those hidden patterns we've been discussing. Unlike supervised learning, there's no "answer key" or "teacher." The models must rely on the inherent structure of the data itself. The core principle is to measure the *similarity* or *dissimilarity* between data points. Think of it like grouping similar objects together based on their characteristics, without knowing beforehand what those groups should be.

Here's a simplified, step-by-step breakdown:

1. **Data Preparation: Getting the Data Ready**

   The unlabeled dataset is prepared and preprocessed. This might involve:

   - **Cleaning the Data:** Handling missing values and outliers.

   - **Scaling or Normalizing Features:** Ensuring that all features are on a comparable scale (e.g., preventing a feature measured in thousands from dominating a feature measured in units).

   - **Feature Engineering:** Creating new features from existing ones that might be more informative for the model.

   Example: For our website activity data, this might involve removing incomplete user sessions, scaling the "time spent on page" variable, and creating a new feature like "engagement score" (combining clicks, scrolls, and time spent).

2. **Algorithm Selection: Choosing the Right Tool for the Job**

   The choice of algorithm depends on the type of patterns you're hoping to find and the nature of your data.

   - **Clustering Algorithms:** These group data points into clusters based on their similarity.

     - **K-Means Clustering:** You specify the number of clusters (k) you want to find. The algorithm then iteratively assigns data points to the nearest cluster centroid (the "center" of the cluster).

Example: Segmenting customers into k groups based on their purchase history. A PM might use this to create targeted marketing campaigns for each segment.

- **Hierarchical Clustering:** This builds a hierarchy of clusters, starting with each data point as its own cluster and progressively merging them based on similarity. *Example:* Grouping products based on customer reviews, revealing relationships between products that might not be immediately obvious.

- **Dimensionality Reduction Algorithms:** These reduce the number of variables in a dataset while preserving important information.

  - **Principal Component Analysis (PCA):** Transforms the data into a new set of uncorrelated variables (principal components) that capture the most variance in the data. **Example:** Reducing the number of features used to describe a product (e.g., size, color, material, price) to a smaller set of "principal components" that still capture most of the product's key characteristics. This can be useful for visualization or as input to another model.

  - **t-distributed Stochastic Neighbor Embedding (t-SNE):** Focuses on preserving local distances between data points, making it particularly useful for visualizing high-dimensional data in 2D or 3D. **Example:** Visualizing customer segments on a scatter plot to see how they relate to each other.

  - **Association Rule Mining:** **Example:** find relationships between items in shopping baskets (e.g., "customers who buy diapers also tend to buy baby wipes").

3. **Pattern Discovery: Finding the "Aha!" Moments**
   The chosen algorithm analyzes the data and identifies patterns based on mathematical measures of similarity or dissimilarity.

   - **Clustering Example (K-Means):** The algorithm might calculate the Euclidean distance (straight-line distance) between data points in the feature space. Figure 3-9 illustrates how this process works by showing how data points are grouped into clusters using K-Means. Data points that are close together are grouped into the same cluster.

- **Dimensionality Reduction Example (PCA):** The algorithm finds the directions in the feature space that capture the most variance in the data. These directions become the new "principal components."

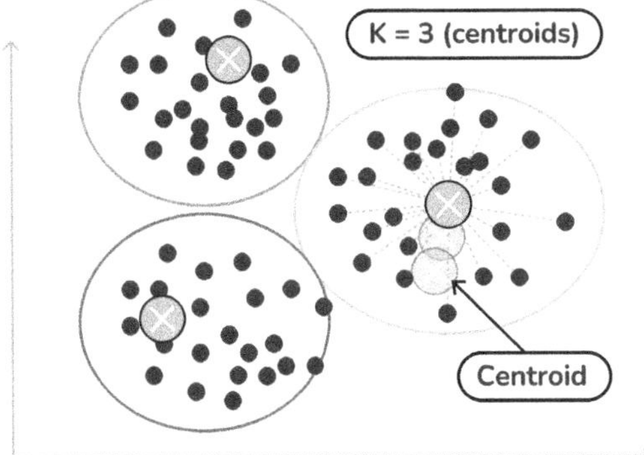

Figure 3-9: How K-Means clustering solves unsupervised ML problems.

4. **Result Interpretation: Making Sense of the Patterns**

   This is where the human element comes back in. The discovered patterns need to be interpreted and evaluated to determine their relevance and usefulness. This often involves:

   - **Visualization:** Creating charts and graphs to visualize the clusters, the reduced dimensions, or the association rules.

   - **Domain Expertise:** Applying your knowledge of the product and the users to understand the meaning of the patterns.

   - **Iteration:** Experimenting with different algorithms and parameters to refine the results.

5. **Application: Turning Insights into Action**

   The discovered patterns are applied to solve the target problem. This might involve:

   - Creating targeted marketing campaigns for different customer segments.

   - Developing new product features based on identified user needs. Figure 3-10 shows how the output of K-Means clustering—initially unlabeled data—can be grouped into meaningful clusters, which are then used to inform business decisions and downstream tasks.

- Improving fraud detection systems by identifying anomalous patterns.

- Personalizing the user experience based on discovered user preferences.

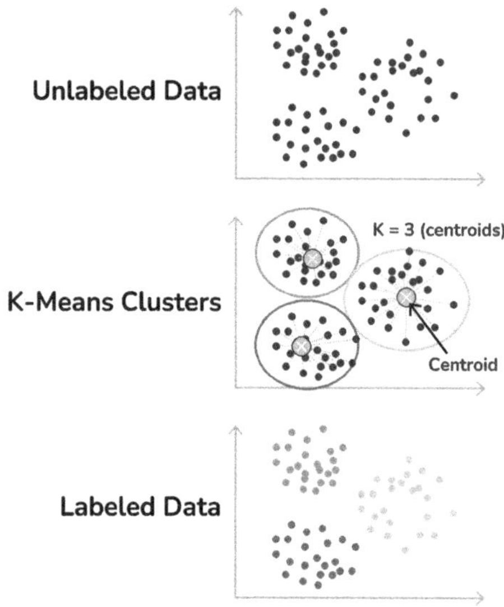

Figure 3-10: K-means clustering example.

Critical Considerations for Product Managers

As a Product Manager working with unsupervised learning, it's important to be aware of several practical challenges and trade-offs that can affect your product's success.

- **No "Right Answer":** Unlike supervised learning, there's no single "correct" answer to compare against in unsupervised learning. Evaluating the results often relies on subjective judgment and domain expertise.

- **Algorithm and Parameter Sensitivity:** The effectiveness of unsupervised learning algorithms can be sensitive to the choice of algorithm and the tuning of its parameters. Experimentation is key.

- **Data Quality Still Matters:** Even though there are no labels, data quality is still critical. Noisy or irrelevant data can lead to misleading patterns.

- **Interpretability:** Some unsupervised learning techniques (like deep learning-based methods) can be difficult to interpret. As a PM, prioritize interpretability when possible, as it will help you understand *why* the model is making certain decisions.

- **Combining with Supervised Learning:** Unsupervised learning is often *not* used in isolation. A common approach is to use unsupervised learning to discover patterns and then use those patterns as input to a supervised learning model. For example, you might use clustering to segment customers and then build a separate supervised learning model to predict churn for *each* segment.

Reinforcement Learning: Learning Through Trial and Error

Let's move on to a fascinating and increasingly important area of Machine Learning: *Reinforcement Learning (RL)*. Think of it like training a puppy. You don't give the puppy a detailed instruction manual on how to sit, stay, or fetch. Instead, you use a system of rewards (treats, praise) and penalties (a gentle "no" or withholding the treat). The puppy tries different actions, observes the consequences, and gradually learns which actions lead to positive outcomes. This is, at its heart, how reinforcement learning works.

Instead of labeled data (supervised learning) or unlabeled data (unsupervised learning), reinforcement learning uses *interaction with an environment*. Figure 3-11 illustrates this concept using a playful analogy—a dog navigating to find rewards (treats) and avoid penalties (like a bath)—to represent how an agent learns optimal behavior through trial and error. We have an "agent" (like our puppy) that takes actions within an "environment" (like your living room) and receives feedback in the form of rewards or penalties. The agent's goal is to learn the best sequence of actions—a *policy*—to maximize its cumulative reward over time. It's all about learning through trial and error, just like that puppy learning to fetch.

Reinforcement learning is particularly well-suited for problems where:

- There's a clear goal or objective.

- The agent needs to make a sequence of decisions, not just a single one.

- The environment is dynamic and potentially uncertain.

- There's a way to provide feedback (rewards and penalties) to the agent.

This makes it a powerful tool for a growing range of applications, including:

- **Game Playing:** This is where RL has seen some of its most impressive successes, with models learning to play games like Go, Chess, and Atari games at superhuman levels.

- **Robotics:** Training robots to perform complex tasks, like walking, grasping objects, or navigating environments.

- **Autonomous Driving:** Teaching self-driving cars to make decisions in real-time, such as lane changes, speed adjustments, and obstacle avoidance.

- **Resource Management:** Optimizing the allocation of resources in complex systems, such as data centers, energy grids, or supply chains. *Think*: dynamically adjusting server allocation to handle fluctuating website traffic.

- **Personalized Recommendations (In Some Cases):** Framing recommendations as a sequential decision-making process, where the system learns to recommend items that maximize user engagement over time.

- **Personalized Notifications:** Optimizing when and how to send notifications, learning what is the best timing.

Imagine you're developing a mobile game. You could use reinforcement learning to train an AI opponent that adapts to the player's skill level and provides a challenging but not frustrating experience. The AI agent would learn through playing the game repeatedly, receiving rewards for winning and penalties for losing. Over time, it would develop a strategy to maximize its chances of winning.

Or, consider a website that wants to optimize the placement of ads. An RL agent could learn to place ads in different locations on the page, receiving rewards for clicks and penalties for ignoring the ads. The agent would learn over time which placements are most effective for different users and different types of content.

Reinforcement learning is about creating agents that can learn to make intelligent decisions in complex, dynamic environments. It's a powerful paradigm that's driving innovation in many areas of product development.

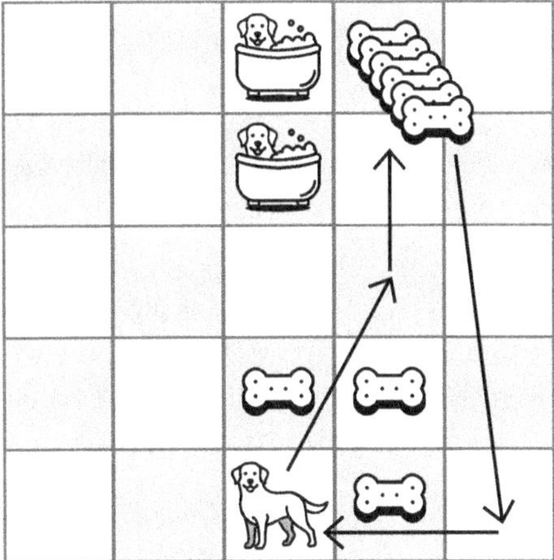

Figure 3-11: With reinforcement learning, we want our Agent (dog) to find the reward (treats) and not the bath!

Technical Deep Dive: How Reinforcement Learning Agents Learn Optimal Policies

Reinforcement learning, at its core, is about an *agent* interacting with an *environment* to learn a *policy*—a strategy—that maximizes its cumulative *reward* over time. This is achieved through algorithms that estimate the "value" of taking a particular action in a given state. It's a bit like learning to play a game by trial and error, keeping track of which moves lead to good outcomes and which lead to bad ones. Figure 3-12 shows how the dog (agent) moves through different states, takes actions, and receives rewards, illustrating how reinforcement learning agents interact with their environment.

Let's break down the key components, using the analogy of training a puppy (our agent) to fetch a ball (the goal):

- **Environment:** This is the world the agent interacts with. In our puppy example, it's the physical space where the puppy is playing, including the ball, the owner, and any obstacles. In a game, it would be the game board, the rules, and the opponent.

- **Agent:** This is the learner and decision-maker. In our example, it's the puppy. In a self-driving car, it would be the car's control system.

- **State (S):** This is a snapshot of the environment at a particular point in time. For the puppy, it might be the puppy's location, the ball's location, and whether the owner is holding the ball. For a chess-playing agent, it would be the position of all the pieces on the board.

- **Action (A):** This is a choice the agent can make. For the puppy, it might be "run forward," "turn left," "bark," "jump," or "pick up ball." For a website optimizing ad placement, it might be "place ad A in slot 1," "place ad B in slot 2," etc.

- **Reward (R):** This is feedback from the environment. For the puppy, a reward might be a treat or praise when it gets closer to the ball or brings it back. A penalty might be a gentle "no" when it runs away. For a game-playing agent, the reward might be winning the game, and the penalty might be losing.

- **Policy (π):** This is the agent's strategy—a mapping from states to actions. It tells the agent what action to take in each state. The goal of RL is to learn the *optimal* policy, the one that maximizes the cumulative reward.

- **Value Function (V or Q):**

  - **V(s):** The value of a state is the expected cumulative reward the agent can achieve starting from that state and following a particular policy.

  - **Q(s, a):** The Q-value (or action-value) is the expected cumulative reward the agent can achieve starting from a given state, taking a specific action, and then following a particular policy. This is important because it tells the agent not just how good a state is, but how good a specific action is in that state.

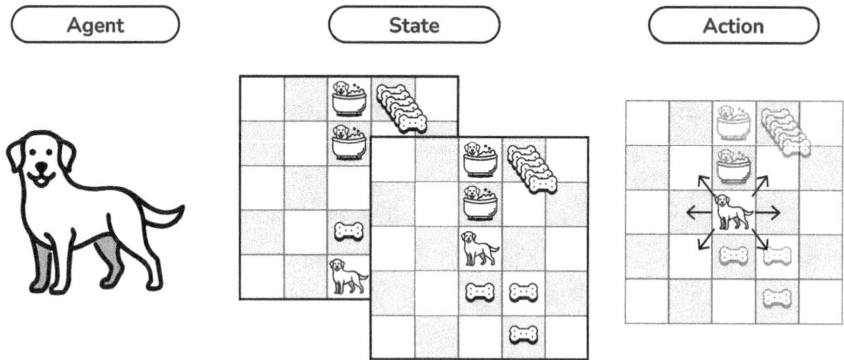

Figure 3-12: An example of Agent(dog) State (where the dog is located), Reward (Treats) and Action (where the dog can move).

The Learning Process: Exploration, Exploitation, and Q-Learning

The agent learns through a cycle of:

1. **Exploration:** Trying out different actions in different states to see what happens. This is like the puppy experimenting with different behaviors to see which ones lead to treats. It's important to explore to discover new and potentially better strategies. Figure 3-13 illustrates the trade-off between exploration (trying new actions) and exploitation (repeating known successful actions), a fundamental challenge in reinforcement learning.

2. **Exploitation:** Choosing the actions that are believed to be best, based on the current knowledge (the current estimates of Q-values). This is like the puppy repeating the actions that have led to treats in the past.

3. **Updating Value Estimates:** After each action and reward, the agent updates its estimates of the value function (V) or the Q-values (Q). A common algorithm for this is *Q-learning*.

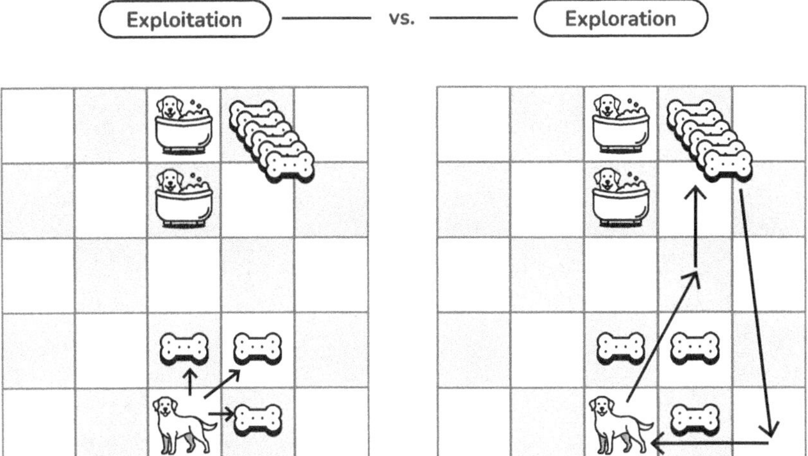

Figure 3-13: Exploitation vs. exploration example.

Q-learning is an algorithm that learns the optimal Q-values. Here's the basic idea:

1. The agent starts with an initial guess for the Q-values (often all zeros).

2. It takes an action in a state, observes the reward and the next state.

3. It updates the Q-value for the previous state and action using the following update rule (simplified):

New Q(s, a) = Old Q(s, a) + Learning Rate * (Reward + Discount Factor * Max Q(s', a') - Old Q(s, a))

Let's break that down:

- **s:** The previous state.

- **a:** The action taken in the previous state.

- **s':** The new state.

- **a':** All possible actions in the new state.

- **Learning Rate:** Controls how much the Q-value is updated based on each new experience.

- **Discount Factor:** A value between 0 and 1 that determines how much the agent cares about future rewards compared to immediate rewards. A higher discount factor means the agent values long-term rewards more.

- **Max Q(s', a'):** Looks at all available actions (a') in the new state and chooses the highest Q-value.

The update rule essentially says: "Adjust the old Q-value based on the immediate reward received *plus* the estimated value of the best possible action in the next state, discounted by how much we care about future rewards."

Over time, through repeated exploration and updates, the Q-values converge to their optimal values, representing the best possible policy (Figure 3-14).

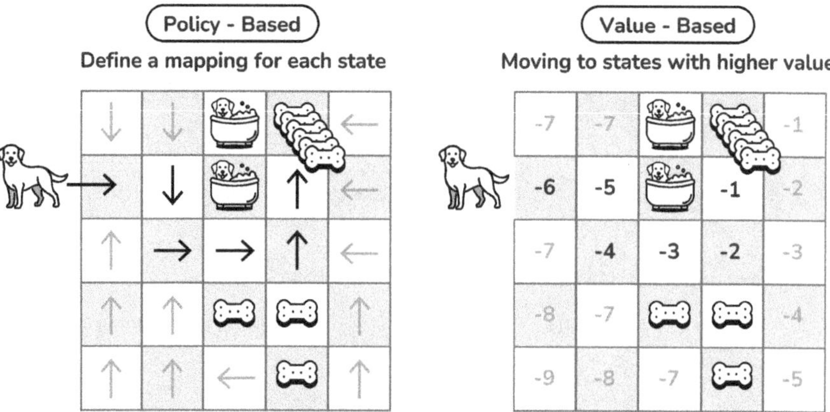

Figure 3-14: Policy is like the agent's brain and dictates what action to take given the state the agent is in. Two ways to find the optimal policy: policy-based and value-based.

Critical Considerations for Product Managers

While reinforcement learning can unlock powerful capabilities, it also introduces unique challenges for product teams. As a PM, you need to be aware of the key risks and design considerations that come with deploying RL in real-world environments.

- **Reward Function Design:** This is *very important.* The reward function defines what the agent is trying to achieve. A poorly designed reward function can lead to unexpected and undesirable behavior. For example, if you reward a robot for moving forward, it might just learn to run in circles! You need to carefully consider the long-term consequences of the reward function.

- **Exploration–Exploitation Trade-Off:** The agent needs to balance exploring new actions (to discover potentially better strategies) with exploiting its current knowledge (to maximize immediate rewards). This is a fundamental challenge in RL.

- **Computational Cost:** Training RL agents can be computationally expensive and time-consuming, especially in complex environments.

- **Safety:** In real-world applications like robotics or autonomous driving, safety is paramount. Ensuring that the agent explores safely and doesn't take actions that could lead to harm is very important.

- **Simulators:** Often, RL agents are trained in simulators before being deployed in the real world. This allows for safe and efficient exploration.

Generative AI: Powering a New Era of Language-Based Applications

We've explored Machine Learning models that predict, classify, and find patterns. Now, we enter a different realm: *Generative AI*, and specifically, *large language models (LLMs)*. These models don't just analyze data; they *create* it. Think of an LLM not as a simple program, but as a sophisticated statistical parrot that has read the entire Internet (and more!). It has absorbed the patterns, structures, and styles of human language to such an extent that it can generate new text that is often indistinguishable from human-written content.

While the "parrot" analogy is helpful, it's also important to remember that LLMs don't "understand" in the human sense. They are incredibly powerful pattern-matching and prediction machines. Given a prompt—a starting piece of text—an LLM can predict the most likely continuation, based on its vast training data. This ability to generate coherent, contextually relevant text is revolutionizing a wide range of applications.

LLMs are more than just fancy text generators. They are becoming foundational components of many products, enabling capabilities like:

- **Intelligent Chatbots and Virtual Assistants:** Creating more natural and engaging conversational experiences. *Think*: customer support bots that can actually understand complex questions and provide helpful answers, not just canned responses.

- **Content Creation and Augmentation:** Assisting writers with drafting articles, generating marketing copy, creating personalized email campaigns, and even writing different kinds of creative content.

- **Code Generation:** Translating natural language descriptions of desired functionality into working code, significantly speeding up the software development process.

- **Data Analysis and Summarization:** Extracting key insights from large text datasets, summarizing lengthy documents, and answering questions about data.

- **Language Translation:** Providing more accurate and nuanced translations between languages.

- **Personalized Learning:** Adapting educational content to individual student needs and learning styles.

- **Accessibility Tools:** Generating descriptions of images for visually impaired users or creating transcripts of audio content.

Imagine a Product Manager using an LLM to:

- **Generate Multiple Variations of ad Copy:** Quickly create different versions of an ad headline and body text, testing which ones resonate best with the target audience.

- **Draft Responses to Common Customer Inquiries:** Automate the creation of personalized and helpful responses to frequently asked questions, freeing up customer support agents to handle more complex issues.

- **Summarize Customer Feedback from Surveys and Reviews:** Quickly identify the key themes and sentiments expressed in large volumes of text data.

- **Create Product Documentation:** Generate initial drafts of user manuals, FAQs, and other documentation based on product specifications.

- **Analyze Competitor's Product Descriptions:** Get insights on how your messaging can be better and more effective.

LLMs are not a magic bullet, and they have limitations (which we'll discuss later). However, their ability to understand and generate human language opens up a vast array of possibilities for product innovation. They represent a fundamental shift in how we interact with computers and how we build software.

Technical Deep Dive: How LLMs Understand and Generate Language

At the heart of most modern LLMs lies the *transformer architecture*, a type of neural network specifically designed to handle sequential data like text. These models don't "understand" language in the way humans do. Instead, they operate on the principle of *statistical pattern-matching and prediction*. They learn to predict the most likely next word in a sequence, given the context of the preceding words. This seemingly simple mechanism, when scaled up to massive models and trained on colossal datasets, produces remarkably human-like text.

Here's a simplified breakdown of the key components and processes:

1. **Tokenization: Breaking Down Text into Units**

   Before an LLM can process text, it needs to break it down into smaller units called *tokens*. These tokens can be words, subwords (parts of words), or even individual characters.

   Example: The sentence "The quick brown fox jumps" might be tokenized as: ["The," "quick," "brown," "fox," "jumps"]. Or, using subword tokenization, it might become: ["The," "quick," "brown," "fox," "jump," "s"].

   The choice of tokenization method affects how the model handles rare words and variations in spelling. Figure 3-15 illustrates how raw text is converted into tokens and then transformed into numerical embeddings that the model can understand.

2. **Embedding: Converting Tokens to Numbers**

   LLMs can't directly process text; they work with numbers. *Embeddings* are numerical representations of tokens. Each token is mapped to a high-dimensional vector (a list of numbers) that captures its semantic meaning (or at least, its statistical relationships with other tokens).

   Example: The word "king" might be represented by a vector like [0.2, **-0.5, 0.9**, ..., 0.1]. The word "queen" might have a similar vector like [0.2, **-0.4, 0.8**, ..., 0.1], reflecting their semantic relationship. Words with very different meanings would have very different vectors.

   These embeddings are learned during the training process.

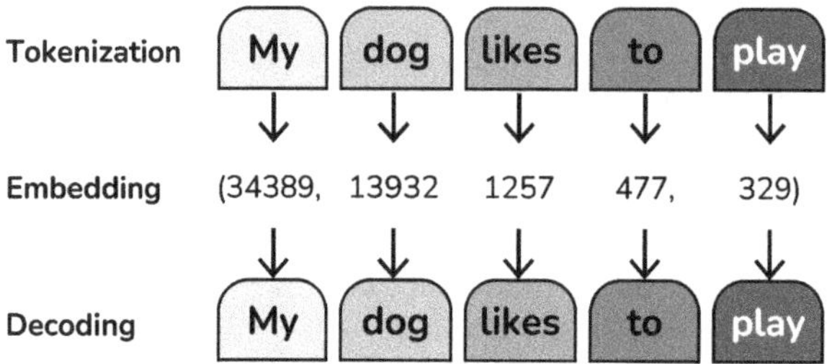

Figure 3-15: Example of tokenization and embedding.

3. **Transformer Layers: The Engine of Contextual Understanding**

   The core of an LLM is a stack of *transformer layers*. Each layer processes the embeddings, taking into account the relationships between *all* the tokens in the sequence. This is where the magic of "contextual understanding" happens.

   The key innovation of the transformer architecture is the *attention mechanism*. This allows the model to weigh the importance of different words in the context when processing a particular word.

   Example: In the sentence "The bank can be a great place to relax if it has benches, but you should not try to deposit money in a river bank," the word "bank" has two very different meanings. The attention mechanism allows the model to focus on the surrounding words ("river" vs. "deposit money") to determine the correct meaning in each case.

Each transformer layer consists of multiple *attention heads*, each of which can learn to focus on different aspects of the context. The output of each transformer layer is a new set of embeddings that incorporate the contextual information.

4. **Prediction: Guessing the Next Word**

   After the embeddings have passed through all the transformer layers, the model makes a prediction about the *next token* in the sequence. It does this by calculating a probability distribution over all the possible tokens in its vocabulary.

   Example: Given the input "The quick brown fox jumps," the model might predict that the next token is "over" with a high probability, "under" with a lower probability, and "the" with a very low probability. Figure 3-16 visualizes this process by showing how the model generates a probability distribution over possible next words.

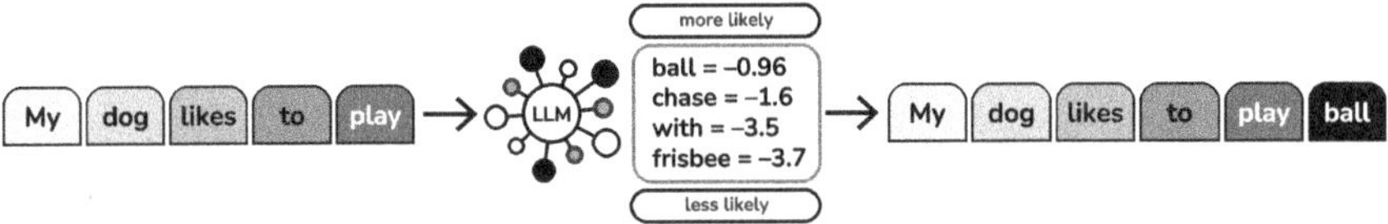

Figure 3-16: Example of an LLM guessing the next word.

5. **Generation: Creating New Text**

   To generate new text, the model starts with a *prompt* (an initial piece of text). It predicts the next token, adds that token to the sequence, and then uses the updated sequence to predict the *next* token, and so on. This is an *autoregressive* process.

   There are different ways to choose the next token from the probability distribution. Figure 3-17 illustrates common decoding strategies—like Greedy Search and Top-K or Nucleus Sampling—used to control the diversity and coherence of generated text.

   - **Greedy Decoding:** Always choose the token with the highest probability. This can lead to repetitive and predictable text.

   - **Temperature Sampling:** Adjusts the probability distribution to make it more or less random. A higher temperature makes the output more diverse but potentially less coherent. A lower temperature makes the output more predictable but potentially more repetitive.

- **Top-K Sampling:** Only considers the *k* most likely tokens.

- **Nucleus (Top-P) Sampling:** Only considers the tokens that make up a certain cumulative probability (e.g., the top 90 percent).

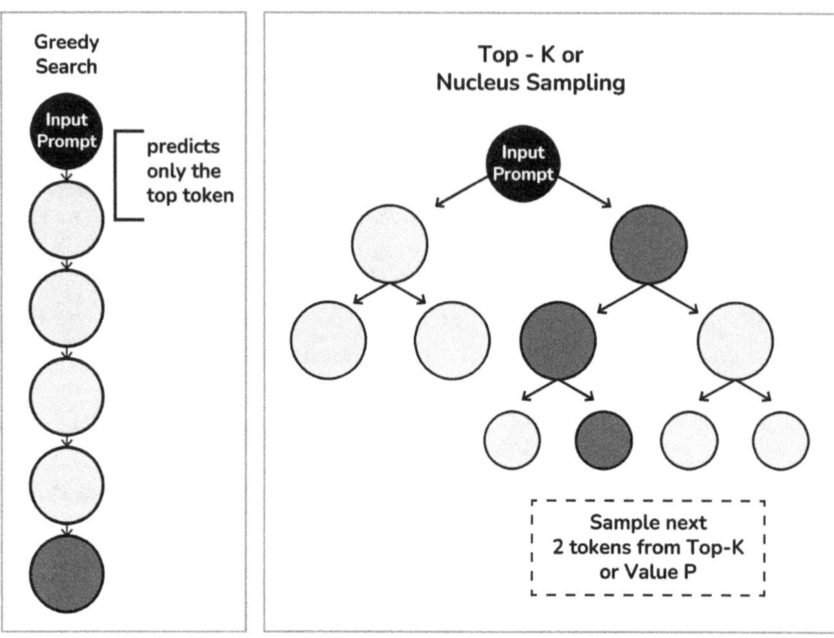

Figure 3-17: Decoding sample strategies for LLMs.

6. **Training.**

   The model is trained by feeding it massive amounts of texts and having it predict the next token. It is a simple, yet very effective, method.

Critical Considerations for Product Managers

While you don't need to become a deep learning expert, understanding the following core concepts will empower you to collaborate more effectively with your technical team and make smarter product decisions when working with LLMs:

- **Transformer Architecture:** Understanding the basic concept of the transformer and the attention mechanism is key for appreciating how LLMs work.

- **Tokenization and Embeddings:** These are fundamental concepts that affect how the model processes and understands language.

- **Autoregressive Generation:** Knowing that LLMs generate text token by token is important for understanding their limitations and potential for errors.

- **Sampling Methods:** Understanding the different sampling methods (greedy, temperature, top-k, top-p) allows you to discuss with your team how to control the creativity and coherence of the generated text.

- **Computational Cost:** Training LLMs require a huge amount of computational resources.

The "Gotchas": A PM's Guide to LLM Limitations and Risks

While the capabilities of LLMs are transformative, they are not without significant challenges. Understanding their inherent limitations is one of the most critical responsibilities of an AI Product Manager. These aren't just technical edge cases; they are fundamental characteristics that will directly impact your product's design, user experience, and potential risks.

By proactively identifying these "gotchas," you can make smarter strategic decisions, mitigate risks before they become major problems, and build more robust and trustworthy AI-powered products. Here are the most important limitations to be aware of:

- **Hallucinations and Factual Inaccuracies:** This is arguably the biggest challenge with LLMs. They can generate text that is fluent, grammatically correct, and seemingly plausible, but *factually incorrect* or completely fabricated. LLMs don't "know" things in the way humans do; they don't have a knowledge base or a connection to reality. They are simply predicting the most likely sequence of words based on their training data.

  - **PM Implication:** Never rely on an LLM for factual accuracy without independent verification. This is especially very important in applications involving health, finance, or legal information. Consider implementing fact-checking mechanisms or providing disclaimers.

- **Bias and Toxicity:** LLMs are trained on massive datasets scraped from the Internet, which inevitably contain biases, stereotypes, and toxic language. As a result, LLMs can reflect and amplify these biases in their generated text, producing outputs that are discriminatory, offensive, or harmful.

- **PM Implication:** Carefully evaluate the potential for bias in your use case. Implement mitigation strategies, such as filtering training data, using techniques to debias the model, and monitoring outputs for harmful content. Consider the ethical implications *before* deployment.

- **Lack of Real-World Understanding:** LLMs have no sensory input, no common sense, and no lived experience. They operate solely on text data. This limits their ability to reason about the physical world, understand cause and effect, or make judgments that require real-world knowledge.

- **PM Implication:** Be wary of using LLMs for tasks that require deep understanding of the physical world, human emotions, or complex social dynamics. They are best suited for tasks that can be accomplished primarily through language manipulation.

- **Contextual Limitations and "Forgetting":** While LLMs can handle relatively long sequences of text, their ability to maintain context over extended conversations or documents is still limited. They may "forget" earlier parts of a conversation or struggle to maintain consistency in a long piece of generated text.

- **PM Implication:** For applications requiring long-term memory or complex reasoning across multiple interactions, consider incorporating mechanisms to track context and ensure consistency.

- **Explainability and Transparency:** LLMs are often described as "black boxes." It can be very difficult to understand *why* a model generated a particular output. This lack of transparency makes it challenging to debug errors, identify biases, or build trust with users.

- **PM Implication:** Prioritize explainability where possible. Consider using techniques that provide some insight into the model's decision-making process. Be transparent with users about the use of LLMs and their limitations.

- **Prompt Sensitivity:** LLMs can be surprisingly sensitive to the way a prompt is phrased. Small changes in wording can lead to dramatically different outputs. This requires careful *prompt engineering*—the art of crafting prompts that elicit the desired results.

- **PM Implication:** Invest time in prompt engineering and testing. Treat prompt design as an iterative process. Be aware that seemingly minor changes to a prompt can have significant consequences.

- **Data Dependence:** LLM models require a vast amount of data to be trained. Deficiencies in the training data can cause a lot of problems to the model.

  - **PM Implication:** The data used in the model must cover most (if not all) of the scenarios intended for the use of the LLM.

- **Over-Reliance and Deskilling:** There's a risk that over-reliance on LLMs could lead to a decline in human skills, such as writing, critical thinking, and problem-solving.

  - **PM Implication:** Consider the long-term impact on users and society. Design products that *augment* human capabilities rather than replacing them entirely. Encourage critical thinking and validation of LLM outputs.

Understanding these limitations is not about dismissing LLMs; it's about using them responsibly and effectively. By being aware of their weaknesses, Product Managers can make informed decisions about when and how to leverage these powerful tools, mitigating risks and maximizing their potential to create positive impact.

Navigating the Nuances of Generative AI: Understanding GenAI Evaluations—Ensuring Quality and Trust

We've introduced Generative AI as a powerful type of ML that can *create* new content—text, images, code, and more. This opens up incredible possibilities for product innovation, but it also introduces *new challenges*. Unlike traditional software with predictable outputs, Generative AI models can produce outputs that are:

- **Variable:** The same input (prompt) can lead to different outputs.

- **Subjective:** The "quality" of the output is often subjective (e.g., is this generated text well-written? Is this generated image aesthetically pleasing?).

- **Potentially Problematic:** The output might be factually incorrect, biased, nonsensical, or even harmful.

This is where *GenAI Evaluations (GenAI Evals)* become absolutely essential. They are the quality control mechanisms for Generative AI.

What Are GenAI Evaluations (and Why Should PMs Care)?

GenAI Evaluations are a set of processes and methodologies used to assess the quality, accuracy, safety, and reliability of Generative AI models. Think of them as rigorous testing procedures specifically designed for AI that *creates*. They are essential to make sure that this powerful technology is fit for a user.

As a Product Manager, you'll find that making GenAI Evals a core part of your development process is essential for several key reasons:

- **De-Risking Product Launches:** You wouldn't launch a new feature without testing it. GenAI Evals are the equivalent for Generative AI features. They help you identify and mitigate potential problems before they impact users.

- **Ensuring User Trust:** Users need to trust that your AI-powered features are reliable and safe. GenAI Evals provide evidence to support that trust.

- **Meeting Ethical and Legal Obligations:** As we discussed in the "Responsible AI" section, there are ethical and legal imperatives to ensure fairness and avoid harm. GenAI Evals help you meet these obligations.

- **Guiding Model Development:** Evals provide valuable feedback to your data science team, helping them improve the model's performance and address its limitations.

- **Making Informed Decisions:** Evals provide the data you need to make informed decisions about how to best integrate Generative AI into your product.

Key Aspects of GenAI Evaluation

GenAI Evals go beyond simple "accuracy" metrics. They focus on a range of qualities, including:

- **Relevance:** Does the output address the user's need or the prompt's intent? (e.g., If you ask a chatbot for help resetting your password, does it provide relevant instructions?)

- **Coherence:** Is the output logically structured, easy to understand, and internally consistent? (e.g., Does a generated text summary make sense as a whole?)

- **Factual accuracy:** Is the generated information correct and verifiable? (e.g., Does a generated news article contain factual errors or "hallucinations"?)

- **Safety:** Is the output free of harmful, biased, or inappropriate content? (e.g., Does a generated image avoid harmful stereotypes?)

- **Diversity:** Does the model generate a variety of outputs, or does it tend to produce repetitive or predictable results? (e.g., Does a product description generator create diverse descriptions, or are they all very similar?)

- **Creativity (Where Applicable):** For creative tasks, how original and imaginative is the output? (e.g., Is a generated song interesting and engaging?)

- **Bias:** Does the model exhibit any biases in its output (e.g., gender bias, racial bias)? (This connects directly back to our earlier discussion of fairness.)

Note that GenAI Evals are not one-size-fits-all. The specific methods used will depend on:

- **The Type of Model:** Evaluating a text generation model is different from evaluating an image generation model.

- **The Intended Application:** The evaluation criteria for a chatbot will be different from those for a code generation tool.

- **The Potential Risks:** High-stakes applications (e.g., medical advice) require more rigorous evaluation than low-stakes applications.

Why GenAI Evaluations Are Essential for Product Managers

We've established *what* GenAI Evals are. Now, let's focus on *why* they are absolutely essential for Product Managers building products with Generative AI. It's not just about technical details; it's about product success, user trust, and responsible innovation.

Here's the breakdown of *why* you need to prioritize GenAI Evals:

Ensuring Quality and Reliability: Delivering on the Promise

The Problem: Generative AI models are inherently variable. The same prompt can produce different outputs. Some outputs might be excellent, while others might be inaccurate, irrelevant, or nonsensical.

The PM's Challenge: You need to ensure a consistent level of quality and reliability in your product. Users won't tolerate a feature that works well sometimes and fails miserably other times.

The Solution (GenAI Evals):
  Measure Consistency: Evals help you quantify how often the model produces high-quality outputs versus low-quality outputs.
  Identify Weaknesses: Evals pinpoint specific areas where the model struggles (e.g., factual accuracy, handling certain types of prompts).
  Example: A product description generator needs to consistently create accurate and compelling descriptions. Evals would reveal if it sometimes invents features or gets facts wrong.

Mitigating Risks and Harms: Protecting Your Users and Your Brand

The Problem: Generative AI models can produce biased, harmful, or offensive content. They can also "hallucinate" (invent) information, leading to misinformation.

The PM's Challenge: You are responsible for ensuring your product is safe, ethical, and compliant with legal regulations.

The Solution (GenAI Evals):
  Detect Bias: Evals, using specific datasets and metrics, can reveal if the model generates biased outputs (e.g., associating certain professions with specific genders).
  Identify Harmful Content: Evals can flag potentially toxic, offensive, or inappropriate outputs.
  Quantify Hallucinations: Evals can measure how often the model invents facts or provides incorrect information.
  Example: An AI-powered writing assistant needs to be rigorously tested to ensure it doesn't generate biased or offensive content, or make false claims.

Building Trust and Confidence: Delivering a Trustworthy Product

The Problem: Users are increasingly (and rightfully) skeptical of AI. They need to trust that your AI-powered features are reliable and unbiased.

The PM's Challenge: You need to build and maintain user trust.

The Solution (GenAI Evals):
  Demonstrate Capabilities: Evals provide evidence of the model's strengths and capabilities. You can use this data (responsibly) in your product messaging.

Acknowledge Limitations: Be transparent about the model's limitations. Evals help you identify and communicate these limitations honestly.

Example: A financial advice chatbot should clearly state that it provides general information, not personalized financial advice, and that its responses should be verified. This transparency, informed by evals, builds trust.

Guiding Model Development and Improvement: Iterating Towards Success

The Problem: You need to know how to improve your AI model. Guesswork isn't enough.

The PM's Challenge: You need to provide data-driven feedback to your data science team to guide their efforts.

The Solution (GenAI Evals):

Identify Specific Weaknesses: Evals pinpoint the areas where the model needs improvement (e.g., specific types of prompts, particular factual domains).

Measure Progress: Evals allow you to track the model's improvement over time, demonstrating the impact of model updates and refinements.

Prioritize Efforts: Help identify and prioritize next steps for improvements.

Example: If evals show that a summarization model struggles with long, complex documents, the data science team can focus on improving its performance in that area.

Meeting Regulatory and Compliance Requirements: Staying on the Right Side of the Law

The Problem: The legal landscape surrounding AI is evolving rapidly. Regulations are emerging that require organizations to demonstrate the safety and fairness of their AI systems.

The PM's Challenge: You need to ensure your product complies with all relevant regulations.

The Solution (GenAI Evals):

Provide Evidence of Compliance: Evals can provide documented evidence that you've taken steps to mitigate bias, ensure accuracy, and protect user privacy.

Example: A company using an AI-powered hiring tool needs to demonstrate compliance with anti-discrimination laws. GenAI Evals, focused on fairness metrics across protected groups, provide critical evidence.

In short, GenAI Evaluations are not an optional extra; they are *fundamental* to responsible and successful AI product development. They are your tool for ensuring quality, mitigating risks, building trust, and driving continuous improvement.

How GenAI Evaluations Are Conducted: Your Toolkit for Assessing AI-Generated Content

We've established why GenAI Evals are essential. Now, let's explore how they're actually done. As a PM, you typically won't be conducting these evaluations yourself, but you must understand the different approaches to guide your team's strategy.

There are three main approaches—Human Evaluation, Automated Metrics, and Hybrid Approaches. The best strategy often involves choosing a method based on the trade-off between scalability (how quickly you can evaluate a large volume of content) and the ability to capture nuance (subjective qualities like creativity or tone). Figure 3-18 illustrates this trade-off, showing where each evaluation type fits.

Human Evaluation: The Gold Standard (with Caveats)

What it is: Real people evaluate the AI-generated content based on specific criteria. This is often considered the "gold standard," especially for subjective qualities.

Why it's valuable: Humans can assess nuances that automated metrics often miss, such as creativity, common sense, and overall quality of experience.

Types of Human Evaluation:
- **Rating Scales:** Evaluators rate outputs on scales (e.g., 1–5 stars for relevance, 1–7 Likert scale for coherence). *Example:* Rating the helpfulness of a chatbot response.
- **Comparative Evaluation:** Evaluators compare outputs from different models (or from the model vs. human-generated content) and choose the best one.
- **Example:** Comparing two different summaries of a news article and choosing the one that's more accurate and informative.

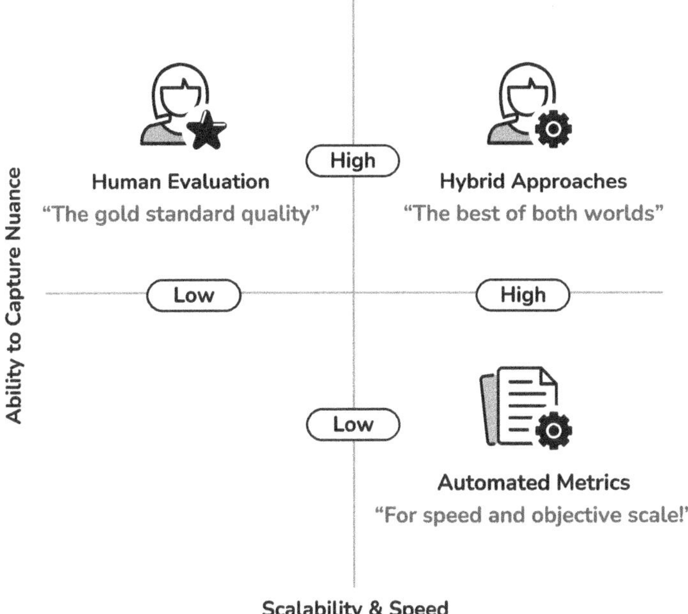

Figure 3-18: A framework for choosing a GenAI evaluation method. The ideal approach depends on the trade-off between the need for scalability and the need to assess subjective, nuanced qualities.

Qualitative Feedback: Evaluators provide written comments and explanations for their ratings. *Example:* Explaining *why* a generated product description is confusing or misleading.

PM's Role:

Define Evaluation Criteria: Work with your team to define *clear, specific, and measurable* criteria for human evaluation. What does "good" look like for this particular feature? This is important for getting consistent results.

Recruit and Train Evaluators: Ensure you have a diverse pool of evaluators who are representative of your target user base. Provide clear instructions and training.

Interpret Results: Understand the limitations of human evaluation (subjectivity, potential bias) and interpret the results in the context of your product goals.

Budget and Timeline: Human evaluation can be time-consuming and costly. Factor this into your project planning.

When to Use: Always. Human evaluation is key to understanding the model.

Automated Metrics: The Fast and Scalable Option

What it is: Algorithms automatically evaluate the AI-generated content based on predefined rules or comparisons to reference data.

Why it's valuable: Fast, scalable, and objective (no human variability). Good for measuring things like fluency, diversity, and (to some extent) factual accuracy.

Common Examples (Simplified):
  Text Generation:
  BLEU/ROUGE: Measure how much the generated text *overlaps* with "reference" (human-written) text. Good for tasks like machine translation or summarization, where there's a "correct" answer. *Think*: How much does the AI's summary match a human-written summary?
  Perplexity: Measures how "surprised" the model is by the text. Lower perplexity generally indicates better fluency. *Think*: How predictable is the generated text, based on what the model has learned?
  Image Generation:
  Inception Score (IS) / Fréchet Inception Distance (FID): Complex metrics that assess the quality and diversity of generated images. *Think:* Do the images look realistic and varied?
  Custom Metrics:
  Often, your data science team will need to create *custom metrics* tailored to your specific product needs. This is where your domain expertise is key to be successful.

PM's Role:
  Understand the Limitations: Recognize that automated metrics are not perfect. They can't fully capture human judgment, especially for subjective qualities.
  Choose Relevant Metrics: Work with your data science team to select metrics that are appropriate for your specific use case.
  Set Thresholds: Define acceptable thresholds for each metric (e.g., "We want a BLEU score of at least X").
  Monitor Trends: Track automated metrics over time to detect any degradation in performance.

When to Use: For all objective, measurable metrics.

Hybrid Approaches: The Best of Both Worlds

What it is: Combining human evaluation and automated metrics to get a more comprehensive and efficient assessment.

Why it's valuable: Leverages the strengths of both approaches: human judgment for nuance and subjectivity, automated metrics for speed and scale.

Common Examples:
- **Automated Pre-Screening:** Use automated metrics to filter out low-quality outputs, so human evaluators can focus on the more challenging cases.
- **Active Learning:** Use automated metrics to identify the most informative examples for human labeling or review. This makes the human effort more efficient.
- **Human-in-the-Loop Refinement:** Use human feedback to improve the automated metrics or to retrain the model.

When to Use: Very often, especially for complex tasks.

Key Considerations for Choosing Your Evaluation Methods

Choosing the right blend of evaluation methods—human, automated, or hybrid—is a critical strategic decision that you, as the Product Manager, will help guide. This isn't a purely technical choice; it involves balancing product goals, available resources, and potential risks. The following table outlines the key considerations to help you and your team make an informed decision and select the most appropriate evaluation strategy for your specific GenAI feature.

CONSIDERATION	DESCRIPTION	PM'S ROLE
Evaluation Criteria	What specific qualities are you trying to assess (relevance, coherence, accuracy, safety, etc.)?	Define clear, measurable criteria that align with your product goals and user needs.
Data Availability	Do you have access to high-quality reference data (for automated metrics)? Can you recruit and train human evaluators?	Ensure the necessary data and resources are available.

Continues

(continued)

CONSIDERATION	DESCRIPTION	PM'S ROLE
Cost and Time	How much time and budget do you have for evaluation? Human evaluation is generally more expensive and time-consuming than automated metrics.	Allocate resources appropriately and prioritize the most critical evaluation methods.
Risk Level	How high are the stakes? For high-stakes applications (e.g., medical advice), more rigorous evaluation (including human review) is essential.	Assess the potential risks and consequences of model errors.
Model Type	Some metrics are specific to certain model types (e.g., BLEU for text generation, FID for image generation).	Understand the limitations of different metrics and choose those that are appropriate for your model type.
Iterative Evaluation	Plan multiple stages of evaluation, using what you find to improve.	Define the evaluation plan, set the schedule and be sure that there's time for model improvements.

In conclusion, choosing the right GenAI evaluation methods is a fundamental part of the product development process. By understanding the different approaches and their trade-offs, you can work effectively with your technical team to ensure that your Generative AI features are high-quality, reliable, and safe. You'll be able to make informed decisions, building products your users will love.

Prompt Engineering: The Art and Science of Talking to AI

You've now explored the landscape of Generative AI and how to evaluate its outputs. But how do you actually *get* those outputs in the first place? This is where *prompt engineering* comes in. Think of prompt engineering as the art and science of crafting effective instructions for Generative AI models, particularly LLMs. Figure 3-19 illustrates how prompt engineering can be used to tailor LLM behavior for specific tasks, guiding the model toward more relevant, accurate, or creative outputs. It's about learning to "talk" to the AI in a way that elicits the desired responses.

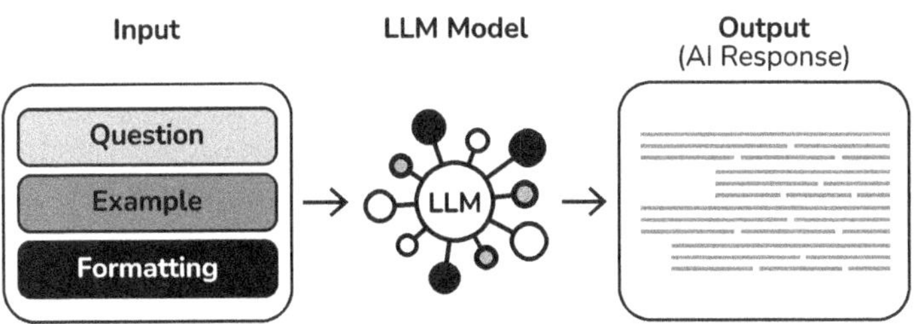

Figure 3-19: With prompt engineering. it's possible to tune an LLM model for specific tasks.

Why Prompt Engineering Matters to Product Managers

As a PM, you might not be writing prompts every day (although you might!), but understanding prompt engineering is a key part of GenAI for several reasons:

- **Feature Design:** You'll be involved in designing features that use prompts, either explicitly (where the user directly enters a prompt) or implicitly (where the prompt is generated behind the scenes based on user actions).

- **Quality Control:** You need to understand how prompt quality impacts the quality of the AI-generated output. Poorly designed prompts lead to poor results.

- **Collaboration with Engineering:** You'll need to communicate effectively with your engineering team about prompt design and optimization.

- **Setting Expectations:** You need to set realistic expectations for what the AI can and cannot do, based on the limitations of prompt engineering.

- **Troubleshooting:** If an AI-powered feature isn't working as expected, understanding prompt engineering can help you diagnose the problem.

The Basics of Prompt Engineering

A prompt is simply the input you give to a Generative AI model. For LLMs, this is typically text. The quality of your prompt has a *huge* impact on the quality of the output.

Keep in mind the following key principles of effective prompt engineering:

1. **Be clear and specific:** Vague prompts lead to vague outputs. Be as specific as possible about what you want the model to do.

   - **Poor Prompt:** "Write something about marketing."

   - **Better Prompt:** "Write a 200-word blog post introduction about the benefits of using AI-powered marketing automation tools for small businesses."

2. **Provide context:** Give the model enough context to understand what you're looking for. This might include background information, examples, or constraints.

   - **Poor Prompt:** "Write a product description."

   - **Better Prompt:** "Write a 50-word product description for a new noise-cancelling wireless headphone, targeting young professionals who work in busy office environments. Highlight the benefits of noise cancellation for focus and productivity."

3. **Specify the desired format and style:** Tell the model *how* you want the output to be formatted and styled.

   - **Poor Prompt:** "Write about customer service."

   - **Better Prompt:** "Write a bulleted list of five tips for providing excellent customer service via email. Use a friendly and professional tone."

4. **Use examples (few-shot learning):** One of the most powerful techniques is to provide a few examples of the desired output. This is called *few-shot learning*.

   Example:

   Prompt:

   Translate the following English sentences to French:

   English: The cat sat on the mat.

   French: Le chat s'est assis sur le tapis.

   English: Where is the nearest train station?

   French: Où se trouve la gare la plus proche ?

English: *I would like to buy a ticket.*

French:

(The model will likely complete the translation correctly.)

5. **Iterate and experiment:** Prompt engineering is an iterative process. Experiment with different prompts, analyze the results, and refine your prompts based on what works best.

6. **Control the output:** LLMs offer parameters to control output:

   - **Temperature:** Controls randomness. Higher values = more creative, but potentially less coherent. Lower values = more predictable, but potentially repetitive.

   - **Top-P (Nucleus Sampling):** Controls diversity by limiting the model to choose from a subset of the most likely next words.

   - **Max Tokens:** Limits the output's length.

To make the principles of effective prompt engineering more concrete, let's look at some side-by-side examples. The following table illustrates how adding specificity, context, and clear instructions can dramatically improve the quality of AI-generated content across several common use cases.

USE CASE	POOR PROMPT	BETTER PROMPT	EXPLANATION
Product Description	"Write a product description."	"Write a 50-word product description for a new smartwatch, targeting fitness enthusiasts. Highlight its heart rate monitoring, GPS tracking, and long battery life. Use an energetic and enthusiastic tone."	The better prompt provides specific context, target audience, desired features, and tone.
Customer Support Email	"Respond to this customer."	"Write a polite and professional email response to the following customer complaint, apologizing for the delayed shipping and offering a 10% discount on their next order. Customer email: [Insert email here]."	The better prompt provides clear instructions, specifies the desired tone, and includes the necessary context (customer email).

Continues

(continued)

USE CASE	POOR PROMPT	BETTER PROMPT	EXPLANATION
Social Media Post	"Write a social media post."	"Write a short, engaging tweet (under 280 characters) promoting our new AI-powered writing assistant. Include a call to action to try the free trial. Use emojis."	The better prompt specifies the platform (Twitter), character limit, desired tone, and call to action.
Code Generation	"Write some code."	"Write a Python function that takes a list of numbers as input and returns the sum of the squares of those numbers. Include a docstring explaining the function's purpose."	The better prompt specifies the programming language, the desired functionality, and the desired format (including a docstring).
Summarization	"Summarize this."	"Write a one-paragraph summary of the following article, focusing on the key findings and conclusions. Article: [Insert article here]."	The better prompts provides specific length, and the focus of the summary.

Prompt Engineering is an *ongoing process*. As a Product Manager, you should:

- **Collaborate Closely with your Data Science/Engineering Team:** They are the experts in prompt engineering techniques.

- **Test and Iterate:** Don't expect to get the perfect prompt on the first try. Experiment with different approaches and use A/B testing to compare results.

- **Monitor User Feedback:** Pay attention to user feedback on the AI-generated content. This can provide valuable insights for improving your prompts.

- **Document and Share:** Document prompts and share with your team.

By understanding the principles of prompt engineering, you can ensure that your Generative AI features deliver high-quality, relevant, and engaging outputs, maximizing their value for your users. This knowledge empowers you to be an active participant in the design and optimization of AI-powered experiences.

Types of Machine Learning: A Recap

Just like there are different tools for different tasks, there are different types of Machine Learning (ML) suited for different product problems. As a PM, you don't need to be an expert in each type, but understanding the *fundamental differences* is key for effective collaboration with your data science team.

Here is a recap of four key types of ML we reviewed:

Supervised Learning: Learning with a Teacher   This is the type we've been focusing on with our fruit example. The model is trained on *labeled data*—data where both the *input features* (e.g., color, shape) and the *correct output* (e.g., fruit type) are known. The model learns to *map* inputs to outputs.

Analogy: Learning with a teacher who provides the correct answers.

Key Applications:
    Classification: Predicting categories (e.g., spam/not spam, fruit type, customer churn/no churn).
    Regression: Predicting continuous values (e.g., house prices, stock prices, customer lifetime value).

PM Relevance: Most common type, used for many prediction tasks.

Unsupervised Learning: Discovering Hidden Patterns   Here, the model is trained on *unlabeled data*—data with only input features, *no* correct answers. The model's goal is to find hidden patterns, structures, or relationships within the data.

Analogy: Exploring a new city without a map—you discover landmarks and neighborhoods on your own.

Key Applications:
    Clustering: Grouping similar data points (e.g., customer segmentation, grouping similar news articles).

Dimensionality Reduction: Simplifying data by reducing the number of features while preserving important information (useful for visualization and speeding up other ML algorithms).
Anomaly Detection: Find outliers.

PM Relevance: Useful for understanding your data, discovering customer segments, and identifying unusual behavior.

Reinforcement Learning: Learning by Doing   This type of ML is inspired by how humans learn through trial and error. The model (often called an "agent") interacts with an *environment*, takes actions, and receives *rewards* or *penalties*. It learns to take actions that maximize its cumulative reward.

Analogy: Training a dog with treats and corrections.

Key Applications:
Game playing (e.g., AlphaGo—a computer program that plays the board game Go).
Robotics (e.g., teaching a robot to walk).
Autonomous driving.
Personalized recommendations (optimizing for long-term engagement).

PM Relevance: Less common in everyday product applications but critical for areas like robotics, gaming, and dynamic optimization.

Generative AI: Creating New Content   Generative AI models go beyond prediction and classification. They *learn the underlying patterns* in a dataset and then *generate new, original content* that resembles the training data.

Analogy: A digital artist learning from countless paintings to create their *own* unique artwork.

Key Applications:
Image Generation: Creating realistic images (e.g., DALL-E 2).
Text Generation: Writing articles, summarizing text, generating code (e.g., ChatGPT, GitHub Copilot).
Music Composition: Creating original musical pieces.

PM Relevance: Revolutionizing content creation, design, and software development. Raises new challenges related to originality, copyright, and potential misuse.

The following table provides a comparative overview of the types of Machine Learning:

FEATURE	SUPERVISED LEARNING	UNSUPERVISED LEARNING	REINFORCEMENT LEARNING	GENERATIVE AI
Primary Goal	Predict outcomes based on labeled data.	Discover hidden patterns.	Learn optimal actions through trial and error.	Create new content.
Data Type	Labeled (features and outcomes).	Unlabeled (features only).	Interaction with an environment.	Labeled or unlabeled (to learn patterns).
PM Applications	Classification, regression.	Customer segmentation, anomaly detection.	Game playing, robotics, personalization.	Image/text generation, content creation.
Key Question for PMs	What outcome do we want to predict?	What hidden insights are in our data?	How can we optimize behavior over time?	How can we generate new and valuable content?
Data Needs	Large, labeled dataset.	Large dataset.	Simulated or real-world environment.	Large dataset (often very large).
Human Interaction	Requires labeled data (often from humans).	Less human interaction during training.	Humans define reward functions.	Human feedback can improve output quality.
Technical Complexity	Moderate	Moderate to High	High	High
Evaluation	Accuracy, precision, recall.	Clustering quality, variance explained.	Cumulative reward.	Quality of generated content (often subjective).

Introduction to Neural Networks and Deep Learning: The Engines of Complex Pattern Recognition

We've explored various types of Machine Learning, from the rule-based simplicity of some AI systems to the sophisticated pattern recognition of unsupervised learning. Now, let's dive into the core technology that powers many of the most advanced AI applications you encounter: *Neural Networks* and *deep learning*.

When you hear terms like "AI-powered image recognition," "natural language understanding," or "self-driving cars," there's a good chance Neural Networks are playing a central role.

Think back to our discussion of LLMs and their transformer architecture. That architecture *is* a type of neural network. In fact, many of the advanced capabilities we've discussed are enabled by these powerful, adaptable models. So, what exactly *are* they?

Neural Networks: Mimicking the Brain's Connections (But Not Really)

At its most basic, a neural network is a computational system inspired by the structure of the human brain (though it's a *very* simplified model). It's a network of interconnected nodes, often called *neurons*, organized in layers. Figure 3-20 contrasts Machine Learning and deep learning workflows, highlighting how deep learning uses multiple layers to extract increasingly complex features from raw data. These neurons are connected by "synapses" (represented by weights) that transmit signals between them. Figure 3-21 illustrates this process by showing how input data moves through hidden layers in a neural network to produce a final prediction. It is important to highlight that a neural network is not a digital replica of the brain, but uses mathematical concepts inspired by it.

Imagine a complex game of telephone. A message (the input data) is whispered from person to person (neuron to neuron). Each person might slightly alter the message based on their own interpretation (the neuron's activation function). By the time the message reaches the end (the output layer), it has been transformed. The "learning" process in a neural network involves adjusting how each person interprets and modifies the message (adjusting the weights of the connections) to ensure the final message is correct.

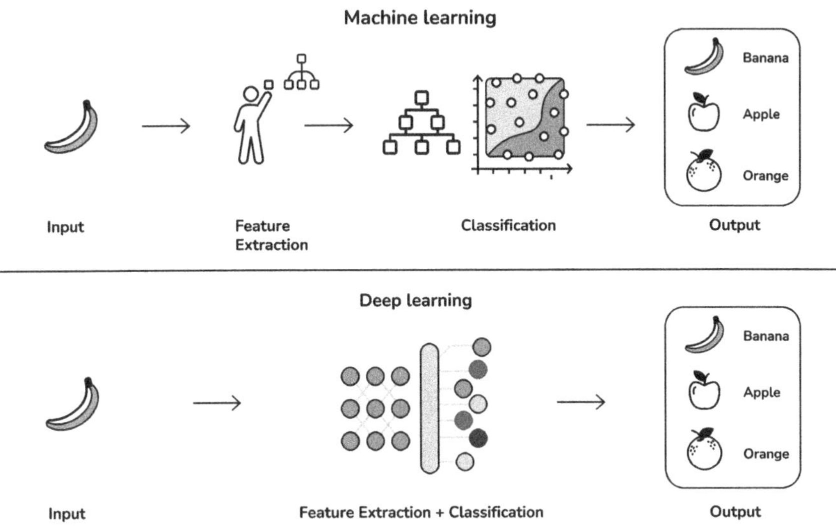

Figure 3-20: Machine learning vs. deep learning steps to make a prediction.

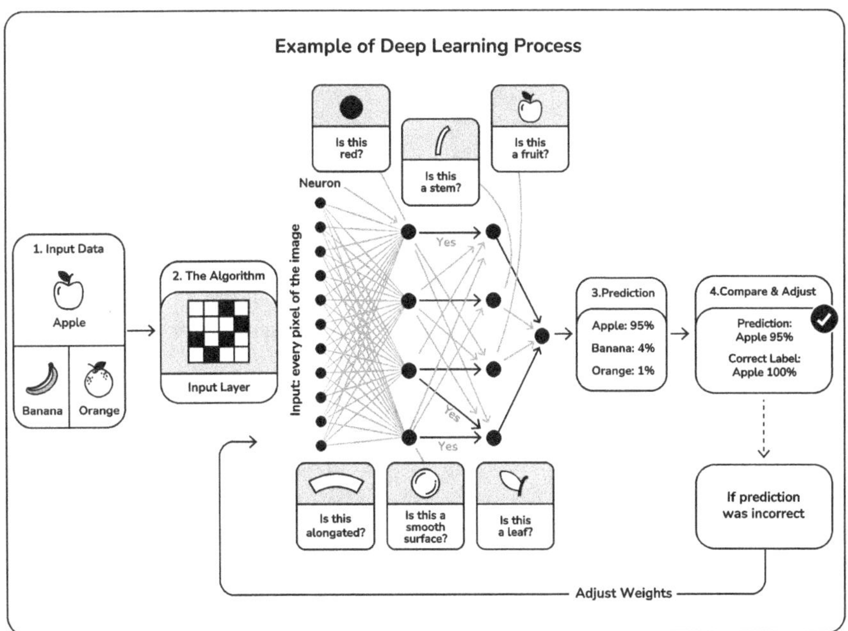

Figure 3-21: Visual example of how a neural network processes inputs through multiple hidden layers to produce an output. Each layer transforms the data to identify increasingly abstract patterns.

Let's break down the key components:

- **Input Layer:** This is where the raw data enters the network. Think of it as the "senses" of the network.

  - **Example:** For an image recognition system, the input layer would receive the pixel values of an image. For a spam filter, it would receive the words in an email.

- **Hidden Layers:** These are the layers between the input and output layers, where the real processing happens. The network transforms the input data through a series of calculations, extracting increasingly abstract and complex features. Figure 3-22 visualizes this transformation, showing how input features are refined layer by layer to support accurate predictions. The more hidden layers a network has, the "deeper" it is—hence "Deep Learning".

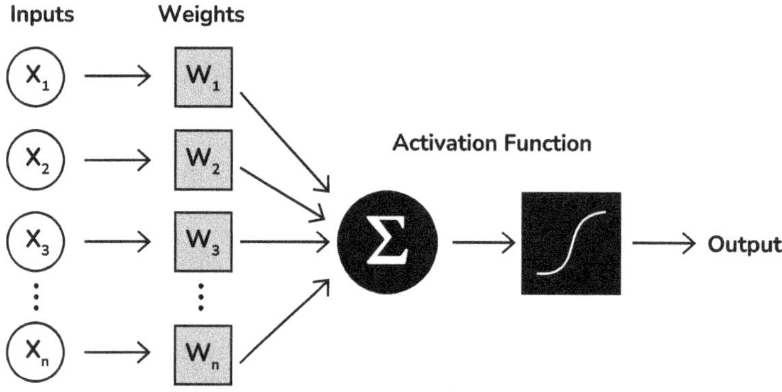

Figure 3-22: A diagram of a single artificial neuron, the fundamental building block of a neural network. It calculates a weighted sum of its inputs and then applies an activation function to produce its output.

  - **Example:** In an image recognition system, the first hidden layer might detect simple features like edges and corners. Subsequent layers might combine these features to detect shapes, and even deeper layers might recognize objects like faces or cars.

- **Output Layer:** This layer produces the final result or prediction.

  - **Example:** In an image recognition system, the output layer might indicate the probability that the image contains a cat, a dog, or a car. In a spam filter, it would output the probability that the email is spam.

How Neural Networks Learn: Adjusting the Connections

The power of a neural network lies in its ability to *learn* from data. This learning happens by adjusting the *weights* of the connections between the neurons. Think of these weights as volume knobs that control the strength of the signal passing between neurons.

Imagine you're trying to teach a child to identify different types of fruit. You show them an apple and say "apple." Initially, the child might not know what an apple is. But as you show them more apples, and correct them when they make mistakes ("That's a banana, not an apple"), they gradually learn to associate the visual features of an apple with the word "apple."

A neural network learns in a similar way, but through a mathematical process called *backpropagation*. Here's the basic idea:

1. **Input and Prediction:** The network receives an input (e.g., an image of an apple) and makes a prediction (e.g., "banana").

2. **Error Calculation:** The prediction is compared to the correct answer (the label "apple"). The difference between the prediction and the correct answer is the *error*.

3. **Weight Adjustment:** The network then adjusts the weights of the connections between the neurons to reduce this error. The adjustments are made in a way that makes it *more likely* to predict "apple" the next time it sees a similar image.

4. **Iteration:** This process is repeated many times, with the network being fed with many different examples. Over time, the weights are fine-tuned, and the network becomes increasingly accurate at its task.

The key to deep learning's success is its ability to automatically learn complex, hierarchical representations of data. The hidden layers act as *feature extractors*, discovering the most relevant features for the task without needing to be explicitly programmed. This is a major advantage over traditional Machine Learning approaches, which often require manual feature engineering. This is also why they can be used in so many different scenarios.

Technical Deep Dive: The Mechanics of Neural Networks and Deep Learning

Let's get a better understanding of how Neural Networks actually work, without getting bogged down in complex math. We'll focus on the key ideas and use analogies to make them more intuitive.

1. **Activation Functions: The "Decision-Makers"**

   ■ **What they are:** Imagine each neuron in the hidden layers as a tiny decision-maker. It receives signals from other neurons, and it needs to decide whether to "fire" (send a strong signal) or not. Figure 3-23 illustrates this basic structure of a single neuron. The activation function is like the rule the neuron uses to make this final "fire" or "don't fire" decision.

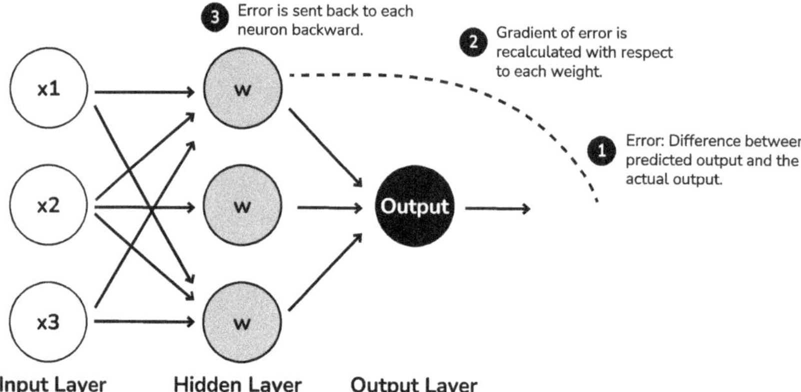

Figure 3-23: Backpropagation adjusts the weights of the neural network layers.

   ■ **Why they're important:** They introduce *non-linearity*. Think of it like this: if every neuron just passed along the signal it received (without an activation function), the whole network would be like a single, simple calculation. Activation functions allow the network to learn much more complex patterns, like those found in images, language, or user behavior.

   ■ **Simple Analogy:** Imagine a light switch with a dimmer. A simple on/off switch is like a network *without* an activation function (linear). The dimmer switch, which allows for a range of brightness levels, is like an activation function (non-linear). The dimmer allows for much more nuanced control.

2. **Backpropagation: Learning from Mistakes**

   ■ **How it works:** Backpropagation is the process the network uses to learn. It's like a feedback loop. The network makes a prediction, compares it to the correct answer, and then adjusts the connections between its neurons to make better predictions in the future.

- **The Chain Reaction:** The adjustment starts at the output layer (where the prediction is made) and works its way backward through the network, layer by layer. It's like tracing back the steps that led to a mistake to figure out where things went wrong.

- **Simple Analogy:** Imagine you're learning to shoot a basketball. You take a shot and miss. You analyze *why* you missed (too much force, wrong angle, etc.) and adjust your next shot accordingly. Backpropagation is like that analysis and adjustment process, but for the network.

3. **Gradient Descent: Finding the "Sweet Spot"**

- **What it is:** Gradient descent is the method used to adjust the connections (weights) between neurons. It's like finding the "sweet spot" on a golf club or the perfect focus on a camera lens. The goal is to find the set of weights that minimizes the network's errors.

- **The "Rolling Ball" Analogy:** Imagine a ball rolling down a hilly landscape. The ball naturally rolls downhill, seeking the lowest point. Gradient descent is like that—it guides the network's weights towards the values that produce the lowest error (the "bottom of the hill"). Figure 3-24 illustrates the concept of a ball rolling down a hilly landscape to find the best minimum (global minimum).

- **Learning Rate:** This is like the size of the steps the ball takes as it rolls downhill. Small steps are more precise but slower; large steps are faster but might overshoot the bottom.

4. **Network Architectures: Different Blueprints for Different Tasks**

There are different types of neural network architectures designed for different tasks.

- **Feedforward Networks:** The simplest type, where information flows in one direction. Good for tasks like classifying emails as spam or not spam.

- **Convolutional Neural Networks (CNNs):** These are like specialized image-processing networks. They're very good at recognizing patterns in images, like identifying objects in photos.

- **Recurrent Neural Networks (RNNs):** These are designed to handle sequences of data, like text or stock prices. They have a "memory" that allows them to consider past information when processing new information.

- **Transformers:** The architecture that powers models such as LLMs, they excel on understanding context on long texts.

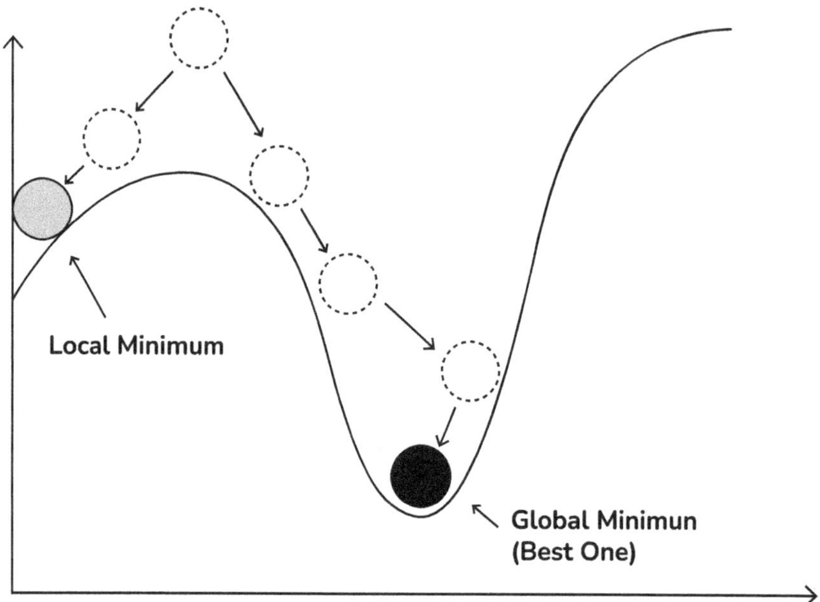

Figure 3-24: An example of gradient descent with a local minimum and a global minimum. We want to optimize models for global minimums.

Challenges in Deep Learning

While deep learning unlocks powerful capabilities, it also presents unique challenges that Product Managers should be aware of. Understanding these hurdles is key to setting realistic timelines and collaborating effectively with your technical teams:

- **Vanishing/Exploding Signals:** Sometimes, the signals passing through the network can become too weak or too strong, making it hard for the network to learn. It's like trying to hear a whisper in a noisy room (vanishing) or trying to have a conversation during a rock concert (exploding).

- **Overfitting:** The model learns the training data *too well*, including the noise and irrelevant details. It's like memorizing the answers to a specific test instead of understanding the underlying concepts. It performs well on the training data but poorly on new, unseen data.

- **Underfitting:** The model is too simple and cannot understand the patterns present in the data.

- **Computational Cost:** Training these networks, especially very large ones, can take a lot of computing power and time.

Now that we've explored AI in depth, let's look at the *process* of building and deploying these models. This is the AI *lifecycle*.

Chapter Summary and Key Takeaways

This chapter armed you with strategic fluency by zooming out from technical mechanics to the product landscape. You can now articulate the very important relationship between the broad goal of Artificial Intelligence (creating intelligent behavior) and the specific methods of Machine Learning (learning from data) used to achieve it. We contrasted the adaptability and power of ML with simpler, rule-based systems, emphasizing your critical role as a PM in choosing the right approach for the problem at hand. You now understand that ML's key advantage is its dynamic adaptability, allowing your products to improve over time as they learn from real-world data.

Key Takeaways

- You think of AI as the *goal* (intelligent behavior) and ML as a powerful *means* to achieve it.

- You recognize that not all AI is ML and that a simpler, rule-based system can sometimes be the right, most effective solution.

- You understand that the core advantage of ML is adaptability—the ability for your product to learn and improve over time.

- Your strategic advantage comes from knowing which approach (rule-based, ML, Deep Learning) is the best fit for the user's problem.

Onward: Mapping the Process

With a clear strategic understanding of the "what" and "why" of AI, you can now map out the end-to-end process of bringing an AI product to life. The next chapter will detail **The AI Lifecycle** from a Product Manager's perspective.

The AI Lifecycle

As a PM working with AI, you don't need to *execute* every step of the data science lifecycle, but you *must* understand it. As shown in Figure 4-1, this lifecycle is the roadmap for building and deploying AI models, from initial idea to ongoing maintenance. Knowing this process allows you to:

- **Collaborate Effectively:** Work effectively with your data science and engineering teams.

- **Set Realistic Expectations:** Understand the time, resources, and data required for each stage.

- **Prioritize Features:** Make informed decisions about which AI features to prioritize based on feasibility and impact.

- **Manage Risks:** Identify potential roadblocks and mitigate them early.

- **Ensure Alignment:** Keep the AI development aligned with overall product strategy and user needs.

Think of the data science lifecycle as a structured recipe for creating AI-powered solutions. Each step is critical for a successful outcome.

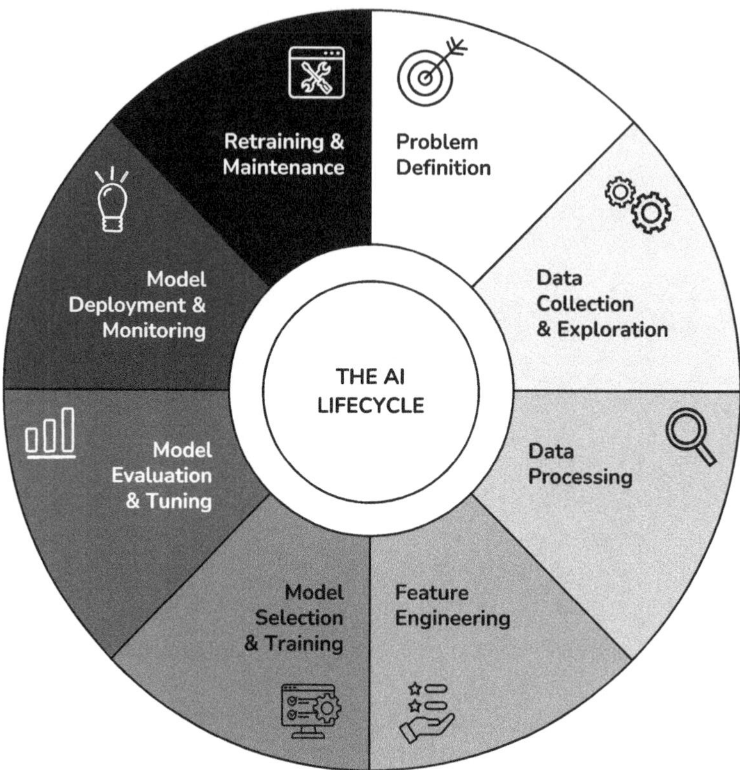

Figure 4-1: The AI lifecycle

This chapter presents a breakdown of the key stages, with a focus on the PM's perspective.

Problem Definition and Business Understanding: The "Why"

This is where *you*, the PM, play a *critical* role. You define the "why" behind the AI initiative. This involves:

- **Identifying the User Problem:** What user needs are we addressing?

- **Defining the Business Goal:** How will solving this problem benefit the business (e.g., increase revenue, reduce costs, improve user engagement)?

- **Setting Measurable Objectives:** How will we measure success? (e.g., reduce customer churn by X percent, increase click-through rates by Y percent).

- **Defining Key Questions:** What specific questions do we need the AI model to answer?

Example: A subscription-based streaming service wants to reduce customer churn. The problem is that users are canceling their subscriptions. The *business goal* is to retain more subscribers. A *measurable objective* might be to reduce churn by 15 percent within the next quarter. A *key question* for the AI model could be: "Which users are most likely to cancel their subscription in the next 30 days?"

PM's role: Lead this phase. Work with stakeholders to define the problem, goals, and objectives. Ensure alignment with overall product strategy.

Data Collection and Exploration: Understanding Your Ingredients

Now we need the data. This involves:

- **Identifying Data Sources:** Where can we find the data we need (e.g., databases, APIs, user activity logs)?

- **Gathering Data:** Collecting the relevant data.

- **Exploring the Data:** Understanding the data's characteristics, identifying missing values, outliers, and potential biases.

Example: For the churn prediction problem, we'd collect data on user demographics, viewing history, subscription plan, payment history, customer service interactions, and any other relevant information. Exploration might reveal that users who watch fewer than five hours of content per month are more likely to churn.

PM's role: Collaborate with data engineering and data scientists to identify and access relevant data sources. Understand the limitations and potential biases of the data.

Data Preprocessing: Preparing the Ingredients

Raw data is rarely ready for modeling. This stage involves:

- **Cleaning the Data:** Handling missing values, correcting errors, and removing inconsistencies.

- **Transforming the Data:** Converting data types, scaling numerical features, and encoding categorical variables.

Example: In the churn prediction example, we might need to:

- Handle missing values in user demographics (e.g., impute missing age based on other users with similar characteristics).

- Convert date formats to a consistent standard.

- Scale numerical features (e.g., viewing hours) to a common range.

PM's role: Understand the implications of data preprocessing decisions on model performance and potential biases. Ensure data quality and privacy are prioritized.

Feature Engineering: Crafting the Inputs for Success

Feature engineering is the process of creating *new* features from existing ones, or transforming existing features, to improve model performance. It's about making the data more informative and easier for the model to learn from. Think of it as combining and transforming your ingredients to create a more flavorful dish.

- **Why It's Important:** Well-engineered features can significantly boost model accuracy and make the model more interpretable.

Example: In our churn prediction example, we might:

- **Create a "Recency" Feature:** How long ago did the user last interact with the service? (This is derived from existing interaction timestamps).

- **Create a "Frequency" Feature:** How often does the user use the service (e.g., average sessions per week)?

- **Create a "Content Diversity" Feature:** How many different genres of content does the user watch?

- **Create a Feature Combining Time of the Day and Day of the Week (Is It Weekend, or Weekday, and Morning, Afternoon, or Night).**

PM's role:

- **Provide Domain Knowledge:** You have valuable insights into user behavior and the product. Share this knowledge with your data science team to help them brainstorm relevant features.

- **Understand Feature Importance:** Ask your data science team which features are most important for the model's predictions. This can inform product decisions (e.g., if "Recency" is a strong predictor of churn, you might focus on re-engagement campaigns).

- **Suggest Features:** You are close to the users and can provide meaningful suggestions.

Model Selection and Training: Choosing the Right Algorithm

This stage involves selecting the appropriate machine learning algorithm and training it on the prepared data. Think of choosing the right tool for the job: a hammer for nails, a screwdriver for screws.

- **Model Selection:** The choice of algorithm depends on:
  - **The Type of Problem:** Classification (predicting categories), regression (predicting continuous values), clustering (grouping similar data points), etc.
  - **The Characteristics of the Data:** The size, dimensionality, and distribution of the data.
  - **Interpretability Requirements:** Do we need to understand *why* the model is making certain predictions? (Some models, like decision trees, are more interpretable than others, like neural networks).
- **Training:** The chosen algorithm learns the patterns and relationships between the features and the target variable (in supervised learning) using the training data.

Example: For our churn prediction problem (a classification task), we might consider algorithms like:

- **Logistic Regression:** A relatively simple and interpretable model.

- **Decision Trees:** Easy to visualize and understand.

- **Random forests:** An ensemble of decision trees, often more accurate than individual trees.

- **Gradient Boosting Machines (GBMs):** Another powerful ensemble method.

- **Neural Networks:** More complex models that can capture non-linear relationships, but often less interpretable.

PM's role:

- **Understand the Trade-offs:** Discuss the pros and cons of different algorithms with your data science team. Consider factors like accuracy, interpretability, and computational cost.

- **Define Success Metrics:** Reiterate the key performance indicators (KPIs) that the model should optimize (e.g., precision, recall, F1-score for churn prediction).

- **Prioritize:** Give inputs on what to prioritize (e.g., accuracy over interpretability).

Model Evaluation and Tuning: Ensuring Quality

After training, we rigorously evaluate the model's performance using the *testing data* (data the model *hasn't* seen during training). This is like giving the student a final exam.

- **Evaluation Metrics:** We use metrics like accuracy, precision, recall, F1-score (which we covered earlier), and others depending on the specific problem.

- **Tuning:** If the model's performance isn't satisfactory, we *tune* its hyperparameters (settings that control the learning process) or even try a different algorithm. This is an iterative process.

Example: We evaluate our churn prediction model on the testing data. We might find that it has high accuracy but low recall (meaning it misses many users who are actually about to churn). We might then tune the model's hyperparameters (e.g., adjust the threshold for classifying a user as "high risk of churn") to improve recall, even if it slightly reduces precision.

PM's role:

- **Understand the Metrics:** Know what the key evaluation metrics mean and how they relate to your product goals.

- **Prioritize Improvements:** Based on the evaluation results, work with your data science team to prioritize areas for improvement. Focus on the metrics that matter most for your business.

- **Iterate:** Recognize that model development is an iterative process. Be prepared for multiple rounds of evaluation and tuning.

Model Deployment and Monitoring: Bringing AI to Life (and Keeping It Healthy)

Deployment is where your AI model goes from being a theoretical construct to a *working part of your product*. Monitoring ensures it *continues* to perform well in the real world.

- **Deployment:** This involves integrating the trained model into your product infrastructure. This could mean:

  - Embedding the model in a mobile app.

  - Deploying it as a web service (API) that other systems can access.

  - Integrating it into a backend system for automated decision-making.

- **Monitoring:** This is *critical* and ongoing. We track key performance metrics (the same ones used during evaluation) to detect any degradation in performance over time. We also monitor for:

  - **Data Drift:** Changes in the input data distribution (e.g., new customer demographics, changing user behavior).

  - **Concept Drift:** Changes in the relationship between the features and the target variable (e.g., what predicts churn might change over time).

  - **System Health:** Ensuring the infrastructure supporting the model is functioning correctly.

Example: Our churn prediction model is deployed as a web service. Every time a user interacts with the streaming service, their data is sent to the model, which predicts their churn risk. This risk score might trigger interventions (e.g., offering a discount) to retain the user. We continuously monitor the model's accuracy, precision, and recall, as well as the distribution of user features. If we see a significant drop in accuracy or a shift in user demographics, it's a signal that we may need to retrain the model.

PM's role:

- **Define Deployment Requirements:** Work with engineering to specify how the model will be integrated into the product.

- **Establish Monitoring Dashboards:** Collaborate with data science and engineering to create dashboards that track key performance metrics and alert you to any issues.

- **Set Alert Thresholds:** Define thresholds for performance metrics that trigger alerts (e.g., if accuracy drops below a certain level).

- **Plan for Fallbacks:** What happens if the model goes down or performs unexpectedly? Have a plan in place (e.g., a simpler rule-based system, human intervention).

Retraining and Maintenance: Keeping Your Model Up-to-Date

AI models are not "set it and forget it." They require ongoing maintenance and retraining to stay accurate and relevant.

- **Retraining:** Periodically retraining the model with *new data* is essential to adapt to changing conditions (data drift, concept drift). The frequency of retraining depends on the specific application and how quickly the underlying data changes.

- **Maintenance:** This includes tasks like:
  - Updating software dependencies.
  - Ensuring compatibility with other systems.
  - Addressing any security vulnerabilities.

Example: We might retrain our churn prediction model every month with the latest user data. We might also need to retrain it if we introduce a major new feature to the streaming service, as this could significantly impact user behavior.

PM's role:

- **Schedule Retraining:** Work with the data scientists to establish a schedule for retraining the model (e.g., monthly, quarterly, or based on performance triggers).

- **Budget for Maintenance:** If applicable to your organization, allocate resources for ongoing maintenance and updates.

- **Prioritize Data Collection:** Ensure you continue to collect the data needed for retraining.

- **Consider Feedback Loops:** If user feedback indicates the model isn't working, understand why.

Chapter Summary and Key Takeaways

You can now visualize the entire end-to-end AI lifecycle. This chapter provided you with a structured roadmap, tracing the journey from an initial business problem to a deployed and maintained AI model. We walked through the eight critical stages, from the Problem Definition where you set the course, through the data-intensive stages of collection and feature engineering, into the core of model training and evaluation, and finally to the very important post-launch phases of deployment, monitoring, and retraining. You now see AI development not as a mysterious black box, but as a structured, iterative process where you play a vital role.

Key Takeaways

- You act as the strategic guide, providing critical input at the start (Problem Definition) and end (Evaluation/ROI) of the lifecycle, while adding essential product context throughout.

- You view the lifecycle as a continuous loop, where insights from monitoring feed back into future iterations and product improvements.

■ You recognize that data is the central thread connecting nearly every stage of the process, making data strategy a core PM concern.

■ You know the work truly begins at deployment, and you plan for the ongoing monitoring and maintenance required for long-term success.

Onward: Exploring the AI PM Roles

With a clear understanding of the end-to-end process, it's now time to explore the "who." Part II will focus on the different AI PM specializations, helping you to chart your own course.

AI PM Specializations

The world of AI Product Management is evolving rapidly. As AI becomes increasingly integrated into products, the demands on PMs are changing. While the core principles of product management remain constant—understanding user needs, defining strategy, and delivering value—the *application* of those principles in the context of AI requires new skills and perspectives.

Part II introduces three distinct, yet interconnected, AI Product Manager specializations: the AI-Experiences PM, the AI-Builder PM, and the AI-Enhanced PM. These are *not* mutually exclusive job titles; rather, they represent different *areas of focus* within the broader AI PM landscape. A single PM might have responsibilities that span multiple roles, particularly in smaller organizations. However, understanding these specializations will help you:

- **Identify your strengths and interests:** Where do you naturally gravitate? Which role aligns best with your existing skills and career aspirations?

- **Focus your learning:** By understanding the key responsibilities and skills associated with each role, you can target your learning and development efforts more effectively.

- **Chart your career path:** Whether you're looking to specialize in a particular area or broaden your skillset, this framework provides a roadmap for growth.

- **Understand your team:** Understand how to better work with other PMs.

Before we dive into the details of each role, it's important to emphasize that *collaboration* is key in any role. Regardless of your specialization, you'll need to work closely with data scientists, engineers, designers, and other stakeholders. These roles are about defining areas of expertise, not creating silos.

The Three AI PM Personas (A Sneak Peek):

1. **AI-Experiences PM**: The champion of the user experience. This PM focuses on *how* AI-powered features are presented to and interacted with by users. They are experts at translating user needs into AI-powered solutions. *Think:* UX design for AI.

2. **AI-Builder PM**: The architect of the AI infrastructure. This PM focuses on building and managing the underlying AI platforms, models, and frameworks that *enable* AI-powered features. *Think:* Platform and tools for AI.

3. **AI-Enhanced PM**: The power user of AI. This PM leverages AI tools and techniques to improve their *own* product management workflows and decision-making. *Think:* AI as a PM's personal assistant.

Let's explore each role in more detail.

AI-Experiences PM: Shaping User Interaction with AI

The AI-Experiences PM focuses on how users interact with and experience AI-powered features within a product. They bridge the gap between the technical capabilities of AI and the needs and expectations of end users. While they don't build the AI models themselves, they are experts at designing and integrating AI functionality to create seamless, intuitive, and valuable user experiences. They ensure the AI enhances, rather than complicates, the user journey.

This role is critical because even the most sophisticated AI is ineffective if users can't understand it, use it, or trust it. The AI-Experiences PM ensures that AI-powered features are not just functional, but also user-friendly, engaging, and aligned with user needs. This drives adoption and ensures the AI truly improves the product.

This PM collaborates closely with Data Scientists and Engineers (who build the underlying AI models), UX Designers (who craft the user interface), and other Product Managers (who may focus on different aspects of the product). They represent the user's perspective throughout the AI development process.

The AI-Experiences PM role frequently involves balancing potentially conflicting priorities: leveraging the most advanced AI capabilities while maintaining a simple, user-friendly experience; maximizing personalization while avoiding bias and ensuring fairness; and driving innovation while upholding responsible and ethical AI principles. Successfully navigating these trade-offs is key.

A *highly effective* AI-Experiences PM combines deep user empathy with a strong understanding of AI's capabilities *and limitations*. They are creative problem-solvers, excellent communicators, and strong advocates for user-centered design principles. They envision how AI cannot just solve problems, but also create intuitive and valuable experiences.

Let's explore the specific responsibilities that define this critical role.

Key Responsibilities: Shaping the AI User Experience

The AI-Experiences PM is responsible for ensuring that AI-powered features are seamlessly integrated into the product and deliver a positive user experience. This involves a range of responsibilities, from initial ideation to ongoing optimization:

Identifying and Prioritizing AI-Driven Feature Opportunities:

- **Action:** Proactively identify user needs and pain points that can be addressed with AI, leveraging user research, data analysis, and competitive analysis.

- **Action:** Prioritize these opportunities based on user impact, business value, and technical feasibility. This involves making informed trade-offs and aligning with the overall product roadmap.

- **Example:** Identifying that users struggle to find relevant content in a large knowledge base and prioritizing the development of an AI-powered search feature.

Defining User-Centric Requirements for AI Features:

- **Action**: Translate user needs and business goals into clear, detailed requirements for AI-powered features. This goes beyond simply stating "build a recommendation system"; it involves specifying what the system should recommend, how it should present those recommendations, and how user feedback will be incorporated.

- **Action**: Define measurable success metrics (KPIs) that reflect user satisfaction and business impact.

- **Example**: Defining requirements for a personalized learning path feature, specifying the target user segments, the desired learning outcomes, the types of content to be recommended, and the user interface for presenting the learning path.

Designing Intuitive and Engaging AI Interactions:

- **Action:** Collaborate closely with UX designers to create user interfaces that are intuitive, engaging, and transparent. This includes designing how users will interact with AI-powered features, how AI outputs will be presented, and how users can provide feedback.

- **Action:** Ensure that AI-powered features are seamlessly integrated into existing user workflows, minimizing disruption and maximizing usability.

- **Example:** Designing the interaction flow for a chatbot, ensuring it's easy to use, provides helpful responses, and seamlessly transitions to a human agent when necessary.

Championing Ethical and Responsible AI Practices:

- **Action**: Proactively address ethical considerations throughout the product development lifecycle. This includes identifying and mitigating potential biases in AI models, ensuring user privacy, and promoting transparency.

- **Action**: Collaborate with legal and compliance teams to ensure that AI-powered features comply with all relevant regulations.

- **Example**: Ensuring that a personalized recommendation system does not discriminate against any particular group of users and that user data is handled responsibly.

Leading Experimentation and Validation (A/B Testing):

- **Action:** Design and execute A/B tests and other experiments to validate the impact of AI-powered features on user behavior and key metrics.

- **Action:** Analyze experiment results and iterate on feature design and model performance based on data-driven insights.

- **Example:** A/B testing different versions of an AI-powered product description generator to determine which version leads to higher click-through rates and conversions.

Monitoring Performance and Driving Continuous Improvement:

- **Action:** Continuously monitor the performance of AI-powered features in production, tracking key metrics and user feedback.

- **Action:** Identify areas for improvement and work with the data science and engineering teams to iterate on the model and the user experience.

- **Example:** Tracking the accuracy and user satisfaction of an AI-powered spam filter and identifying opportunities to reduce false positives and false negatives.

Communicating with Stakeholders:

- **Action:** Clearly communicate the vision, strategy, and progress of AI initiatives to stakeholders (including engineering, design, marketing, sales, and leadership).

- **Action:** Advocate for AI-powered features and secure buy-in from stakeholders.

- **Example:** Presenting the results of A/B tests to stakeholders, demonstrating the impact of AI on key business metrics and advocating for continued investment in AI initiatives.

Managing User Expectations and Handling Uncertainty:

- **Action:** Proactively manage user expectations about the capabilities and limitations of AI-powered features. This involves clear communication, transparent design, and providing appropriate feedback mechanisms.

- **Action:** Design user experiences that gracefully handle situations where the AI is uncertain or makes an error. This might involve providing fallback options, offering explanations, or allowing users to easily override the AI's suggestions.

- **Example:** For a chatbot, clearly indicating when the bot is unsure of an answer and providing an option to connect with a human agent. For a recommendation system, allowing users to easily provide feedback on the relevance of recommendations. For a text generation feature, providing a disclaimer that the generated content may not be factually accurate.

These responsibilities highlight the multifaceted nature of the AI-Experiences PM role. It's a blend of user advocacy, strategic thinking, design sensibility, data analysis, and effective communication. The AI-Experiences PM is the driving force behind creating AI-powered products that are not just technically impressive, but also truly valuable and delightful for users.

Day-to-Day Activities

As shown in Figure 5-1, the daily work of an AI-Experiences PM is dynamic and multifaceted, blending user-centric design, data analysis, strategic planning, and constant collaboration. It's a role that demands both creative problem-solving and a rigorous, data-driven approach. Here's a glimpse into the kinds of activities that might fill their days:

Figure 5-1: A snapshot of the daily responsibilities of an AI-Experiences PM, highlighting how they leverage AI tools, collaborate with cross-functional teams, and manage product workflows throughout the day

One of the most important aspects of the role is staying deeply connected to the user. This might involve:

- **Analyzing User Feedback:** The AI-Experiences PM regularly reviews user feedback from various sources—app store reviews, customer support tickets, in-app surveys, user forums—to identify recurring themes, pain points, and unmet needs related to AI-powered features. For example, they might notice users consistently praising the accuracy of personalized recommendations but expressing confusion about *why* certain items were recommended.

- **Conducting User Research:** This could involve running usability tests on new AI-powered features, conducting user interviews to understand user expectations and perceptions of AI, or analyzing user session recordings to identify areas of friction in the user journey. The PM might discover, through interviews, that users are hesitant to trust AI-generated summaries of complex documents, leading to a design change that emphasizes transparency and explainability.

- **Monitoring User Behavior:** The AI-Experiences PM uses analytics dashboards to monitor user interactions with AI features: click-through rates, conversion rates, time spent on tasks, feature adoption rates, and other relevant metrics. They look for patterns and anomalies that might indicate areas for improvement.

Collaboration and communication are also central to the AI-Experiences PM's work:

- **Collaborating with Data Science:** The PM works closely with data scientists, providing them with the "product context" for their work. This involves communicating user needs, defining success metrics, and providing feedback on model performance *from a user perspective*. They might discuss the trade-offs between different model evaluation metrics (precision vs. recall) or brainstorm new features to improve model accuracy. A key part of this collaboration is discussing the *limitations* of the current models and setting realistic expectations for what's achievable.

- **Collaborating with Engineering:** The PM works with engineers to ensure that AI-powered features are seamlessly integrated into the product and that the user experience is smooth and intuitive.

This might involve discussing the technical feasibility of different design options, troubleshooting integration issues, or planning the rollout of new features.

- **Collaborating with Design:** The PM partners with UX/UI designers to create user interfaces that are both visually appealing and effective in communicating the AI's capabilities and limitations. This includes designing how AI outputs are presented to the user, how users can provide feedback, and how uncertainty or errors are handled. They might A/B test different design options to see which one leads to better user engagement.

- **Stakeholder Communication:** The AI-Experiences PM regularly communicates with stakeholders (leadership, marketing, sales) to provide updates on AI initiatives, present A/B testing results, and advocate for continued investment in AI. They need to be able to explain complex AI concepts in a clear and concise way, demonstrating the value of AI for both users and the business.

Strategic planning and experimentation are also key activities:

- **Prioritizing and Roadmapping:** AI-Experiences PMs are constantly evaluating new AI opportunities and prioritizing them based on user impact, business value, and technical feasibility. They incorporate these priorities into the product roadmap, ensuring that AI initiatives are aligned with the overall product strategy.

- **Designing and Running A/B Tests:** A/B testing is a core part of the AI-Experiences PM's toolkit. They design and execute experiments to rigorously evaluate the impact of AI features on user behavior and key metrics. This might involve testing different versions of a recommendation algorithm, different prompt engineering strategies for an LLM, or different user interface designs for presenting AI-generated content.

- **Staying Up-to-Date with Current AI/ML Trends and Tools:** New tools are constantly being launched that may help improve internal processes, or improve the customer experience.

The AI-Experiences PM is a constant learner, a user advocate, a data interpreter, and a strategic thinker. Their days are filled with a diverse range of activities, all focused on ensuring that AI-powered features deliver real value and a positive experience for users.

Required Skills and Knowledge: The AI-Experiences PM Toolkit

To excel as an AI-Experiences PM, you'll need a blend of core product management skills, a solid understanding of AI concepts, and strong communication and collaboration abilities. This section outlines the key skills and knowledge areas, categorized for clarity, and indicates the level of proficiency needed.

Core Product Management Craft and Practices

Building successful AI-powered products requires more than technical fluency—it demands mastery of core product management practices, adapted to the unique challenges of AI. The following table outlines how foundational PM skills translate into the AI context, with specific examples and behavioral indicators that distinguish effective AI Product Managers.

SKILL	PROFICIENCY LEVEL	HOW IT'S APPLIED (AI-EXPERIENCES PM)
User Research and Analysis	Working Knowledge	Conducting user interviews, surveys, and usability tests to understand user needs and pain points related to AI features. Analyzing user behavior data to identify opportunities for AI-powered improvements. Creating user personas and journey maps to guide AI feature development.
Ideation and Solution Design	Working Knowledge	Brainstorming and conceptualizing AI-powered features that address user needs and align with product strategy. Applying design thinking principles to create intuitive and engaging AI interactions.
Prioritization & Roadmapping	Working Knowledge	Prioritizing AI features based on user impact, business value, technical feasibility, and ethical considerations. Integrating AI initiatives into the product roadmap and managing dependencies.

SKILL	PROFICIENCY LEVEL	HOW IT'S APPLIED (AI-EXPERIENCES PM)
Requirements Definition	Working Knowledge	Writing clear and detailed product requirements documents (PRDs) and user stories for AI features, specifying functionality, user interactions, and success metrics.
Data Analysis and Interpretation	Working Knowledge	Analyzing data from user research, A/B tests, and model performance metrics to identify trends, draw conclusions, and make data-driven decisions. Understanding key metrics like click-through rates, conversion rates, user satisfaction, precision, recall, and F1-score.
Experimentation (A/B Testing)	Working Knowledge	Designing and executing A/B tests to evaluate the impact of AI features on user behavior and key metrics. Interpreting experiment results and iterating on feature design based on data.
Go-to-Market Strategy and Execution	Foundational	Collaborating with marketing and communications teams to develop launch plans for AI-powered features. Crafting messaging that highlights the user benefits of AI without overhyping capabilities. Monitoring user adoption and feedback post-launch.

Engineering Foundations for PMs

AI Product Managers must bridge the gap between product goals and engineering constraints. While they aren't expected to write code, understanding core engineering principles—such as system architecture, APIs, and infrastructure trade-offs—is essential. The following table outlines the key engineering concepts every AI PM should grasp to collaborate effectively and make sound technical decisions.

SKILL	PROFICIENCY LEVEL	HOW IT'S APPLIED (AI-EXPERIENCES PM)
Software Development Methodologies	Foundational	Understanding Agile/Scrum principles to collaborate effectively with engineering teams and manage AI feature development within iterative sprints.
Key Technical Concepts (APIs, Algorithms, System Architecture)	Foundational	Having a basic understanding of how AI models are deployed and integrated into products (e.g., via APIs). Understanding the basic concepts of different algorithms (without needing to code them) to communicate effectively with data scientists.
Working with AI Infrastructure	Foundational	Understanding the basics of how and where AI models are hosted (e.g., cloud, on-premises), and how factors like latency might impact the user experience.

Essential Leadership and Collaboration Skills

Leading AI product development requires more than technical and strategic acumen—it demands strong leadership and cross-functional collaboration. AI PMs must align diverse teams, communicate uncertainty, and drive consensus across disciplines. The following table outlines the critical leadership and collaboration behaviors that enable AI PMs to guide teams effectively and influence outcomes at scale.

SKILL	PROFICIENCY LEVEL	HOW IT'S APPLIED (AI-EXPERIENCES PM)
Communication and Storytelling	Working Knowledge	Clearly communicating the vision, strategy, and value proposition of AI features to both technical and non-technical audiences. Explaining complex AI concepts in a user-friendly way.

SKILL	PROFICIENCY LEVEL	HOW IT'S APPLIED (AI-EXPERIENCES PM)
Collaboration and Cross-Functional Teamwork	Working Knowledge	Working closely with data scientists, engineers, designers, marketers, and other stakeholders to bring AI features to life. Facilitating communication and alignment across teams.
Problem-Solving and Decision-Making	Working Knowledge	Identifying and solving problems that arise during the development and deployment of AI features. Making data-driven decisions and balancing competing priorities (e.g., user needs, technical feasibility, business goals).
Influence and Persuasion	Foundational	Advocating for user-centric AI solutions and securing buy-in from stakeholders. Influencing product strategy and resource allocation for AI initiatives.
Adaptability and Learning Agility	Working Knowledge	Staying up-to-date with the rapidly evolving field of AI and adapting to new technologies and best practices.

AI Lifecycle and Operational Awareness

To design great AI-powered experiences, a Product Manager must understand the practical realities of the AI lifecycle. This operational awareness—from understanding data requirements to knowing how models are deployed and evaluated—is what allows a PM to create features that are not only innovative but also feasible, reliable, and responsible. The following table breaks down the essential lifecycle and operational skills for the AI-Experiences PM.

SKILL	PROFICIENCY LEVEL	HOW IT'S APPLIED (AI-EXPERIENCES PM)
Understanding AI and GenAI's Unique Capabilities	Working Knowledge	Identifying opportunities to leverage AI's strengths (e.g., personalization, automation, prediction) to solve user problems. Understanding the limitations of AI and setting realistic expectations.

Continues

(continued)

SKILL	PROFICIENCY LEVEL	HOW IT'S APPLIED (AI-EXPERIENCES PM)
DataOps and Management	Foundational	Understanding the data requirements for AI features and working with data engineering to ensure data quality and availability. Understanding data privacy and ethical considerations.
Productionization Considerations	Foundational	Understanding the basics of deploying and monitoring AI models in a production environment. Collaborating with engineering on rollout plans and monitoring strategies.
Ethics and Compliance	Working Knowledge	Ensuring that AI features are developed and deployed ethically and in compliance with relevant regulations. Identifying and mitigating potential biases in AI models and data.
Prompt Engineering (for LLMs)	Working Knowledge	(If applicable to the product) Crafting effective prompts to elicit desired responses from LLMs. Iterating on prompts based on user feedback and model performance.
GenAI Evals understanding	Working Knowledge	Understanding the different methods to evaluate Generative AI models.

Illustrative Example: A Day in the Life of an AI-Experiences PM

To bring the AI-Experiences PM role to life, let's walk through a hypothetical day, highlighting the diverse range of activities and interactions that might be involved. This isn't a rigid schedule, but rather a snapshot of the dynamic and multifaceted nature of the work.

Morning

- **8:30 AM–9:00 AM: Review User Feedback and Performance Metrics—**
  The day starts by reviewing user feedback on the AI-powered "Smart Compose" feature in the company's email product. The PM scans app store reviews, support tickets, and in-app feedback forms, looking for recurring themes and patterns. They also check the key performance metrics dashboard, noting a slight dip in the "Smart Compose" acceptance rate (the percentage of users who accept the AI-generated suggestions).
  Skills Used: Data Analysis and Interpretation, User Research and Feedback Analysis.

- **9:00 AM–10:00 AM: Stand-Up Meeting with the "Smart Compose" Team—**
  The PM participates in the daily stand-up meeting with the data scientists, engineers, and designers working on the "Smart Compose" feature. They share the user feedback trends and the dip in the acceptance rate, prompting a discussion about potential causes and solutions. The data science team suggests exploring whether recent changes to the underlying language model might be responsible.
  Skills Used: Communication and Collaboration, AI Fluency, Problem-Solving.

- **10:00 AM–11:00 AM: Design Review for a New AI-Powered Feature—**
  The PM joins a design review session for a new AI-powered feature: a "Meeting Summarizer" that will automatically generate summaries of meeting transcripts. The UX designer presents wireframes and prototypes, and the PM provides feedback from a user perspective, focusing on clarity, usability, and how the AI's output will be presented. They discuss how to handle potential errors or uncertainties in the summaries and how to allow users to provide feedback.
  Skills Used: User-Centric AI Design, Communication and Collaboration, Understanding AI Capabilities.

- **11:00 AM–12:00 PM: Prompt Engineering Workshop—**
  The PM attends a workshop led by a data scientist on prompt engineering techniques for large language models. They learn

about different prompting strategies and experiment with crafting prompts to elicit desired responses from the "Meeting Summarizer" model.

Skills Used: Prompt Engineering, AI Fluency, Continuous Learning.

Afternoon

- **1:00 PM–2:00 PM: A/B Test Planning—**
The PM works with a data analyst to design an A/B test to evaluate a new version of the "Smart Compose" feature. They define the hypothesis, select the target metric (acceptance rate), determine the sample size, and plan the rollout strategy. They discuss how to segment users to see if the feature performs differently for different groups.
Skills Used: Experimentation (A/B Testing), Data Analysis and Interpretation, Collaboration.

- **2:00 PM–3:00 PM: Roadmap Prioritization Meeting—**
The PM leads the product roadmap prioritization meeting, advocating for AI-powered feature enhancements based on user research, competitive analysis, and potential business impact. They present data on the success of existing AI features and propose new initiatives, balancing user needs, technical feasibility, and strategic alignment.
Skills Used: Prioritization and Roadmapping, Strategic Thinking, Communication and Storytelling, Influence and Persuasion.

- **3:00 PM–4:00 PM: Review of GenAI Evaluation Metrics—**
The PM meets with the data science team to review the latest evaluation metrics for the "Meeting Summarizer" model. They discuss the model's performance on key metrics like accuracy, coherence, and hallucination rate. They identify areas where the model is struggling and discuss potential strategies for improvement, such as refining the training data or adjusting the model's parameters. They specifically review metrics related to bias and fairness, ensuring the summaries are not perpetuating harmful stereotypes.
Skills Used: Data Analysis, AI Fluency, GenAI Evals understanding.

- **4:00 PM–5:00 PM: Drafting a Product Requirements Document (PRD)—**
The PM starts drafting a PRD for a new AI-powered feature: a "Smart Reply" option for customer support emails. They outline

the user problem, the proposed solution, the functional requirements, the success metrics, and the ethical considerations.
Skills Used: Requirements Definition, User-Centric AI Design, Communication, AI Fluency.

This "day in the life" example illustrates the dynamic and varied
nature of the AI-Experiences PM role. It's a blend of strategic thinking,
user empathy, data analysis, design collaboration, and constant communication. It's a role that requires both a deep understanding of user needs
and a solid grasp of AI's capabilities and limitations. The AI-Experiences
PM is at the forefront of shaping how users interact with and benefit
from the power of artificial intelligence.

Challenges and Complexities

The AI-Experiences PM role is both exciting and challenging. It offers
the opportunity to shape the future of how users interact with AI, but
it also comes with its own set of unique hurdles. Understanding both
the challenges and the rewards is essential for anyone considering this
career path.

Here are some of the common challenges you may face in this role:

- **Balancing Innovation and Usability:** One of the biggest challenges
  is finding the right balance between leveraging cutting-edge AI
  capabilities and creating a user experience that is simple, intuitive,
  and understandable. It's easy to get caught up in the technical
  possibilities of AI, but the AI-Experiences PM must always prioritize the user's needs and ensure that AI enhances, rather than
  complicates, the product.

- **Managing User Expectations:** AI is often hyped, leading to unre-
  alistic expectations from users. The AI-Experiences PM needs to
  carefully manage these expectations, communicating both the
  capabilities and the limitations of AI-powered features. This includes
  being transparent about when and how AI is being used and
  providing clear explanations for AI-driven decisions.

- **Dealing with Uncertainty and Errors:** AI models are not perfect.
  They can make mistakes, generate unexpected outputs, or exhibit
  limitations that users may find frustrating. The AI-Experiences
  PM needs to design experiences that gracefully handle these

situations, providing fallback options, offering explanations, and allowing users to easily provide feedback.

- **Addressing Ethical Concerns:** AI raises a host of ethical concerns, including bias, fairness, privacy, and transparency. The AI-Experiences PM must be a strong advocate for responsible AI development, proactively identifying and mitigating potential ethical risks. This requires staying informed about ethical guidelines and best practices.

- **Keeping Up with a Rapidly Evolving Field:** The field of AI is constantly changing, with new models, techniques, and tools emerging all the time. The AI-Experiences PM needs to be a continuous learner, staying up-to-date with the latest advancements and adapting their strategies accordingly.

- **Data Dependency and Quality:** AI-powered features are heavily reliant on data. The AI-Experiences PM often faces challenges related to data availability, quality, and bias. They need to work closely with data scientists and engineers to ensure that the data used to train and evaluate AI models is representative, accurate, and ethically sourced.

- **Cross-Functional Collaboration:** Successfully launching AI-powered features requires a high-level of coordination between PMs, Data Scientists, ML Engineers, and UX designers.

Despite the hurdles, the role is incredibly rewarding for several reasons:

- **Shaping the Future of User Experience:** AI-Experiences PMs are at the forefront of defining how users interact with AI, creating new paradigms and possibilities for human–computer interaction. This is a unique opportunity to shape the future of technology and have a significant impact on people's lives.

- **Solving Real User Problems:** AI has the potential to solve a wide range of user problems, from automating tedious tasks to providing personalized recommendations to making complex information more accessible. The AI-Experiences PM gets to see the direct impact of their work on users' lives, making their jobs more efficient, enjoyable, or meaningful.

- **Working at the Cutting Edge of Technology:** The AI-Experiences PM role is inherently innovative, involving constant learning and experimentation with new technologies. This is a rewarding experience for those who are passionate about technology and enjoy pushing the boundaries of what's possible.

- **Collaborating with Talented Teams:** AI-Experiences PMs work closely with talented data scientists, engineers, designers, and other professionals, learning from their expertise and contributing to a shared mission. This collaborative environment can be highly stimulating and rewarding.

- **Seeing Tangible Results:** The impact of the AI-Experiences PM's work is often directly measurable through key metrics like user engagement, satisfaction, and task completion rates. Seeing these metrics improve as a result of your efforts is highly gratifying.

- **Driving Product Innovation:** AI-Experiences PMs are key drivers of product innovation, identifying new opportunities to leverage AI and creating features that differentiate their products from the competition.

The AI-Experiences PM role is not for the faint of heart. It requires a unique blend of technical understanding, user empathy, strategic thinking, and resilience. But for those who are up to the challenge, it offers the opportunity to make a significant impact on the world, shaping how users interact with the transformative power of artificial intelligence.

How the AI-Experiences PM Interacts with Other Roles

No AI product is built in a silo. The AI-Experiences PM acts as the central hub or the "conductor" of an orchestra, responsible for bringing together a diverse set of experts to create a harmonious and effective product. Successfully navigating this landscape means understanding not just *who* to talk to, but *what* expertise each role brings and *how* to best collaborate with them.

The stakeholder map in Figure 5-2 provides a high-level overview of this collaborative ecosystem. Let's break down these key relationships.

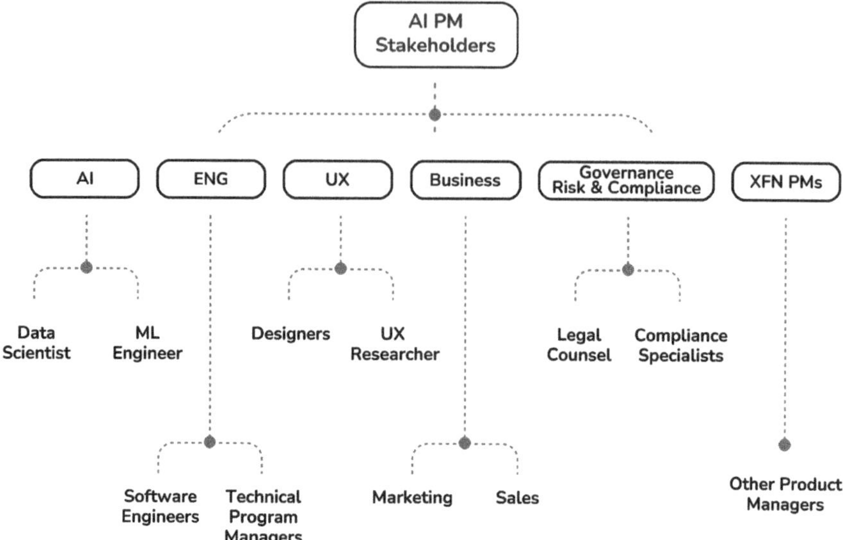

Figure 5-2: The stakeholder ecosystem for an AI Product Manager. The AI PM acts as a central coordinator, collaborating with cross-functional teams including AI/ML specialists, Engineering, UX Design, Business, Governance, and other PMs to successfully guide a product from concept to launch and beyond.

- **Data Scientists:**
  - **Nature of Interaction:** Frequent and close collaboration. The AI-Experiences PM provides the *product vision and user context*, while the data scientists provide the *technical expertise* to build the AI models.
  - **PM Responsibilities**:
    - Clearly communicate user needs, pain points, and desired outcomes.
    - Define success metrics for the AI model (e.g., precision, recall, F1-score).
    - Provide feedback on model performance from a user perspective.
    - Understand the limitations of the model and manage user expectations accordingly.
    - Collaborate on feature engineering, suggesting potential features based on user insights.
    - Help prioritize model development efforts based on user impact and business value.

- **Example:** For a personalized recommendations feature, the PM would work with data scientists to define the target audience, the types of recommendations to be provided, and the success metrics (e.g., click-through rate, conversion rate). The PM would also provide feedback on the relevance and usability of the recommendations from a user perspective.

- **ML Engineers:**

  - **Nature of Interaction:** Close collaboration, particularly during the deployment and monitoring phases. ML Engineers are responsible for taking the trained model and making it work in a production environment.

  - **PM Responsibilities:**

    - Communicate the performance requirements for the deployed model (e.g., latency, throughput).

    - Collaborate on the rollout strategy (e.g., A/B testing, phased rollout).

    - Work with ML Engineers to establish monitoring dashboards and alerts.

    - Understand the infrastructure implications of different design choices.

  - **Example:** For a real-time fraud detection system, the PM would work with ML Engineers to ensure that the model can process transactions quickly enough to prevent fraud without causing unacceptable delays for legitimate users.

- **UX Designers:**

  - **Nature of Interaction:** Extremely close collaboration. The AI-Experiences PM and UX Designer work together to design the *user interface and interactions* for AI-powered features.

  - **PM Responsibilities:**

    - Define the user flows and interaction patterns for AI features.

    - Ensure that AI outputs are presented to users in a clear, understandable, and trustworthy way.

    - Design mechanisms for user feedback and control.

    - Address ethical considerations in the design (e.g., transparency, explainability).

- **Example:** For a chatbot, the PM and UX Designer would collaborate on the chatbot's personality, conversation flow, and how it handles errors or uncertainty.

- **Software Engineers and Technical Program Managers:**

  - **Nature of Interaction**: Collaborate on integrating the AI models onto the experience.

  - **PM Responsibilities**:

    - Define the requirements.

    - Make sure the AI features are aligned with the rest of the product.

    - Help testing the integration.

  - **Example:** Collaborating with engineers to ensure the outputs from a recommendation model are displayed correctly in the user interface, and working with TPMs to track dependencies across backend and frontend systems during rollout.

- **Marketing:**

  - **Nature of Interaction:** Collaboration on go-to-market strategy and messaging.

  - **PM Responsibilities**:

    - Communicate the value proposition of AI-powered features to the marketing team.

    - Ensure that marketing materials accurately reflect the capabilities and limitations of the AI.

    - Gather user feedback from marketing campaigns.

  - **Example:** Working with marketing to create a campaign that highlights the benefits of an AI-powered personalized recommendation feature, without overpromising or misleading users.

- **Sales:**

  - **Nature of Interaction:** Providing sales teams with the information and tools they need to effectively sell AI-powered products.

  - **PM Responsibilities**:

    - Educate sales teams on the capabilities and limitations of AI features.

- Develop sales materials that highlight the value proposition of AI.

- Gather feedback from sales teams on customer perceptions and needs.

- **Example:** Providing sales teams with a demo of an AI-powered customer support chatbot and explaining how it can help them close deals.

- **Legal/Compliance:**

  - **Nature of Interaction:** Ensuring that AI-powered features comply with all relevant regulations (e.g., data privacy laws, anti-discrimination laws).

  - **PM Responsibilities**:

    - Understand the legal and regulatory landscape for AI.

    - Work with legal and compliance teams to assess and mitigate risks.

    - Ensure that data is collected and used ethically and responsibly.

  - **Example:** Consulting with legal counsel to ensure that an AI-powered hiring tool complies with anti-discrimination laws.

- **Other Product Managers:**

  - **Nature of Interaction:** Collaboration, especially with AI-Builder PM.

  - **PM Responsibilities**:

    - Share best practices.

    - Understand how models can be used.

  - **Example:** Working with the AI-Builder PM to understand the capabilities and limitations of a new personalization model, then applying that knowledge to design a tailored onboarding experience in your own product area.

The AI-Experiences PM acts as a central point of alignment and communication between these different roles, ensuring that everyone is working together towards a common goal: building AI-powered products that deliver exceptional user experiences. This requires strong communication skills, a collaborative mindset, and a deep understanding of both the technical and user-facing aspects of AI but also communicating often with Leadership and making sure the plans are communicated across orgs.

Chapter Summary and Key Takeaways

You have now done a deep dive into the AI-Experiences PM specialization, the role that acts as the essential advocate for the user in the world of artificial intelligence. You've explored how this PM translates user needs into concrete AI opportunities, collaborates deeply with UX designers to craft intuitive interactions, and uses rigorous experimentation like A/B testing to validate that a feature truly delivers value. You understand the balancing act this role requires: managing user expectations around a probabilistic technology while grounding powerful, personalized experiences in ethical principles like fairness and transparency. Ultimately, your mission in this role is to shape the "last mile" of AI interaction, ensuring that complex technology enhances the user journey rather than complicating it.

Figure 5-3 summarizes the core aspects of this role—from its mission to its essential skills.

Key Takeaways

- **You always start with the user.** Your primary focus is on understanding user needs and pain points to design effective AI features that are valuable and intuitive.

- **You are a cross-functional translator.** This role requires close collaboration with data scientists, engineers, and designers to translate user needs into feasible product experiences.

- **You have "AI Fluency," not necessarily technical mastery.** You understand the capabilities and limitations of AI to guide product design, but your core focus remains on the user experience.

- **You are the owner of responsible UX.** As the user advocate, you are the primary champion for ensuring the user-facing aspects of AI are fair, transparent, and handle uncertainty gracefully.

Onward: Architecting the AI Foundation

Now that you've explored the user-facing role of the AI-Experiences PM, you'll turn your attention to the architects behind the scenes. The next chapter will detail the role of the AI-Builder PM, who is responsible for creating the foundational platforms that make these experiences possible.

AI - EXPERIENCES PM
Shaping user interaction with AI

Role Summary 

Bridges the gap between AI technology and end-users. Designs and integrates AI features for seamless, intuitive and valuable user experiences.

Why it matters? 

Ensures AI-powered features are user-friendly, engaging, and aligned with user needs.

Collaboration 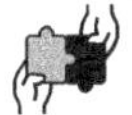

Works closely with ML/AI experts, designers, and other PMs.

Key Trade - Offs 

- Complexity vs. Usability
- Personalization vs. Fairness
- Innovation vs. Ethics

Essential Skils & Mindset 

- Deep user empathy
- Understanding of AI
- Creative problem-solving

Figure 5-3: A summary of the AI-Experiences PM role, highlighting its core focus, key collaborators, trade-offs, and essential skills

AI-Builder PM: Architecting the Foundation of Intelligent Systems

The AI-Builder PM is the strategic and technical leader responsible for the foundational AI capabilities within an organization. They usually don't focus on individual user-facing features (that's the AI-Experiences PM's domain). Instead, they build and manage the platforms, models, and frameworks that empower other teams to create AI-powered products. Think of them as the architects and builders of the AI infrastructure—the people who lay the groundwork for AI innovation.

This role is critical because a robust and scalable AI foundation is essential for long-term success with AI. The AI-Builder PM ensures that the organization has the tools and resources it needs to develop and deploy AI solutions efficiently and effectively. They are the enablers, making it possible for others to build AI-powered experiences.

The AI-Builder PM works closely with data scientists and Machine Learning Engineers (who build and train the specific models), with Software Engineers (who integrate the models and platforms into products), and with AI-Experiences PMs (who define the user-facing features). They translate high-level business needs and product strategies into a technical roadmap for AI infrastructure.

This role comes with its own set of inherent challenges. The AI-Builder PM must balance the need for cutting-edge AI capabilities with the practical constraints of scalability, maintainability, and cost. They must also navigate the complexities of data governance, model versioning, and ensuring the long-term reliability of the AI infrastructure. Furthermore, they must keep an eye on, and define a plan for, evaluating their models, especially if those models are Generative AI models.

A highly effective AI-Builder PM possesses a strong technical background, coupled with strategic product vision. They are excellent communicators, able to bridge the gap between technical teams and business stakeholders. They are proactive problem-solvers, constantly seeking ways to improve the AI infrastructure and empower other teams to build innovative AI solutions.

Let's now examine the specific responsibilities that characterize this foundational role.

Key Responsibilities: Building and Managing the AI Foundation

The AI-Builder PM is responsible for creating and maintaining the underlying AI infrastructure that powers AI-driven products and features across the organization. This encompasses a wide range of responsibilities, from strategic planning to technical oversight:

- **Defining and Owning the AI Platform Strategy and Roadmap:**
    - **Action:** Develop and maintain a strategic roadmap for the internal AI platform, aligning it with the overall business objectives and the needs of various product teams. This is *not* just a technical roadmap; it's a *product* roadmap for the AI platform itself.
    - **Action:** Define the platform's capabilities, architecture, and key features, ensuring it is scalable, reliable, secure, and cost-effective.
    - **Example:** Defining the roadmap for an internal AI platform to include support for new model types (e.g., LLMs), improved model deployment workflows, and enhanced monitoring capabilities.

- **Driving the Development and Deployment of Foundational AI Models:**

  - **Action:** Lead the development and deployment of reusable AI models that can be leveraged by multiple product teams. These are "foundational" models that address common needs across the organization.

  - **Action:** Define requirements for these models, collaborate with data scientists on model development, and oversee the deployment process, ensuring models are well-documented and easily accessible.

  - **Example:** Building a company-wide churn prediction model (as an API) that different product teams can integrate into their products, rather than each team building their own. Other examples: customer lifetime value prediction, fraud detection, product categorization.

- **Overseeing the Development of AI Frameworks and Tooling:**

  - **Action:** Identify needs and define requirements for internal AI frameworks and tools that streamline the AI development process for other teams. This is about making it *easier* for others to build AI.

  - **Action:** Oversee the development and maintenance of these frameworks, ensuring they are user-friendly, well-documented, and integrated with the AI platform.

  - **Example:** Creating a standardized framework for A/B testing AI models, providing templates and tools that simplify the experimentation process for all product teams. Another example: a framework for building and deploying GenAI agents.

- **Managing AI Infrastructure and MLOps:**

  - **Action:** Define the strategy and oversee the implementation of the AI infrastructure and MLOps practices. This ensures that models can be deployed, monitored, and updated efficiently and reliably.

  - **Action:** Collaborate with engineering and operations teams to ensure the infrastructure is scalable, secure, and cost-effective.

- **Example:** Defining the requirements for model monitoring dashboards, setting up automated retraining pipelines, and establishing processes for model versioning and rollback.

- **Establishing Data Governance and Compliance:**

  - **Action:** Work with legal, security, and compliance teams to establish and enforce data governance policies for AI projects. This ensures that data is used ethically, responsibly, and in compliance with all relevant regulations.

  - **Action:** Define processes for data access, usage, and storage, ensuring data privacy and security.

  - **Example:** Implementing policies for data anonymization, defining data retention periods, and establishing procedures for handling data breaches.

- **Managing GenAI Evaluations and Ensuring Model Quality:**

  - **Action:** Define and oversee the implementation of a robust GenAI evaluation process, ensuring that generative models used across the organization meet quality, safety, and ethical standards.

  - **Action:** Collaborate with data scientists and ethicists to select appropriate evaluation metrics and establish benchmarks for model performance.

  - **Example:** Establishing a process for regularly evaluating LLMs used in customer support chatbots for accuracy, coherence, and potential bias.

- **Driving Collaboration and Knowledge Sharing:**

  - **Action:** Foster a collaborative environment for AI development, facilitating communication and knowledge sharing between data scientists, engineers, product managers, and other stakeholders.

  - **Action:** Promote best practices for AI development and deployment, ensuring consistency and efficiency across teams.

  - **Example:** Organizing workshops and training sessions on AI/ML concepts and tools, creating internal documentation and wikis, and establishing regular communication channels.

- **Performance and Optimization Strategy:**
  - **Action:** Ensure AI systems are performing optimally in production and that best practices are shared across teams.

These responsibilities highlight the strategic and technical nature of the AI-Builder PM role. It's a role that requires a deep understanding of AI, strong leadership skills, and the ability to collaborate effectively with a wide range of stakeholders. The AI-Builder PM is the driving force behind building a solid foundation for AI innovation across the organization.

Day-to-Day Activities

The day-to-day activities of an AI-Builder PM are a mix of strategic planning, technical oversight, cross-functional collaboration, and hands-on problem-solving. They are constantly balancing the needs of different product teams, the constraints of the existing infrastructure, and the long-term vision for the AI platform. These diverse responsibilities can be grouped into five core pillars of activity, as shown in Figure 6-1. Here's a more detailed glimpse into their world:

- **Strategic Planning and Roadmapping:**
  - **Reviewing Requests for New AI Capabilities:** The PM analyzes requests from various product teams for new AI models, features, or platform enhancements. This involves understanding the underlying business needs and assessing the feasibility and potential impact of each request.
  - **Prioritizing Platform Development:** Based on the requests and the overall AI strategy, the PM prioritizes development efforts for the AI platform, balancing short-term needs with long-term goals. This might involve making trade-offs between building new features, improving existing infrastructure, and addressing technical debt.
  - **Developing and Maintaining the AI Platform Roadmap:** The PM creates and updates the roadmap for the AI platform, communicating the plan to stakeholders and ensuring alignment with business objectives.

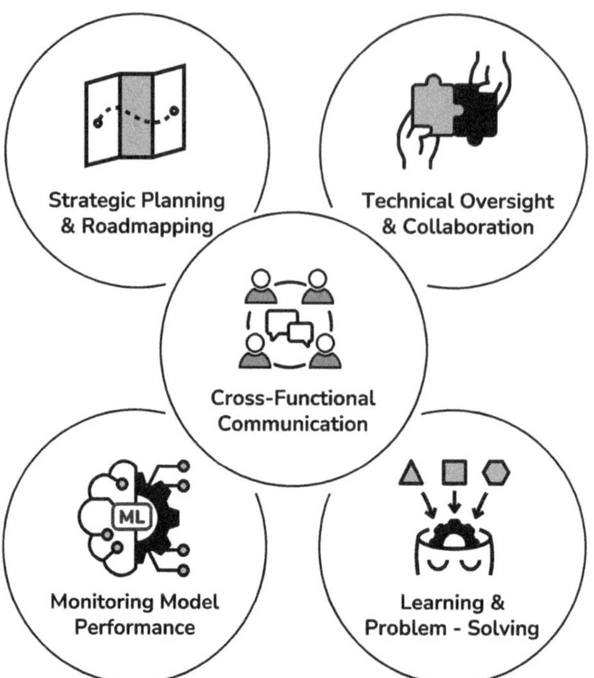

Figure 6-1: The five core pillars of an AI-Builder PM's daily activities, which range from high-level strategic planning and cross-functional communication to detailed technical oversight and performance monitoring

- **Technical Oversight and Collaboration:**

  - **Meetings with Data Scientists and ML Engineers:** The PM regularly meets with the technical teams building the AI models and platform. These meetings might involve discussing model performance, reviewing architecture designs, troubleshooting technical issues, or planning upcoming sprints.

  - **Reviewing Model Performance Metrics:** The PM monitors the performance of deployed AI models, looking for signs of degradation or opportunities for improvement. This might involve analyzing metrics like accuracy, latency, throughput, and cost.

  - **Collaborating with DevOps/MLOps Engineers:** The PM works with DevOps and MLOps engineers to ensure the smooth deployment, monitoring, and maintenance of AI models and infrastructure. This might involve discussing infrastructure requirements, setting up automated deployment pipelines, or troubleshooting production issues.

- **Reviewing Documentation and API Specifications:** The PM ensures that AI models and platform features are well-documented, with clear API specifications, making it easy for other teams to integrate them into their products.

- **Cross-Functional Communication and Alignment:**

  - **Presenting the AI Platform Roadmap to Stakeholders:** The PM regularly communicates the AI platform roadmap and progress to stakeholders, including product leadership, engineering teams, and other PMs. This involves explaining the platform's capabilities, benefits, and future plans.

  - **Gathering Feedback from Product Teams:** The PM actively solicits feedback from other product teams on their experiences using the AI platform, identifying areas for improvement and new feature requests.

  - **Advocating for AI Platform Adoption:** The PM encourages other product teams to leverage the AI platform, showcasing its benefits and providing support and guidance.

- **Staying Informed and Problem-Solving:**

  - **Learning about New AI Tools:** Some tools can help improve productivity.

  - **Troubleshooting Production Issues:** When problems arise with deployed AI models or infrastructure, the PM works with the technical teams to diagnose and resolve the issues, minimizing impact on users.

  - **Researching New Technologies:** The PM stays up-to-date on the latest advancements in AI and cloud computing, evaluating new technologies and tools that could potentially improve the AI platform.

The AI-Builder PM's days are filled with a diverse range of activities, requiring a strong blend of technical understanding, strategic thinking, and collaboration. They are constantly working to improve the AI foundation, empower other teams, and drive AI innovation across the organization.

Required Skills and Knowledge: The AI-Builder PM's Technical and Strategic Toolkit

The AI-Builder PM role demands a unique blend of technical expertise, strategic thinking, and product management acumen. This section outlines the essential skills and knowledge areas, categorized for clarity, and indicates the required proficiency level. We'll use the following proficiency levels, as shown in Figure 6-2:

- **Foundational:** Basic understanding of the concept; able to participate in discussions and understand implications.

- **Working Knowledge:** Able to apply the skill in common scenarios; can work independently on most related tasks.

- **Expert:** Deep understanding and mastery of the skill; can lead initiatives and mentor others.

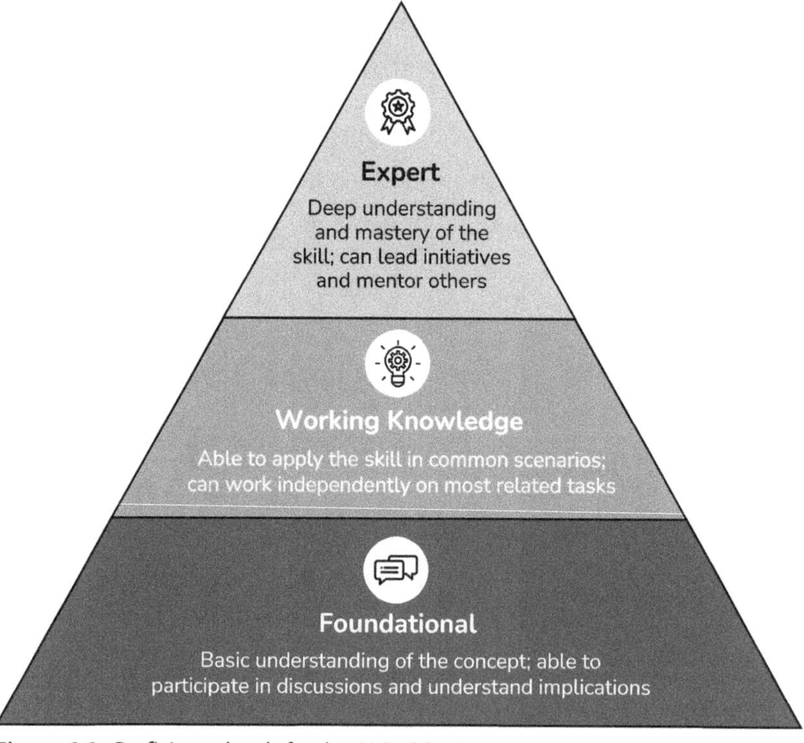

Figure 6-2: Proficiency levels for the AI-Builder PM

Core Product Management Craft and Practices

While the AI-Builder PM role is highly technical, success is built upon a rock-solid foundation of core product management principles. These skills are applied in a unique context: the "product" is a platform, the "users" are internal development teams, and the "features" are scalable AI capabilities. The following table outlines how these foundational PM skills are adapted for the strategic work of building the AI-powered backbone of an organization.

SKILL	PROFICIENCY LEVEL	HOW IT'S APPLIED (AI-BUILDER PM)
Strategic Thinking and Visioning	Expert	Defining the long-term vision and strategy for the AI platform, aligning it with business goals and anticipating future needs. Identifying opportunities to create reusable AI models and frameworks that can benefit multiple product teams.
Prioritization and Roadmapping	Expert	Prioritizing platform features, model development, and infrastructure improvements based on strategic value, technical feasibility, and resource constraints. Creating and maintaining the AI platform roadmap, communicating it to stakeholders, and managing dependencies.
Requirements Definition	Working Knowledge	Defining clear and detailed requirements for AI platforms, models, and frameworks, translating business needs and user stories into technical specifications.
Data Analysis and Interpretation	Working Knowledge	Analyzing data on platform usage, model performance, and infrastructure costs to identify trends, track progress, and make data-driven decisions. Understanding key metrics like API latency, model accuracy, and resource utilization.
Experimentation (A/B Testing)	Foundational	Understanding the principles of A/B testing and how it can be applied to evaluate different versions of AI models or platform features. (While the AI-Experiences PM might lead A/B testing, the AI-Builder PM needs to understand the process.)

Continues

(continued)

SKILL	PROFICIENCY LEVEL	HOW IT'S APPLIED (AI-BUILDER PM)
Go-to-Market Strategy and Execution	Foundational	Less directly relevant for this role, as the "customers" are typically internal teams. However, some basic understanding of GTM is helpful for communicating the value of the AI platform to internal stakeholders.

Engineering Foundations for PMs

To effectively architect foundational AI capabilities, the AI-Builder PM must possess a technical fluency that goes beyond that of a typical product manager. They don't need to write production code, but they must be able to hold their own in deep technical discussions about system architecture, algorithms, and infrastructure. This engineering foundation is essential for earning credibility with technical teams and making sound strategic decisions, as detailed in the following table.

SKILL	PROFICIENCY LEVEL	HOW IT'S APPLIED (AI-BUILDER PM)
Software Development Methodologies	Foundational	Understanding Agile/Scrum principles to collaborate effectively with engineering teams and manage AI platform development within iterative sprints.
Key Technical Concepts (APIs, Algorithms, System Architecture)	Working Knowledge	Understanding the technical architecture of AI platforms and models, including APIs, algorithms, data pipelines, and underlying infrastructure. This enables effective communication with technical teams and informed decision-making about platform design.
Working with AI Infrastructure	Expert	Deep understanding of cloud computing platforms (AWS, GCP, Azure), containerization (Docker, Kubernetes), and other infrastructure components relevant to AI. Making strategic decisions about infrastructure choices to ensure scalability, reliability, and cost-effectiveness.

SKILL	PROFICIENCY LEVEL	HOW IT'S APPLIED (AI-BUILDER PM)
Foundational Model Understanding	Expert	Understanding of foundational AI models and their applications, evaluation and the GenAI Evals processes.

Essential Leadership and Collaboration Skills

Building a centralized AI platform requires exceptional leadership and the ability to unite diverse, highly technical teams around a shared vision. The AI-Builder PM acts as a key influencer and cross-functional leader, driving alignment between data science, engineering, and other product teams. The table below outlines the critical leadership and collaboration skills needed to manage these complex dependencies and guide projects to success.

SKILL	PROFICIENCY LEVEL	HOW IT'S APPLIED (AI-BUILDER PM)
Communication and Storytelling	Working Knowledge	Communicating the vision, strategy, and roadmap for the AI platform to both technical and non-technical audiences. Explaining complex technical concepts in a clear and concise way.
Collaboration and Cross-Functional Teamwork	Expert	Working closely with data scientists, ML engineers, software engineers, DevOps engineers, product managers, and other stakeholders to build and maintain the AI platform.
Problem-Solving and Decision-Making	Expert	Identifying and resolving technical and strategic challenges related to AI platform development and deployment. Making informed decisions under uncertainty.
Influence and Persuasion	Working Knowledge	Advocating for the AI platform and securing buy-in from stakeholders. Influencing technical decisions and resource allocation.

Continues

(*continued*)

SKILL	PROFICIENCY LEVEL	HOW IT'S APPLIED (AI-BUILDER PM)
Adaptability and Learning Agility	Working Knowledge	Staying up-to-date with the rapidly evolving field of AI and adapting to new technologies and best practices. Being able to quickly learn and integrate new information.

AI Lifecycle and Operational Awareness

Beyond core PM and engineering skills, the AI-Builder PM must have a deep, operational awareness of the entire AI lifecycle. They are responsible for the systems that manage everything from data pipelines to model monitoring and retraining. The following table breaks down the essential AI-specific operational skills required to build and maintain a robust and reliable AI ecosystem.

SKILL	PROFICIENCY LEVEL	HOW IT'S APPLIED (AI-BUILDER PM)
Understanding AI and GenAI's Unique Capabilities	Expert	Deep understanding of various AI/ML techniques and their strengths and weaknesses. Identifying opportunities to leverage AI to solve business problems and create reusable AI capabilities.
DataOps and Management	Working Knowledge	Understanding data pipelines, data governance, and data privacy best practices. Ensuring that the AI platform has access to the necessary data and that data is used responsibly.
Productionization Considerations	Expert	Deep understanding of MLOps principles and practices. Designing and implementing processes for deploying, monitoring, and maintaining AI models in a production environment.

SKILL	PROFICIENCY LEVEL	HOW IT'S APPLIED (AI-BUILDER PM)
Ethics and Compliance	Working Knowledge	Ensuring that the AI platform and foundational models comply with ethical guidelines and legal regulations. Addressing potential biases in data and models.
Prompt Engineering (for LLMs)	Foundational/ Working Knowledge	(If applicable to the platform) Understanding the basics of prompt engineering and how it can be used to interact with LLMs. Might involve creating guidelines or tools for other teams using LLMs via the platform.
GenAI Evals understanding	Expert	Deep understanding of the different evaluation methods.

Illustrative Example: A Day in the Life of an AI-Builder PM

To provide a concrete understanding of the AI-Builder PM role, let's walk through a hypothetical day. This is not a rigid schedule, but rather a snapshot of the dynamic and multifaceted nature of the work. As Figure 6-3 illustrates, the day is a blend of strategic planning, technical collaboration, and forward-looking research.

Morning:

- **8:30 AM–9:00 AM: Review Platform Performance Metrics and Alerts—**
  The day begins by reviewing dashboards that track the performance of the AI platform and its key components (e.g., foundational models, APIs, data pipelines). The PM checks for any anomalies, performance degradations, or alerts triggered overnight. They notice a slight increase in latency for the product recommendation API and flag it for investigation by the engineering team.

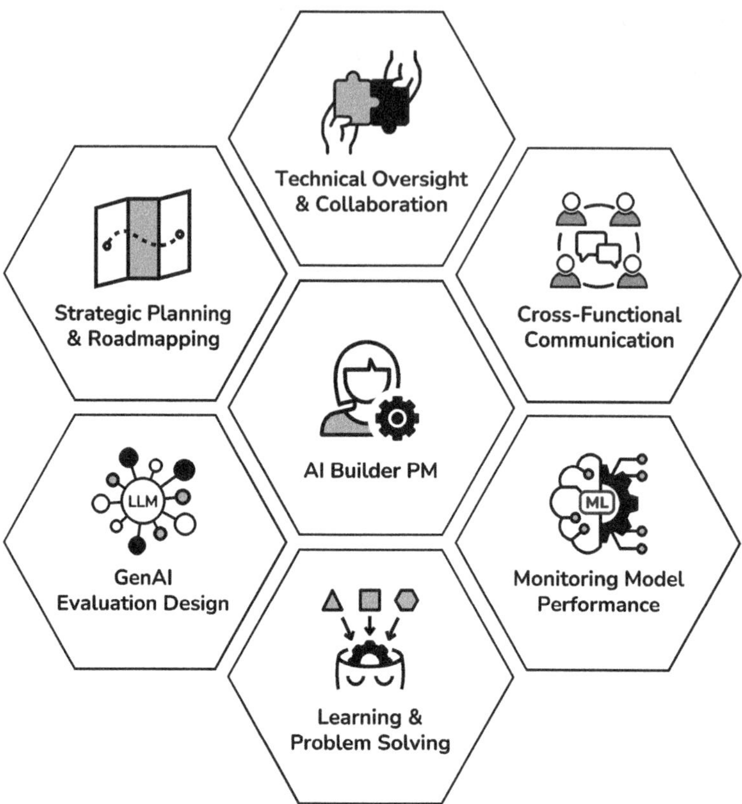

Figure 6-3: A snapshot of the core activities that define a day for an AI-Builder PM, balancing platform strategy, technical collaboration, and governance

Skills Used: Data Analysis and Interpretation, Foundational Model Understanding, Working with AI Infrastructure, Problem-Solving.

■ **9:00 AM–10:00 AM: Stand-up with the Platform Engineering Team—**
The PM participates in the daily stand-up meeting with the platform engineering team. They discuss progress on ongoing projects, address any roadblocks, and prioritize tasks for the day. The team discusses the latency issue flagged earlier and plans a diagnostic investigation.
Skills Used: Communication and Collaboration, Project Management, Technical Fluency.

■ **10:00 AM–11:00 AM: Meeting with Data Science Team—New Model Request—**
The PM meets with the lead data scientist from a product team that wants to integrate a new natural language processing (NLP)

model into their feature. They discuss the requirements for the model (input data, desired output, performance expectations), the feasibility of integrating it with the existing AI platform, and the timeline for development and deployment. The PM asks clarifying questions about the model's potential for bias and how the team plans to mitigate it.

Skills Used: Strategic Thinking, Deep ML Knowledge, Communication and Collaboration, Data Expertise, Ethical Considerations and Bias Mitigation.

▪ **11:00 AM–12:00 PM: Reviewing and Prioritizing Platform Feature Requests—**
The PM reviews a backlog of feature requests for the AI platform, submitted by various product teams. These requests range from support for new data sources to enhancements to the A/B testing framework. The PM prioritizes the requests based on strategic alignment, potential impact, and technical feasibility, updating the platform roadmap accordingly.

Skills Used: Prioritization and Roadmapping, Strategic Thinking, User Understanding.

Afternoon:

▪ **1:00 PM–2:30 PM: Working Session: Designing a New GenAI Evaluation Framework—**
The PM leads a working session with data scientists and ML engineers to design a standardized framework for evaluating generative AI models (GenAI Evals) across the organization. They discuss the different evaluation metrics to be used, how to collect human feedback, and how to automate the evaluation process as much as possible. The focus is on creating a reusable framework that can be applied to various GenAI applications.

Skills Used: GenAI Evals Management, Deep ML Knowledge, Collaboration, Problem-Solving.

▪ **2:30 PM–3:30 PM: Reviewing Documentation for a New API Endpoint—**
The PM reviews the documentation and API specifications for a newly deployed foundational model (a sentiment analysis API). They ensure that the documentation is clear, comprehensive, and easy to understand for other product teams who will be integrating with this API.

Skills Used: API Design and Development, Communication, Technical Fluency.

- **3:30 PM–4:30 PM: Meeting with Legal and Compliance—** The PM meets with representatives from the legal and compliance teams to discuss data governance policies for the AI platform. They review upcoming changes to data privacy regulations and discuss how to ensure the platform remains compliant.
  Skills Used: Data Governance and Compliance, Communication and Collaboration.

- **4:30 PM–5:00 PM: Catching Up on Industry News—** The PM dedicates some time to learn about new tools and research papers.
  Skill Used: Adaptability and Learning Agility.

This "day in the life" example demonstrates the breadth and depth of the AI-Builder PM role. It's a role that requires a strong technical foundation, strategic thinking, and excellent communication and collaboration skills. The AI-Builder PM is a key driver of AI innovation, enabling other teams to build and deploy AI-powered products efficiently and effectively. They are constantly balancing short-term needs with long-term vision, ensuring the AI platform remains a valuable asset for the entire organization.

Challenges and Complexities

The AI-Builder PM role is a challenging but highly rewarding one. It offers the opportunity to shape the technical foundation of AI within an organization, but it also demands a unique blend of technical expertise, strategic thinking, and leadership skills. Understanding both the challenges and rewards is key to assessing whether this is the right path for you.

Here are some of the common challenges you may face in this role:

- **Balancing Competing Priorities:** The AI-Builder PM often faces the challenge of balancing competing priorities from different product teams, all vying for access to the AI platform and its resources. They must make difficult trade-offs between supporting existing features, developing new capabilities, and addressing technical debt.

- **Managing Technical Complexity:** Building and maintaining a robust and scalable AI platform is inherently complex. The AI-Builder PM needs to understand the technical intricacies of the platform, anticipate potential problems, and work closely with engineering teams to resolve issues. This requires a strong technical foundation and the ability to quickly learn new technologies.

- **Keeping Up with the Pace of Innovation:** The field of AI is rapidly evolving, with new models, frameworks, and tools emerging constantly. The AI-Builder PM needs to stay abreast of these advancements and evaluate their potential impact on the AI platform. This requires continuous learning and a willingness to experiment with new approaches.

- **Ensuring Platform Adoption:** A beautifully engineered AI platform is useless if no one uses it. The AI-Builder PM needs to actively promote the platform within the organization, demonstrating its value to other product teams and encouraging its adoption. This requires strong communication and advocacy skills.

- **Data Governance and Security:** The AI-Builder PM is responsible for ensuring that the AI platform adheres to strict data governance and security policies. This involves working closely with legal and compliance teams to protect sensitive data and comply with relevant regulations.

- **Defining and Measuring Platform Success:** Unlike user-facing features, where success can be measured by direct user feedback and metrics like click-through rates, the success of an AI *platform* is often indirect. The AI-Builder PM needs to define metrics that reflect the platform's impact on *other* teams' ability to build and deploy AI solutions (e.g., time to deploy a new model, number of teams using the platform, cost savings from automation).

- **Managing Expectations:** Different stakeholders may have different expectations. The PM must make sure that everyone is aligned.

Despite the hurdles, the role is incredibly rewarding for several reasons:

- **Driving AI Innovation at Scale:** The AI-Builder PM has the opportunity to drive AI innovation across the *entire organization*, not just within a single product or feature. They empower other teams to leverage the power of AI, amplifying their impact.

- **Building a Foundation for the Future:** The AI-Builder PM is responsible for creating a solid technical foundation for future AI development, enabling the organization to adapt and innovate quickly. This is a highly strategic and impactful role.

- **Working with Cutting-Edge Technology:** The AI-Builder PM role is inherently technical, involving constant learning and experimentation with the latest AI models, frameworks, and tools. This is a rewarding experience for those who are passionate about technology and enjoy solving complex technical challenges.

- **Enabling Other Teams to Succeed:** The AI-Builder PM plays a critical role in empowering other product teams to build AI-powered features. They provide the tools, infrastructure, and support that enable these teams to succeed. This is a highly collaborative and rewarding aspect of the role.

- **Shaping the Organization's AI Strategy:** The AI-Builder PM has a significant influence on the organization's overall AI strategy, helping to define the direction of AI development and ensure that AI investments are aligned with business goals.

- **Seeing Broad Impact:** While the AI-Experiences PM focuses on the user-facing aspects of a *specific* feature, the AI-Builder PM sees the impact of their work across *multiple* products and teams. This provides a broader sense of accomplishment.

The AI-Builder PM role is demanding, requiring a unique combination of technical depth, strategic vision, and leadership skills. It's a role for those who enjoy building complex systems, solving challenging technical problems, and enabling others to succeed. But for those with the right skills and passion, it offers the opportunity to make a significant and lasting impact on the organization's ability to leverage the transformative power of artificial intelligence.

How the AI-Builder PM Interacts with Other Roles

The AI-Builder PM doesn't operate in isolation. Their success depends on close collaboration with a variety of other roles within the organization. Here's a breakdown of the key interactions:

- **Data Scientists:**
  - **Interaction:** The AI-Builder PM collaborates with data scientists on the development and deployment of foundational AI models. They provide product requirements, prioritize model features, and ensure that models are designed for reusability and scalability. Data scientists, in turn, provide technical expertise, build and train the models, and evaluate their performance.

- ■ **Key Dependency:** The AI-Builder PM *depends* on data scientists for the technical implementation of the AI models.

■ **Machine Learning (ML) Engineers:**

- ■ **Interaction:** The AI-Builder PM works closely with ML engineers to deploy, monitor, and maintain AI models and the AI platform. ML engineers are responsible for the operational aspects of MLOps.

- ■ **Key Dependency:** The AI-Builder PM *depends* on ML engineers to ensure the platform is reliable, scalable, and performant.

■ **Software Engineers:**

- ■ **Interaction:** The AI-Builder PM collaborates with software engineers to integrate AI models and platform features into various products and applications. This often involves defining APIs and ensuring seamless integration.

- ■ **Key Dependency:** The AI-Builder PM *depends* on software engineers to actually integrate the platform's capabilities into end-user products.

■ **UX Designers:**

- ■ **Interaction:** While the AI-Builder PM doesn't directly manage user-facing design, they *may* collaborate with UX Designers on the design of internal tools and dashboards for the AI platform itself (making it user-friendly for *internal* users—other PMs, data scientists, etc.). They might also provide technical guidance to UX Designers working on AI-Experiences features.

- ■ **Key Dependency:** The success of the platform's adoption often depends on UX Designers creating intuitive and efficient interfaces for its internal tools and dashboards.

■ **Other Product Managers (Especially AI-Experiences PMs):**

- ■ **Interaction:** This is a *critical* relationship. The AI-Builder PM acts as a service provider to other PMs, particularly AI-Experiences PMs. They gather requirements, provide support, and ensure the AI platform meets the needs of different product teams.

- ■ **Key Dependency:** The AI-Builder PM *depends* on other PMs to adopt and utilize the AI platform. The AI-Experiences PMs are the "customers" of the AI-Builder PM.

- **Marketing/Sales:**
  - **Interaction:** The AI-Builder PM may need to explain to internal stakeholders how the platform works.
  - **Key Dependency**: The AI-Builder PM provides information that may help other teams understand the product better.

- **Legal/Compliance:**
  - **Interaction:** The AI-Builder PM works with legal and compliance teams to ensure that the AI platform and its data usage adhere to all relevant regulations and ethical guidelines.
  - **Key Dependency:** The AI-Builder PM *depends* on legal/compliance for guidance on data governance, privacy, and ethical considerations.

- **Executive Leadership**
  - **Interaction:** The AI-Builder PM regularly communicates the strategic vision, progress, and business impact of the AI platform to executive leadership through reports, presentations, and roadmap reviews.
  - **Key Dependency**: The AI-Builder PM depends on executive leadership for strategic alignment, resource allocation, and buy-in for the long-term vision of the AI platform.

The AI-Builder PM acts as a central hub, connecting technical teams (data science, engineering) with product teams and ensuring that AI capabilities are developed and deployed effectively across the organization. Strong communication, collaboration, and a deep understanding of both technical and business needs are essential for success in this role.

Chapter Summary and Key Takeaways

In this chapter you explored the strategic and highly technical role of the AI-Builder PM. You've seen how this product leader architects the foundational AI capabilities—the platforms, reusable models, and MLOps frameworks—that empower an entire organization. You now understand that their focus is not on a single product feature, but on creating the scalable and reliable infrastructure that enables all future AI-driven innovation. This is a role defined by strategic vision, technical depth, and the ability to enable other teams to succeed.

Figure 6-4 summarizes the core aspects of this foundational role.

AI - BUILDER PM
Architecting the foundation of intelligent systems

Role Summary 

Builds core AI platforms, models, and frameworks to enable AI innovation across the organization.

Why it matters? 

A strong AI foundation is essential for developing and deploying AI solutions efficiently and effectively.

Collaboration 

Works with data scientists, engineers, and AI-experienced PMs to translate product strategy into technical roadmaps.

Key Trade - Offs 

- Cutting-edge vs. scalability
- Maintainability vs. cost
- Data governance vs. agility
- Responsible AI

Essential Skils & Mindset 

- Technical expertise
- Strategic vision
- Communication
- Proactive

Figure 6-4: A summary of the AI-Builder PM role, highlighting its core focus on creating foundational AI capabilities, key collaborators, strategic trade-offs, and essential skills

Key Takeaways

- **Your "product" Is the Platform.** As an AI-Builder PM, your primary customers are internal development teams, and your success is measured by their ability to efficiently build and deploy high-quality AI features.

- **Technical Depth Is Strategic.** This role requires a strong understanding of AI infrastructure, MLOps, and model architecture to make credible strategic decisions and guide technical teams effectively.

- **Your Goal Is to Create Leverage.** The core mission is to build scalable and reusable AI assets that can be used across multiple products, driving efficiency and consistency for the entire organization.

- **You Are an Enabler of Innovation.** In this role, you are a key force multiplier, providing the tools, systems, and governance that accelerate AI development for everyone else.

Onward: Supercharging the PM Workflow

After covering the PMs who build AI experiences and AI platforms, you're now ready to shift focus to a third emerging specialization. The next chapter will explore the AI-Enhanced PM, who uses AI not to build products for others, but to supercharge their own product management workflow.

AI-Enhanced PM: Supercharging Product Management with AI

The AI-Enhanced PM isn't primarily focused on *building* AI products or features *for users*. Instead, they are masters at leveraging AI to *improve their own product management workflows and decision-making*. Think of them as power users of AI, applying its capabilities to become more efficient, data-driven, and strategic. They are the PMs who embrace AI as a personal productivity and insight-generation tool.

This role is becoming increasingly important because AI offers a wealth of tools that can significantly enhance the *practice* of product management itself. The AI-Enhanced PM actively seeks out and adopts these tools, becoming a more effective and impactful product leader.

This PM collaborates with all the usual stakeholders (engineers, designers, marketing, etc.), but their relationship with data scientists and ML engineers is different from the other two PM roles. The AI-Enhanced PM is a *consumer* of AI tools and insights, rather than a direct collaborator on building AI models or platforms. They might provide feedback on internally built AI tools, but their primary focus is on *application*, not *creation*.

The inherent challenges in this role involve staying up-to-date with the rapidly evolving landscape of AI tools, selecting the *right* tools for the job, integrating them effectively into existing workflows, and critically evaluating the outputs of AI to avoid over-reliance or misinterpretation. It also involves championing the use of AI tools within their product teams, fostering a data-driven culture.

A *highly effective* AI-Enhanced PM is a data-savvy, tool-proficient, and adaptable product leader. They are curious, constantly seeking new ways to leverage AI to improve their work. They are also critical thinkers, able to evaluate the outputs of AI tools and avoid blind acceptance. They are champions of AI adoption within their teams, leading by example.

Let's delve into the specific responsibilities that define this increasingly vital role.

Key Responsibilities: Augmenting PM Workflows and Decision-Making with AI

The AI-Enhanced PM is responsible for strategically integrating AI tools and techniques into their own workflow and, by extension, into the workflows of their product team. This involves a proactive and continuous effort to improve efficiency, decision-making, and overall product outcomes.

- **Identifying Opportunities for AI-Powered Workflow Enhancement:**

  - **Action:** Proactively identify areas within the product management process where AI tools can automate tasks, provide insights, or improve decision-making. This requires a deep understanding of both PM workflows and the capabilities of available AI tools.

  - **Example:** Recognizing that competitive analysis is time-consuming and identifying AI-powered tools that can automate the process of gathering and analyzing competitor information.

- **Evaluating and Selecting AI Tools for Product Management:**

  - **Action:** Research and evaluate the landscape of AI-powered tools designed for product management tasks (e.g., market research, user feedback analysis, roadmap prioritization, documentation).

  - **Action:** Select tools based on their capabilities, cost-effectiveness, ease of integration, and alignment with the team's needs.

- ▪ **Example:** Evaluating different AI-powered user feedback analysis tools, comparing their features, accuracy, and pricing to choose the best option for the team.

- ▪ **Integrating AI Tools into PM Workflows:**

  - ▪ **Action:** Seamlessly integrate chosen AI tools into their daily work routines and the workflows of the product team. This involves developing processes and best practices for using the tools effectively.

  - ▪ **Example:** Integrating an AI-powered meeting summarization tool into the team's meeting workflow, establishing guidelines for when and how to use the tool, and ensuring that the summaries are easily accessible to all team members.

- ▪ **Driving Adoption of AI Tools within the Product Team:**

  - ▪ **Action:** Champion the use of AI tools within the product team, providing training, support, and guidance to colleagues. This involves demonstrating the value of the tools and fostering a culture of experimentation.

  - ▪ **Example:** Organizing a workshop to train other PMs on how to use an AI-powered user research analysis tool, sharing best practices and success stories.

- ▪ **Measuring and Optimizing the Impact of AI Tools:**

  - ▪ **Action:** Define metrics to track the impact of AI tools on PM productivity, decision-making quality, and overall product outcomes.

  - ▪ **Action:** Regularly analyze these metrics and identify areas for improvement, optimizing tool usage and workflows based on data-driven insights.

  - ▪ **Example:** Tracking the time saved by using an AI-powered documentation generation tool and measuring the impact on product release cycles.

- ▪ **Staying Current with AI Trends and Best Practices:**

  - ▪ **Action:** Continuously monitor the rapidly evolving AI landscape, identifying new tools, techniques, and best practices that could benefit the product team.

  - ▪ **Example:** Attending webinars on new AI-powered market research tools, reading articles about prompt engineering for LLMs, and experimenting with new AI platforms.

- **Advocating for AI Literacy and Adoption:**
  - **Action:** Promote AI literacy within the broader organization, sharing knowledge and insights with other teams and advocating for the responsible and effective use of AI.
  - **Action:** Help shape processes to improve AI adoption.
  - **Example:** Presenting case studies of how the product team has successfully leveraged AI to improve its workflows, inspiring other teams to explore similar opportunities.
- **Ensuring Responsible and Ethical Use of AI:**
  - **Action**: Make sure that all the tools used follow ethical guidelines.

These responsibilities demonstrate that the AI-Enhanced PM is not just a user of AI tools, but a *strategic adopter and champion* of AI within the product management function. They are constantly seeking ways to leverage AI to improve their own work and the work of their team, ultimately leading to better product decisions and more successful products.

Day-to-Day Activities

The day-to-day activities of an AI-Enhanced PM are a mix of strategic analysis, hands-on tool evaluation, workflow optimization, and data-driven decision-making. They are constantly balancing the potential of new AI tools with the practical needs of their product team, seeking to augment their capabilities without sacrificing critical judgment. These diverse activities can be grouped into five core areas, as shown in Figure 7-1. Here's a more detailed glimpse into their typical activities:

- **Market and Competitive Analysis:**
  - **Using AI-Powered Tools to Monitor Competitor Activity:** The PM might use tools that automatically track competitor websites, social media mentions, and press releases, identifying new feature launches, marketing campaigns, and customer sentiment. This goes beyond manual Google searches, providing automated analysis and alerts.
  - **Analyzing Industry Trends with AI:** Leveraging AI platforms that analyze large datasets of market research reports, news articles, and social media conversations to identify emerging

trends and potential disruptions. This helps inform product strategy and roadmap prioritization.

Figure 7-1: The five core areas of an AI-Enhanced PM's daily activities, which range from high-level market analysis and strategic planning to personal productivity and learning, and user feedback analysis

- **User Research and Feedback Analysis:**

  - **Summarizing and Synthesizing User Feedback**: Using NLP tools to analyze user reviews, survey responses, and support tickets, identifying key themes, pain points, and feature requests. This replaces manual tagging and analysis of qualitative data.

  - **Identifying User Segments with AI**: Applying unsupervised learning techniques (clustering) to user data to identify distinct user segments with different needs and behaviors, even if those segments weren't predefined. This informs personalization strategies.

- **Product Strategy and Planning:**

  - **AI-Assisted Roadmap Prioritization:** Using AI tools that analyze various data points (user feedback, market trends, technical feasibility, business goals) to help prioritize features on the product roadmap. This provides a more data-driven approach to prioritization.

- **Generating Product Ideas with AI:** Experimenting with LLMs to brainstorm new product feature ideas or variations on existing features, using prompts based on user needs and market opportunities.

- **Drafting Product Requirement Documents (PRDs):** PMs can leverage an LLM to create an initial draft of a PRD.

■ **Communication and Collaboration:**

- **Creating Presentations and Reports with AI Assistance**: Using AI tools to generate summaries of data, create visuals, and even draft presentations, saving time and improving communication.

- **Automating Meeting Scheduling and Follow-up**: Using AI-powered scheduling tools to find optimal meeting times for team members and automatically send follow-up emails with action items.

- **AI-Powered Note-Taking and Summarization**: Using tools that transcribe meetings, generate summaries, and extract key decisions and action items, ensuring nothing is missed.

■ **Personal Productivity and Learning:**

- **Automating Routine Tasks:** Using AI-powered tools to automate tasks like email filtering, calendar management, and data entry, freeing up time for more strategic work.

- **Staying Current with AI Advancements:** Dedicating time to reading articles, attending webinars, and experimenting with new AI tools to stay informed about the latest developments in the field.

■ **Team Meetings**

- Sharing insights found by using any of the mentioned AI tools, and making decisions with the team.

The AI-Enhanced PM is constantly seeking ways to *augment* their own capabilities and those of their team with AI. They are not just managing products; they are actively transforming the *process* of product management itself, embracing AI as a powerful tool for innovation and efficiency.

Required Skills and Knowledge: The AI-Enhanced PM's Toolkit

The AI-Enhanced PM needs a blend of core product management skills, a foundational understanding of AI, and a strong aptitude for adopting and integrating new technologies. This section outlines the key skills and knowledge areas, categorized for clarity, and indicates the required proficiency level.

We'll use the following proficiency levels:

- **Foundational**: Basic understanding of the concept; able to participate in discussions and understand implications.

- **Working Knowledge**: Able to apply the skill in common scenarios; can work independently on most related tasks.

- **Expert**: Deep understanding and mastery of the skill; can lead initiatives and mentor others.

Core Product Management Craft and Practices

The AI-Enhanced PM builds upon the foundation of core product management skills, but with a key difference: they actively leverage AI to augment and accelerate these practices. Their goal is to use intelligent tools to become more efficient and insightful in their day-to-day work. The following table outlines how these core skills are transformed when viewed through an AI-powered lens.

SKILL	PROFICIENCY LEVEL	HOW IT'S APPLIED (AI-ENHANCED PM)
Data Analysis and Interpretation	Expert	Analyzing data from various sources (user feedback, market research, competitive analysis) to identify trends, patterns, and insights. Interpreting AI-generated insights and translating them into actionable product decisions.
Experimentation (A/B Testing)	Working Knowledge	Designing and executing A/B tests to evaluate the effectiveness of AI tools and workflows.

Continues

(continued)

SKILL	PROFICIENCY LEVEL	HOW IT'S APPLIED (AI-ENHANCED PM)
User Research and Feedback Analysis	Working Knowledge	Using AI tools to analyze user feedback and identify key themes and pain points. Understanding the limitations of AI-powered analysis and supplementing it with qualitative research when necessary.
Prioritization and Roadmapping	Working Knowledge	Prioritizing product initiatives and incorporating AI tool adoption into the product roadmap.
Requirements Definition	Working Knowledge	Writing clear and concise requirements for integrating AI tools into PM workflows.
Go-to-Market Strategy and Execution	Foundational	Less directly relevant for this role, as the focus is on internal tools. However, a basic understanding is helpful for communicating the value of AI-enhanced workflows to stakeholders.

Engineering Foundations for PMs

While the AI-Enhanced PM is not a technical role, a foundational understanding of key engineering concepts is essential for effectively selecting and integrating AI tools. This knowledge empowers them to assess a tool's capabilities, understand how it connects with existing systems, and collaborate with IT or engineering support when needed. The table below details the necessary level of technical fluency.

SKILL	PROFICIENCY LEVEL	HOW IT'S APPLIED (AI-ENHANCED PM)
Software Development Methodologies	Foundational	Understanding Agile/Scrum principles to effectively manage projects and collaborate with teams using AI tools.
Key Technical Concepts (APIs, Algorithms, System Architecture)	Foundational	Understanding the basic concepts of APIs and how they can be used to integrate AI tools into existing workflows. Having a high-level understanding of different AI algorithms and their capabilities.

SKILL	PROFICIENCY LEVEL	HOW IT'S APPLIED (AI-ENHANCED PM)
Working with AI Infrastructure	Foundational	Understanding the basics of cloud computing and data storage, as many AI tools are cloud-based.

Essential Leadership and Collaboration Skills

For the AI-Enhanced PM, leadership often takes the form of being a change agent and an internal champion for new ways of working. Their role requires strong communication and influence to encourage the adoption of AI tools and data-driven practices within the broader product team. The following table outlines the critical leadership skills needed to drive this transformation.

SKILL	PROFICIENCY LEVEL	HOW IT'S APPLIED (AI-ENHANCED PM)
Communication and Storytelling	Working Knowledge	Communicating the value of AI tools to other PMs and stakeholders. Sharing best practices and success stories to encourage adoption. Explaining the insights derived from AI-powered analysis in a clear and concise way.
Collaboration and Cross-Functional Teamwork	Working Knowledge	Working with other PMs, data analysts, and IT teams to integrate AI tools into existing workflows.
Problem-Solving and Decision-Making	Working Knowledge	Identifying and solving problems related to AI tool integration and usage. Making data-driven decisions based on insights from AI-powered analysis.
Influence and Persuasion	Working Knowledge	Advocating for the adoption of AI tools within the product team and the broader organization. Securing buy-in for investment in AI tools and training.

Continues

(continued)

SKILL	PROFICIENCY LEVEL	HOW IT'S APPLIED (AI-ENHANCED PM)
Adaptability and Learning Agility	Expert	Staying up-to-date with the rapidly evolving landscape of AI tools and technologies. Being willing to experiment with new tools and adapt workflows as needed. This is a defining characteristic of the AI-Enhanced PM.

AI Lifecycle and Operational Awareness

An AI-Enhanced PM must be an intelligent consumer of AI, which requires an awareness of the broader AI lifecycle and its operational realities. Understanding the capabilities, limitations, and ethical considerations of AI tools is very important for using them responsibly and effectively. The following table breaks down the essential AI-specific awareness needed to leverage these tools successfully.

SKILL	PROFICIENCY LEVEL	HOW IT'S APPLIED (AI-ENHANCED PM)
Understanding AI and GenAI's Unique Capabilities	Working Knowledge	Identifying opportunities to leverage AI's strengths (e.g., automation, pattern recognition, content generation) to improve PM workflows. Understanding the limitations of AI and avoiding over-reliance on AI-generated outputs.
DataOps and Management	Foundational	Understanding the data requirements of different AI tools and ensuring that data is accessible and usable.
Productionization Considerations	Foundational	Understanding the basic principles of deploying and maintaining software, as they apply to integrating AI tools.

SKILL	PROFICIENCY LEVEL	HOW IT'S APPLIED (AI-ENHANCED PM)
Ethics and Compliance	Working Knowledge	Ensuring that AI tools are used ethically and in compliance with relevant regulations. Being aware of potential biases in AI-powered analysis and taking steps to mitigate them.
Prompt Engineering (for LLMs)	Working Knowledge	Effectively using LLMs and other generative AI tools by crafting clear and specific prompts. Understanding how to control the output of these models.
GenAI Evals Understanding	Working Knowledge	Understanding how Generative AI is evaluated.

Illustrative Example: A Day in the Life of an AI-Enhanced PM

To understand the AI-Enhanced PM role in practice, let's walk through a hypothetical day, showcasing the diverse range of activities and interactions that might be involved. This is not a rigid schedule, but rather a snapshot of how an AI-Enhanced PM might leverage AI tools to improve their workflow and decision-making. This PM works for a company that develops a popular project management SaaS platform.

Morning:

- **8:30 AM–9:00 AM: Competitive Landscape Analysis—**
  The day starts by using an AI-powered competitive intelligence tool. Instead of manually searching for competitor news and updates, the tool automatically aggregates relevant information from various sources (news articles, social media, company websites). The tool also uses NLP to summarize key developments and highlight potential threats and opportunities. The PM reviews the AI-generated summary, noting that a major competitor has just released a new feature similar to one on the PM's roadmap.

Skills Used: Data Analysis and Interpretation, AI Tool Proficiency, Strategic Thinking.

▪ **9:00 AM–9:30 AM: User Feedback Review—**
The PM uses an AI-powered sentiment analysis tool to analyze the latest batch of user feedback from in-app surveys and support tickets. The tool automatically categorizes feedback by topic and sentiment (positive, negative, neutral). The PM quickly identifies a recurring theme of user frustration with the platform's reporting features.
Skills Used: User Research & Feedback Analysis, AI Tool Proficiency, Data Literacy.

▪ **9:30 AM–10:30 AM: Sprint Planning Meeting—**
The PM participates in the bi-weekly sprint planning meeting with the engineering and design teams. They use an AI-powered project management tool (integrated into their existing platform) that analyzes historical sprint data to predict task completion times and identify potential bottlenecks. The PM uses these insights to guide the discussion and ensure the team commits to a realistic and achievable sprint goal. They also use a collaborative document where an LLM is embedded, so they use it for note-taking and summarizing.
Skills Used: Communication and Collaboration, Data Analysis and Interpretation, Workflow Optimization, AI Tool Proficiency.

▪ **10:30 AM–12:00 PM: Synthesizing User Research with AI Tools—**
Following up on the user feedback theme discussed in sprint planning, the PM uses an AI tool like NotebookLM to upload several recent user interview transcripts. They ask the tool to summarize the key pain points related to the platform's reporting features and to identify any direct quotes that highlight user frustration. This provides powerful qualitative evidence to support the PRD they will draft later in the day.
Skills Used: User Research and Feedback Analysis, AI Tool Proficiency, Data Literacy.

Afternoon:

▪ **1:00 PM–2:00 PM: Drafting a PRD—**
The PM is drafting a PRD for a new feature. They use an LLM (like ChatGPT or a specialized writing assistant) to help brainstorm different approaches to the feature, generate initial drafts

of user stories, and refine the language of the document. The PM critically evaluates the AI-generated content, making edits and additions as needed.

Skills Used: Requirements Definition, AI Tool Proficiency, Critical Evaluation, Communication.

- **2:00 PM–3:00 PM: Roadmap Prioritization Exercise—**
The PM uses an AI-powered prioritization tool that analyzes data from various sources (user feedback, market research, internal metrics) to help rank potential features for the next quarter's roadmap. The tool considers factors like user impact, business value, and technical feasibility. The PM reviews the AI's recommendations, adjusts the rankings based on their own product judgment, and prepares a presentation for the leadership team.
Skills Used: Prioritization and Roadmapping, Data Analysis and Interpretation, AI Tool Proficiency, Strategic Thinking.

- **3:00 PM–4:00 PM: Exploring New AI Tools—**
The PM dedicates time to exploring a new AI-powered user research platform that claims to automate the process of user interview analysis. They sign up for a free trial, test the platform with some sample data, and evaluate its potential value for their team.
Skills Used: Adaptability and Learning Agility, Tool Proficiency, Critical Evaluation.

- **4:00 PM–4:30 PM: Team Training Session Prep—**
The PM prepares a short presentation for the product team on how to effectively use the new AI-powered summarization tool they've integrated into their workflow. They focus on practical tips and best practices, demonstrating how the tool can save time and improve communication.
Skills Used: Communication and Collaboration, Tool Proficiency, Change Management.

- **4:30 PM–5:00 PM: Review and Plan—**
The PM takes some time to review dashboards that show relevant data related to the use of AI tools.
Based on their review, they make some adjustments on tomorrow's plan.

This "day in the life" example illustrates how the AI-Enhanced PM seamlessly integrates AI tools and techniques into their daily workflow, leveraging AI to improve efficiency, gain deeper insights, and make more informed decisions. They are not just a *user* of AI; they are a *strategic adopter* and *champion* of AI within the product management function. They are constantly seeking new ways to leverage AI to enhance their own work and the work of their team, ultimately contributing to the development of better products.

Examples of AI Tools

The landscape of AI tools is evolving at an incredible pace, with new applications emerging weekly. Therefore, the following list is not meant to be an exhaustive or permanent set of recommendations, but rather a snapshot of the types of powerful tools that AI-Enhanced PMs are using today to accelerate their work. The key is to develop a mindset of continuous exploration to find the tools that best fit your needs.

These tools generally fall into several categories:

- **For Ideation, Writing, and Planning:** Tools that act as a brainstorming partner or writing assistant.
  - **Gemini, Claude, ChatGPT:** Large Language Models excellent for generating ideas, drafting PRDs, writing user stories, summarizing text, and planning projects.

- **For Research and Real-Time Insights:** Tools that can synthesize information from the live Internet.
  - **Perplexity, Grok:** Act as "answer engines" that can provide real-time information, research topics, and offer cited sources for market analysis.

- **For Information Distillation and Learning:** Tools designed to help you analyze and understand large sets of documents.
  - **NotebookLM:** A research assistant that can answer questions and generate insights from your own source documents (like user interviews, research papers, etc.).

- **For Meeting and Workflow Productivity:** Tools designed to automate common, time-consuming tasks.
  - **Granola, Otter.ai:** Take notes, transcribe meetings, and generate summaries with action items.
  - **SuperWhisper:** Real-time dictation to quickly get thoughts onto paper.

- **For Prototyping and UI Generation:** Tools that can accelerate the design and development process.

    - **Bolt + Cursor:** AI-powered tools to help build MVPs and working code prototypes faster.

    - **v0.dev, Lovable:** Generate working user interfaces from natural language prompts, allowing for rapid UI prototyping.

Challenges and Complexities

The AI-Enhanced PM role is on the cutting edge of product management, offering significant opportunities to boost productivity and improve decision-making. However, like any role that embraces new technologies, it comes with its own set of challenges. Understanding both sides of the coin is essential for success.

Here are some of the common challenges you may face in this role:

- **Tool Selection Overload:** The landscape of AI-powered tools for PMs is rapidly expanding. It can be overwhelming to choose the *right* tools, evaluate their effectiveness, and avoid getting bogged down in "shiny object syndrome." The PM needs to be discerning and focus on tools that genuinely address their needs.

- **Integration Complexity:** Integrating AI tools into existing PM workflows can be complex, requiring technical expertise and careful planning. Data compatibility, API integrations, and workflow adjustments can present significant hurdles.

- **Data Dependency and Quality:** Many AI tools rely on data, and the quality of that data directly impacts the quality of the insights generated. The AI-Enhanced PM may face challenges related to data access, data cleanliness, and data bias.

- **Over-Reliance on AI:** It's important to remember that AI is a *tool*, not a replacement for human judgment. Over-relying on AI-generated insights without critical evaluation can lead to poor decisions. The AI-Enhanced PM needs to maintain a healthy skepticism and always validate AI outputs.

- **"Black Box" Concerns:** Some AI tools are "black boxes," meaning it's difficult to understand *why* they are producing certain outputs.

This lack of transparency can make it challenging to trust the results or troubleshoot problems.

- **Keeping Up with the Pace of Change:** The field of AI is evolving at an incredibly rapid pace. The AI-Enhanced PM needs to be a continuous learner, constantly updating their knowledge and skills to stay ahead of the curve.

- **Driving Adoption within the Team**: Convincing other PMs to adopt new AI tools and change their established workflows can be a challenge. The AI-Enhanced PM needs to be a strong advocate for AI and demonstrate its value through concrete results.

- **Measuring the ROI of AI Tools:** It's important to ensure that the investment made on tools is worth it.

Despite the hurdles, the role is incredibly rewarding for several reasons:

- **Increased Productivity and Efficiency:** AI tools can automate many routine PM tasks, freeing up time for more strategic work, such as user research, product visioning, and stakeholder communication. This is a direct and tangible benefit.

- **Data-Driven Decision-Making:** AI-powered analytics can provide deeper insights into user behavior, market trends, and competitive landscapes, enabling PMs to make more informed and data-driven decisions.

- **Enhanced Creativity and Innovation:** AI tools can help PMs brainstorm new ideas, explore different solutions, and generate creative content, fostering innovation.

- **Improved Product Outcomes:** By leveraging AI to improve their own workflows and decision-making, AI-Enhanced PMs can ultimately contribute to the development of better, more user-centric products.

- **Becoming a Thought Leader:** The AI-Enhanced PM is often seen as a pioneer and innovator within their organization, shaping the future of product management and driving the adoption of AI best practices.

- **Personal and Professional Growth:** The AI-Enhanced PM role offers a unique opportunity for continuous learning and professional growth in a rapidly evolving field.

The AI-Enhanced PM role is not without its challenges, but it offers significant rewards for those who are willing to embrace the opportunities of AI. It's a role for PMs who are passionate about technology, data, and continuous improvement. By strategically integrating AI into their work, AI-Enhanced PMs can elevate their own performance, empower their teams, and drive product innovation.

How the AI-Enhanced PM Interacts with Other Roles

The AI-Enhanced PM's collaborative role is unique. They act less as a director of a specific AI feature and more as a "force multiplier" for their entire product team. Their interactions are focused on two key areas: first, leveraging AI-generated insights to inform and align stakeholders, and second, championing the adoption of new tools and workflows to make the entire team more efficient and data-driven.

Understanding these key interactions reveals how the AI-Enhanced PM drives value not by building AI products, but by transforming the product management process itself. Here's a breakdown of the most important relationships:

- **Other Product Managers (Especially AI-Experiences and AI-Builder PMs):**
  - **Interaction:** The AI-Enhanced PM shares insights and best practices on using AI tools for product management. They might champion the adoption of specific tools across the PM organization. They may also provide feedback on internally built AI tools (if those tools are used by PMs). They may get insights from AI-Builder PMs.
  - **Key Dependency:** The AI-Enhanced PM benefits from the work of the AI-Builder PM (if an internal AI platform exists) and can inform the work of the AI-Experiences PM by showcasing the potential of AI-driven insights.
- **Data Scientists:**
  - **Interaction:** The AI-Enhanced PM *consumes* insights and tools developed by data scientists, but typically doesn't directly collaborate on model building. They might provide feedback on the usability of data analysis tools or request specific analyses to be performed. They might also share insights gleaned from AI-powered tools *with* data scientists, potentially sparking new research directions.

- **Key Dependency:** The AI-Enhanced PM *depends on* data scientists for access to high-quality data analysis and, potentially, for the development of internal AI-powered tools for PMs.

- **ML Engineers:**

  - **Interaction:** Direct interaction with ML engineers is typically limited; however, the AI-Enhanced PM may collaborate with them when providing feedback on the performance or usability of internal MLOps tools and deployment platforms.

  - **Key Dependency:** The AI-Enhanced PM has an indirect dependency on ML engineers, as the reliability and performance of the AI tools they use often rely on the underlying infrastructure and MLOps practices that ML engineers maintain.

- **Software Engineers:**

  - **Interaction:** The AI-Enhanced PM might work with software engineers to integrate AI-powered tools into existing PM workflows (e.g., integrating a user feedback analysis tool into the company's CRM).

  - **Key Dependency:** The AI-Enhanced PM *depends on* software engineers for the technical implementation of any workflow integrations involving AI tools.

- **UX Designers:**

  - **Interaction:** Interaction with UX designers is less frequent than for an AI-Experiences PM. The primary collaboration occurs when the AI-Enhanced PM provides feedback on the usability and design of internal AI-powered tools used by the product team, rather than on user-facing product interfaces.

  - **Key Dependency:** Indirect—relies on good UX design for the tools they use.

- **Marketing/Sales:**

  - **Interaction:** The AI-Enhanced PM might use AI-powered tools for market research, competitive analysis, or lead scoring, which could inform marketing and sales strategies. They might also share insights gleaned from AI-powered user feedback analysis.

  - **Key Dependency:** May use insights generated by the AI-Enhanced PM to inform their strategies.

- **Legal/Compliance:**
  - **Interaction:** The AI-Enhanced PM ensures that the AI tools they use comply with all relevant regulations and ethical guidelines, particularly regarding data privacy.
  - **Key Dependency:** The AI-Enhanced PM *depends on* legal/compliance for guidance on data usage and ethical considerations.
- **Executive Leadership:**
  - **Interaction**: Interaction with executive leadership involves providing regular updates and reports on the measurable impact of AI tools on team productivity and decision-making, as well as advocating for continued investment.
  - **Key Dependency**: The PM's ability to drive team-wide efficiency is dependent on securing buy-in and budget approval from executive leadership for acquiring new AI tools and implementing training programs.

The AI-Enhanced PM is a *power user and advocate* for AI within the product management organization. They are less about *building* AI and more about *leveraging* it to improve their own work and the work of their peers. They are a bridge between the potential of AI and the practical realities of day-to-day product management.

Skill Comparison: AI-Experiences PM, AI-Builder PM, and AI-Enhanced PM

The following table provides a comparative overview of the key skills and knowledge areas required for each of the three AI Product Manager specializations we've discussed: AI-Experiences PM, AI-Builder PM, and AI-Enhanced PM. This is *not* a rigid checklist; the specific skills and required proficiency levels will vary depending on the organization, the product, and the specific responsibilities of the role. However, it serves as a valuable guide for understanding the core competencies of each specialization and for identifying areas for your own professional development.

The "How It's Applied" column for each role provides specific examples of how that skill is used in the context of that PM specialization. This is critical for understanding the *practical application* of each skill, beyond just a theoretical definition.

SKILL CATEGORY	SKILL	AI-EXPERIENCES PM	HOW IT'S APPLIED (AI-EXPERIENCES)	AI-BUILDER PM	HOW IT'S APPLIED (AI-BUILDER)	AI-ENHANCED PM	HOW IT'S APPLIED (AI-ENHANCED)
Core Product Management	User Research and Analysis	Working Knowledge	Conducting user interviews, surveys, usability tests to understand needs related to AI features. Analyzing user behavior.	Foundational	Understanding needs of internal teams who will use the AI platform.	Working Knowledge	Using AI tools to analyze user feedback, identify trends, and segment users.
	Ideation and Solution Design	Working Knowledge	Brainstorming and conceptualizing AI-powered features. Applying design thinking.	Working Knowledge	Defining features and capabilities of the AI platform and reusable models.	Working Knowledge	Identifying opportunities to use AI tools to improve PM workflows.
	Prioritization and Roadmapping	Working Knowledge	Prioritizing AI features based on impact, value, and feasibility. Integrating AI into the product roadmap.	Expert	Prioritizing platform features, model development, and infrastructure improvements.	Working Knowledge	Using AI tools to assist with roadmap prioritization.
	Requirements Definition	Working Knowledge	Writing PRDs and user stories for AI features, specifying functionality, user interactions, and success metrics.	Working Knowledge	Writing clear and concise requirements for the platform and models to be used.	Working Knowledge	Writing clear and concise requirements to improve and optimize the AI tools to be used.

SKILL CATEGORY	SKILL	AI-EXPERIENCES PM	HOW IT'S APPLIED (AI-EXPERIENCES)	AI-BUILDER PM	HOW IT'S APPLIED (AI-BUILDER)	AI-ENHANCED PM	HOW IT'S APPLIED (AI-ENHANCED)
	Data Analysis and Interpretation	Working Knowledge	Analyzing data from user research, A/B tests, and model performance metrics.	Working Knowledge	Analyzing data on platform usage, model performance, and infrastructure costs.	Expert	Using AI tools to analyze large datasets, identify trends, and generate insights for product decisions.
	Experimentation (A/B Testing)	Working Knowledge	Designing and executing A/B tests to evaluate AI features.	Foundational	Understanding A/B testing principles to evaluate different versions of AI models or platform features.	Working Knowledge	Using AI tools to design and analyze A/B tests more efficiently.
	Go-to-Market Strategy and Execution	Foundational	Collaborating on launch plans for AI features. Crafting messaging that highlights user benefits.	Foundational	Less directly relevant, but some understanding is helpful for communicating platform value internally.	Foundational	Less directly relevant, but some understanding is helpful.
Engineering Foundations	Software Development Methodologies	Foundational	Understanding Agile/Scrum.	Foundational	Understanding Agile/Scrum.	Foundational	Understanding Agile/Scrum.

Continues

(continued)

SKILL CATEGORY	SKILL	AI-EXPERIENCES PM	HOW IT'S APPLIED (AI-EXPERIENCES)	AI-BUILDER PM	HOW IT'S APPLIED (AI-BUILDER)	AI-ENHANCED PM	HOW IT'S APPLIED (AI-ENHANCED)
	Key Technical Concepts (APIs, Algorithms, System Architecture)	Foundational	Understanding basic AI/ML concepts, how models are deployed (APIs), and system architecture implications.	Working Knowledge	Understanding AI platform architecture, API design, and how different algorithms work.	Foundational	Understanding how to use AI tools and APIs.
	Working with AI Infrastructure	Foundational	Understanding the basics of how and where AI models are hosted, and how latency might impact UX.	Expert	Making strategic decisions about infrastructure choices (cloud, on-premises, edge) for scalability, reliability, and cost-effectiveness.	Foundational	Understanding how AI tools are deployed and integrated.
Essential Leadership and Collaboration	Communication and Storytelling	Working Knowledge	Communicating the vision, strategy, and value of AI features. Explaining AI concepts clearly.	Working Knowledge	Communicating the vision, strategy, and roadmap for the AI platform. Explaining complex technical concepts.	Working Knowledge	Communicating the benefits of AI tools and advocating for their adoption.

SKILL CATEGORY	SKILL	AI-EXPERIENCES PM	HOW IT'S APPLIED (AI-EXPERIENCES)	AI-BUILDER PM	HOW IT'S APPLIED (AI-BUILDER)	AI-ENHANCED PM	HOW IT'S APPLIED (AI-ENHANCED)
	Collaboration and Cross-Functional Teamwork	Working Knowledge	Working with data scientists, engineers, designers, marketers, and other stakeholders.	Expert	Working with data scientists, engineers, other PMs, and stakeholders.	Working Knowledge	Collaborating with colleagues to integrate AI tools into shared workflows.
	Problem-Solving and Decision-Making	Working Knowledge	Identifying and solving problems during development and deployment of AI features.	Expert	Identifying and resolving technical and strategic challenges related to AI platform development.	Working Knowledge	Using AI-driven insights to make data-driven decisions and solve product problems.
	Influence and Persuasion	Foundational	Advocating for user-centric AI solutions and securing buy-in.	Working Knowledge	Advocating for the AI platform and securing buy-in from stakeholders.	Working Knowledge	Advocating for the adoption of AI tools within the product team.
	Adaptability & Learning Agility	Working Knowledge	Staying up-to-date with the AI field.	Working Knowledge	Staying up-to-date with the AI field.	Expert	Staying up-to-date with the rapidly evolving landscape of AI tools.

Continues

(*continued*)

SKILL CATEGORY	SKILL	AI-EXPERIENCES PM	HOW IT'S APPLIED (AI-EXPERIENCES)	AI-BUILDER PM	HOW IT'S APPLIED (AI-BUILDER)	AI-ENHANCED PM	HOW IT'S APPLIED (AI-ENHANCED)
AI Lifecycle and Operational Awareness	Understanding AI and GenAI Capabilities	Working Knowledge	Identifying opportunities to leverage AI's strengths. Understanding limitations.	Expert	Deep understanding of various AI/ML techniques and their strengths and weaknesses.	Expert	Identifying opportunities to leverage AI to improve PM workflows. Understanding limitations of AI tools.
	DataOps and Management	Foundational	Understanding data requirements for AI features and working with data engineering on data quality.	Working Knowledge	Understanding data pipelines, data governance, and data privacy.	Foundational	Understanding data requirements for AI tools.
	Productionization Considerations	Foundational	Understanding deployment and monitoring of AI models.	Expert	Designing and implementing processes for deploying, monitoring, and maintaining AI models.	Foundational	Understanding the basic principles of deploying and maintaining software.
	Ethical Considerations and Bias Mitigation	Working Knowledge	Ensuring AI features are ethical and fair. Addressing potential biases.	Working Knowledge	Collaborating with stakeholders to make sure that ethical practices are followed.	Working Knowledge	Ensuring that AI tools are used responsibly and ethically within the product team.

SKILL CATEGORY	SKILL	AI-EXPERIENCES PM	HOW IT'S APPLIED (AI-EXPERIENCES)	AI-BUILDER PM	HOW IT'S APPLIED (AI-BUILDER)	AI-ENHANCED PM	HOW IT'S APPLIED (AI-ENHANCED)
	Prompt Engineering (for LLMs)	Working Knowledge	Crafting effective prompts for LLMs.	Foundational/ Working Knowledge	Understanding prompt engineering to guide internal use of LLMs.	Working Knowledge	Effectively using LLMs and other generative AI tools by crafting clear and specific prompts. Understanding how to control model output.
	GenAI Evals understanding	Working Knowledge	Understanding the different methods to evaluate Generative AI models and their outputs.	Expert	Defining and overseeing the GenAI Evals process, ensuring model quality and safety.	Working Knowledge	Understanding the limitations and potential biases of AI-generated content and critically evaluating the outputs of AI tools.

Chapter Summary and Key Takeaways

This chapter introduced you to the AI-Enhanced PM, the modern product leader who strategically uses AI tools to augment their own workflows and decision-making. You've explored how this persona acts as a "force multiplier," leveraging AI for everything from market research and user feedback analysis to roadmap prioritization. You understand that their focus is on transforming the *process* of product management itself through the intelligent adoption of new tools.

Figure 7-2 illustrates the core aspects of this efficiency-focused role.

AI - BUILDER PM
Supercharging product management with AI

Role Summary 

Leverages AI tools to optimize product management workflows and decision-making.

Why it matters? 

AI boosts PM efficiency, insight and strategic impact.

Collaboration 

Works with cross-functional teams, consumes AI insights rather than builds models.

Key Challenges 

- Tool overload vs. focused productivity
- Integration into workflow
- Critical evaluation of outputs
- Championing adoption

Essential Skils & Mindset 

- Data-savvy
- Tool-proficient
- Adaptable
- Critical thinker
- AI advocate

Figure 7-2: A summary of the AI-Enhanced PM role, highlighting its core focus on leveraging AI for productivity, key challenges, and essential skills

Key Takeaways

- You view AI as a tool for augmentation, enhancing your existing skills and efficiency rather than replacing your critical judgment and strategic thinking.

- Your primary focus is on internal processes. The main impact of this role is on improving the speed and quality of your own team's work to drive better and faster product decisions.

- Your role demands adaptability and continuous learning to keep up with the rapidly evolving landscape of AI tools and best practices.

- You act as a champion for adoption, leading by example to demonstrate the value of using AI in the PM workflow and encouraging your peers.

Onward: From Theory to Action

Now that you have a comprehensive understanding of the different AI PM roles and have likely identified which persona resonates most with you, it's time to put this knowledge into action. The next chapter will equip you with a series of frameworks for identifying and evaluating AI opportunities in any product.

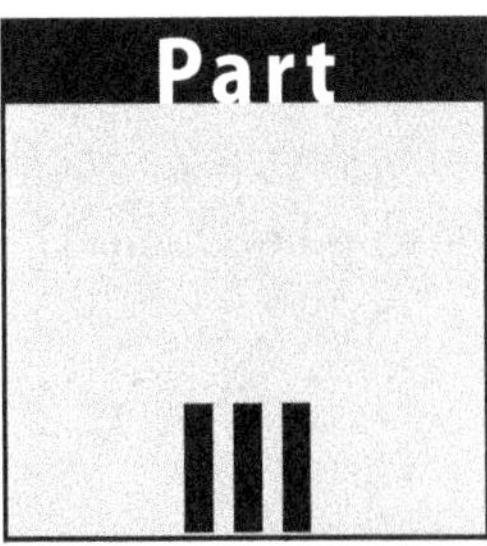

Connecting the Dots Between AI/ML Knowledge and PM Craft

Now that you've built a strong foundation in AI/ML (Part I) and explored the specialized roles of AI Product Managers (Part II), it's time to put that knowledge into action. Part III bridges your technical understanding with the core responsibilities of product management. You'll learn how to identify AI opportunities in your product, align teams across disciplines, translate complex capabilities into user value, and integrate AI thinking into every stage of the product development lifecycle—from strategy to execution to ethical evaluation.

In Part III, you'll explore:

- Frameworks for AI opportunity discovery and user journey analysis.

- Practical strategies for applying AI to enhance product features and create predictive or automated capabilities.

- Ethical, feasibility, and evaluation considerations that every AI PM must master.

- Techniques for ideation and A/B testing in AI contexts, plus an end-to-end case study to bring it all to life.

By the end of Part III, you'll be equipped with the tools and mindset to lead AI-powered product development with confidence—bridging the gap between AI literacy and impactful execution.

Identifying and Evaluating AI Opportunities

You've now built a foundational understanding of the core concepts and technologies behind AI and Machine Learning. You know the difference between supervised and unsupervised learning; you understand the power of neural networks; and you're aware of the capabilities and limitations of LLMs. It's time to move from theory to practice. This chapter is all about developing an "AI-first" mindset as a Product Manager—learning to identify and evaluate opportunities to leverage AI to solve user problems and enhance your product.

Uncovering Potential Use Cases—Mining Your Product for AI Gold

The first step in building successful AI-powered products isn't to jump on the latest technology trend. It's to *start with the problem*. Just like any good product development process, we begin by deeply understanding user needs, pain points, and opportunities for improvement. However, now we're doing it with an "AI lens"—looking for problems that are particularly well-suited to AI solutions. Think of it like prospecting for gold: you need to know where to look and what to look for.

The key is to identify *data-rich problems*. AI, and particularly Machine Learning, thrives on data. The more data you have, and the more relevant that data is to the problem, the better the chances of building a successful AI solution. But "data-rich" doesn't just mean "lots of data." It means data that contains *patterns* and *relationships* that can be learned by an AI model.

Let's explore the types of problems that are often good candidates for AI solutions, and how to identify them within your own product:

Recognizing Data-Rich Problem Areas

Think about areas within your product where users interact with data, generate data, or where data could be used to improve their experience. These are your prime prospecting grounds:

- **Repetitive Tasks: The Automation Gold Mine:** AI excels at automating tasks that are repetitive, predictable, and involve processing or analyzing data. Look for areas where users are performing the same actions over and over again, especially if those actions are tedious or time-consuming. This is low-hanging fruit for AI.

  - **Example 1 (Project Management Tool):** Imagine a project management tool where users manually assign tags to tasks based on keywords in the task description (e.g., "marketing," "design," "development"). This is repetitive and prone to human error. An AI could be trained to automatically tag tasks based on their content, saving users time and improving consistency. This leverages *supervised learning*, with the existing tags serving as the labeled data.

  - **Example 2 (Customer Support Portal):** Customer support agents often spend significant time searching for relevant knowledge base articles or past tickets to help resolve customer issues. An AI-powered search engine, using *natural language processing (NLP)*, could understand the *meaning* of the customer's query (not just the keywords) and surface the most relevant information much faster. This goes beyond simple keyword matching.

  - **Example 3 (E-Commerce Platform):** Product catalog managers often manually categorize new products into existing categories.

An AI, trained on existing product data (descriptions, images, etc.), could automatically suggest or even assign categories, significantly speeding up the cataloging process.

- **Pattern Recognition: Finding the Needles in the Haystack:** AI is incredibly powerful at identifying patterns, trends, and anomalies in data that humans might miss. This is particularly useful when dealing with large datasets or subtle patterns.

  - **Example 1 (Content Recommendation):** A news app or streaming service can use AI to analyze user behavior (articles read, videos watched, songs listened to) to identify patterns in their preferences. This allows the system to recommend content that the user is likely to enjoy, increasing engagement. This often uses *unsupervised learning* (clustering users with similar tastes) and *supervised learning* (predicting click-through rates).

  - **Example 2 (Fraud Detection):** Financial institutions use AI to detect fraudulent transactions in real-time. The AI model is trained on vast amounts of transaction data, learning to identify subtle patterns that indicate fraudulent activity (unusual purchase amounts, locations, times, etc.). This is a classic example of *anomaly detection*, a type of *unsupervised learning*.

  - **Example 3 (Predictive Maintenance):** In a manufacturing setting, sensors on machines generate vast amounts of data. An AI model can analyze this data to predict when a machine is likely to fail, allowing for proactive maintenance and preventing costly downtime.

- **Personalization Opportunities: Delivering Tailored Experiences:** AI can analyze user behavior, preferences, and demographics to create personalized experiences that are more relevant and engaging. This goes beyond simple rule-based personalization ("If a user is in Group A, show them Content X") to dynamic, AI-driven tailoring.

  - **Example 1 (E-Learning Platform):** An AI-powered e-learning platform can track a student's progress, identify areas where they're struggling, and recommend personalized learning materials and exercises. This creates a more effective and engaging learning experience.

  - **Example 2 (Personalized Notifications):** A mobile app can use AI to learn when and how to best send notifications to users. Instead of bombarding users with generic notifications, the AI can personalize the timing, content, and frequency of notifications based on individual user behavior, increasing engagement and reducing churn.

■ **Example 3 (Smart To-Do App):** The app can learn when you are more productive, what tasks you tend to procrastinate, and much more. Based on this, the AI can suggest optimal times, tasks, or reminders.

■ **Data Analysis Bottlenecks: Streamlining Insights:** If users are spending significant time manually analyzing data to make decisions, AI can often streamline this process, providing faster and more insightful results.

■ **Example 1 (Financial Reporting):** Finance teams often spend hours manually collecting data from various sources, cleaning it, and generating reports. An AI could automate this entire process, freeing up the team to focus on higher-level analysis and strategic decision-making.

■ **Example 2 (Marketing Analytics Dashboard):** Instead of requiring marketers to manually sift through data to understand campaign performance, an AI-powered dashboard could automatically identify key trends, anomalies, and insights, providing actionable recommendations.

Analyzing Existing Data Sources

To identify these data-rich problems, you need to become a data detective. Here are some key sources to investigate:

■ **User Behavior Data:** Dive deep into user interaction logs, clickstream data, and usage patterns. Look for:

■ **Frequent Actions:** What tasks are users performing most often?

■ **Points of Friction:** Where are users getting stuck, abandoning workflows, or making errors?

■ **Search Queries:** What are users searching for? Are they finding what they need?

■ **Navigation Patterns:** How are users navigating through your product? Are there common paths or dead ends?

- **Content Data:** If your product involves content (text, images, audio, video), analyze it for patterns and opportunities.

  - **Common Themes and Topics:** What are the most common topics discussed in user-generated content or your product's content library?

  - **Sentiment Analysis:** What is the overall sentiment (positive, negative, neutral) expressed in user reviews, comments, or support tickets?

  - **Image and Video Analysis:** If your product uses images or videos, can AI be used to automatically tag, categorize, or analyze them?

- **Performance Data:** Analyze metrics related to the performance of your product and its features.

  - **Response Times:** Are there areas where your product is slow or unresponsive?

  - **Error Rates:** Are there features or workflows with high error rates?

  - **Conversion Rates:** Where are users dropping off in key funnels?

- **Feedback Data:** Don't underestimate the value of qualitative data. Analyze user feedback, support tickets, reviews, and survey responses.

  - **Common Complaints:** What are the most frequent complaints or pain points reported by users?

  - **Feature Requests:** What features or improvements are users asking for?

  - **Unmet Needs:** Are there any unmet needs or problems that users are expressing?

Asking the Right Questions

As you analyze your data and think about your product, ask yourself these key questions:

- Where are users spending the most time and effort? (Focus on time-saving opportunities.)

- Where are users making the most errors? (Focus on improving accuracy and reducing frustration.)

- Where are users explicitly asking for more personalization or automation? (Listen to your users!)

- What data do we have that could be used to solve these problems? (Identify your data assets.)

- What patterns might exist in our data that we're currently missing? (Think about potential insights from unsupervised learning.)

- What predictions could we make that would improve the user experience? (Think about potential applications of supervised learning.)

- What repetitive tasks are good candidates to be automated?

- If we had perfect information about our users and their needs, what would we do differently? (This helps you think big and identify potential AI applications.)

By systematically exploring these problem areas, analyzing your existing data, and asking the right questions, you'll be well on your way to uncovering valuable AI opportunities within your product. This framework is about becoming a proactive problem-solver, using AI as a powerful tool to enhance your product and deliver exceptional user experiences.

AI/ML Capability Matching: Connecting Problems to Solutions

You've identified potential "gold mines"—data-rich problems within your product that might be amenable to AI solutions. Now it's time to choose the right tools for the job. Think of this section as your AI toolkit, filled with different capabilities that can be applied to address specific types of challenges. Just like a carpenter wouldn't use a hammer to saw a board, you need to understand the strengths of each AI/ML technique to select the most appropriate one.

Remember, this isn't about becoming a technical expert. It's about understanding the *capabilities* of different AI/ML approaches so you can have informed conversations with your engineering team and make strategic product decisions.

Understanding Your AI/ML Toolkit: Key Capabilities

Here's a breakdown of the core AI/ML capabilities you'll likely encounter, along with examples of how they can be applied to product problems:

- **Classification: Putting Things in Their Place**

  - **What It Is:** Categorizing data into predefined groups or classes. Think of it like sorting mail into different bins.

  - **When to Use It:** Any time you need to automatically categorize information, label data, or make a decision between a set of predefined options.

  - **Examples:**

    - **Spam Filtering:** Classifying emails as "spam" or "not spam" (a classic example of *supervised learning*), as shown in Figure 8-1.

    - **Customer Support Ticket Routing:** Automatically categorizing incoming support tickets (e.g., "technical issue," "billing question," "feature request") and routing them to the appropriate team.

    - **Document Type Identification:** Automatically identifying the type of document uploaded by a user (e.g., invoice, contract, resume, report).

    - **Image Tagging:** Automatically tagging images with relevant keywords (e.g., "cat," "dog," "car").

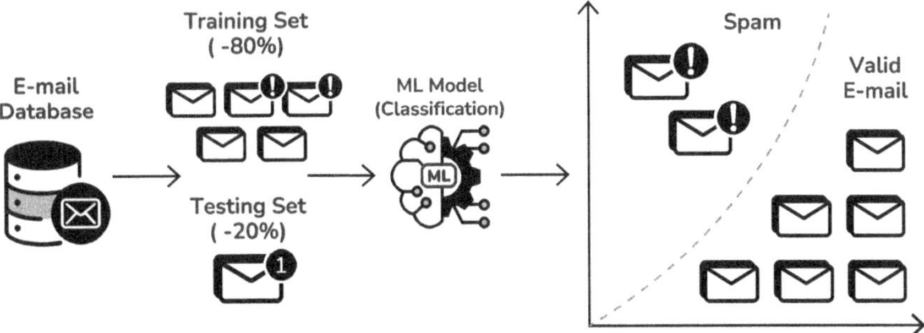

Figure 8-1: An illustration of a spam filter, a classic example of an AI classification model. The model analyzes an incoming email and automatically categorizes it as either 'spam' or 'not spam' based on learned patterns.

- **Clustering: Finding Hidden Groups**
  - **What It Is:** Grouping similar data points together *without* pre-defined categories. It's like discovering natural groupings within your data.
  - **When to Use It:** When you want to understand the underlying structure of your data, discover hidden segments, or identify anomalies.
  - **Examples:**
    - **Customer Segmentation:** Dividing your customer base into distinct groups based on their behavior, demographics, or purchasing patterns, *without* predefining those groups, as shown in Figure 8-2. This allows for more targeted marketing and personalized experiences. (This is a prime example of *unsupervised learning*.)
    - **Identifying User Personas:** Discovering different types of users based on their interaction with your product, even if you didn't explicitly define those personas beforehand.
    - **Grouping Similar Products:** In an e-commerce setting, grouping products together based on their features, descriptions, or customer reviews, even if they don't belong to the same predefined category.

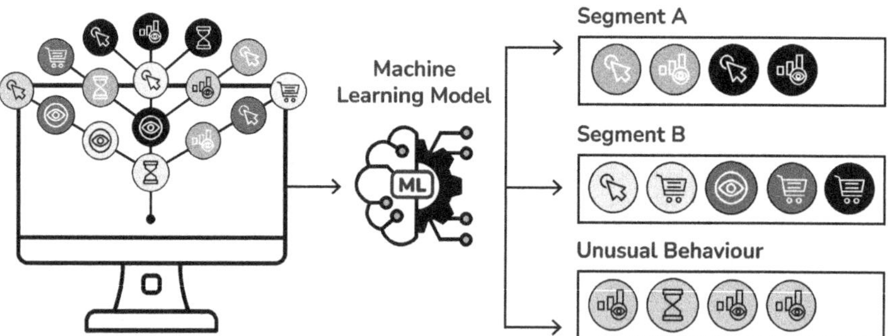

Figure 8-2: An illustration of customer segmentation, a common application of unsupervised learning. The model identifies hidden patterns in user data to automatically group customers into distinct segments, enabling more targeted product strategies and personalized experiences.

- **Generation: Creating Something New**
  - **What It Is:** Using AI, particularly Large Language Models (LLMs), to create new content, such as text, images, audio, or even code. To do this, these models first break down vast amounts of information into smaller pieces called tokens—like words or parts of words. By learning the statistical relationships between these tokens, the models can then generate new, original content. Figure 8-3 illustrates this initial step of processing text. This is where AI moves from analysis to creation.
  - **When to Use It:** When you need to automate content creation, personalize content at scale, or provide creative assistance to users.
  - **Examples:**
    - **Generating Marketing Copy:** Creating variations of ad headlines, email subject lines, or product descriptions.
    - **Summarizing Text:** Condensing long articles, documents, or customer support conversations into concise summaries.
    - **Creating Personalized Email Responses:** Drafting replies to customer inquiries based on the content of the email.
    - **Generating Code Snippets:** Assisting developers by generating code based on natural language descriptions of the desired functionality.
    - **Creating Variations of Images:** Based on existing images or text descriptions.

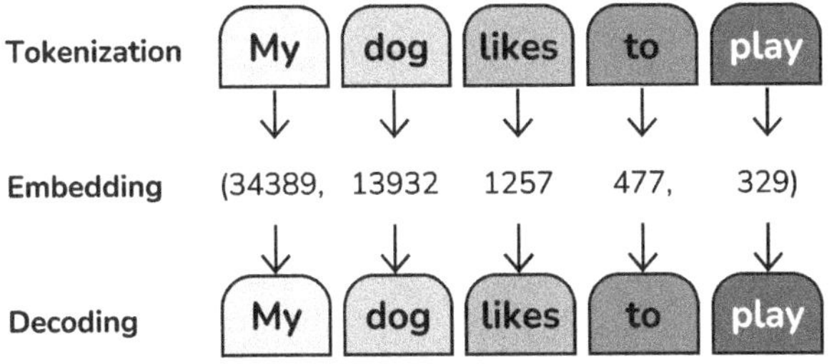

Figure 8-3: A simplified view of how LLMs process text. Input text is first broken down into smaller units called "tokens" and then converted into numerical "embeddings" before being used by the model to generate new content.

- **Recommendation: Guiding Choices**
  - **What It Is:** Suggesting relevant items or content to users based on their past behavior, preferences, or the behavior of similar users. This common approach, known as collaborative filtering, is illustrated in Figure 8-4.
  - **When to Use It:** When you want to increase engagement, drive sales, or help users discover new content or features.
  - **Examples:**
    - **Product Recommendations:** Suggesting products that a user might be interested in based on their past purchases or browsing history (like Amazon's "Customers who bought this also bought. . ." feature).
    - **Content Recommendations:** Recommending articles, videos, or music based on a user's past consumption patterns (like Netflix or Spotify).
    - **Feature Recommendations:** Suggesting features within your product that a user might find helpful based on their current task or workflow.

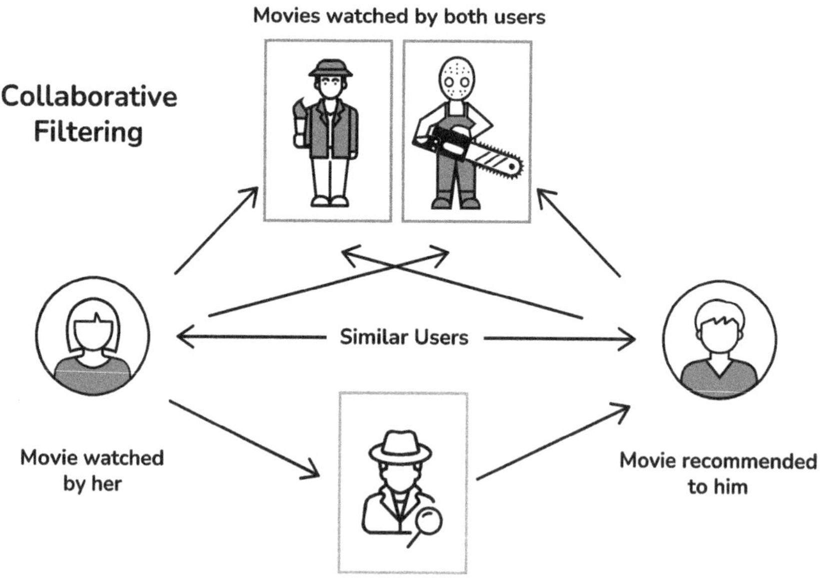

Figure 8-4: Collaborative filtering is a method used in recommendation systems that predicts a user's preferences by analyzing the preferences of other users with similar tastes.

- **Anomaly Detection: Spotting the Unusual**
  - **What It Is:** Identifying data points that deviate significantly from the norm. It's like finding the outliers or the exceptions, as shown in Figure 8-5.
  - **When to Use It:** When you need to detect fraud, identify system errors, or flag unusual behavior.
  - **Examples:**
    - **Fraudulent Transaction Detection:** Identifying unusual spending patterns that might indicate a fraudulent credit card transaction.
    - **System Monitoring:** Detecting unusual activity on a server or network that might indicate a security breach or a system malfunction.
    - **Manufacturing Defect Detection:** Identifying products that deviate from quality standards based on sensor data or image analysis.

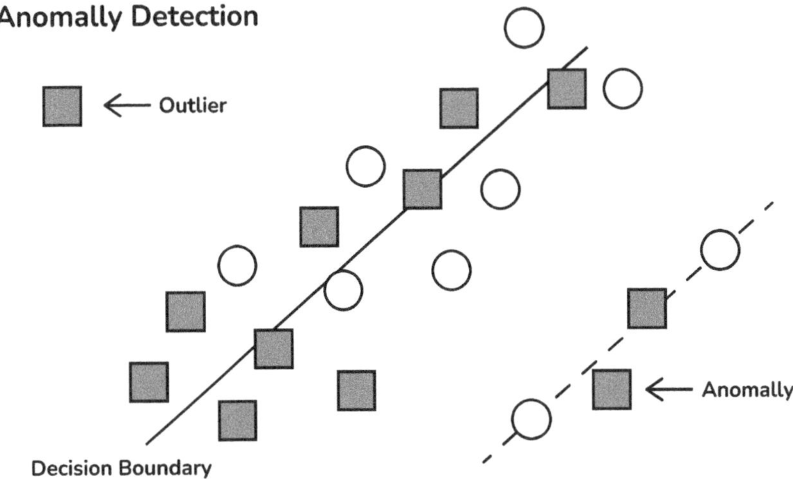

Figure 8-5: An example of anomaly detection. The model learns the pattern of "normal" data points and flags any outlier that deviates significantly from that pattern, a technique very important for tasks like fraud detection or system monitoring.

Matching Capabilities to Problems: A Practical Approach

Here's a simple way to think about matching capabilities to problems:

IF THE PROBLEM INVOLVES...	CONSIDER THESE AI/ML CAPABILITIES...
Forecasting or predicting	Prediction models (e.g., regression, time series analysis)
Categorizing data	Classification models (e.g., logistic regression, decision trees, support vector machines, neural networks)
Grouping similar data points	Clustering models (e.g., K-means, hierarchical clustering)
Generating new content	Generative AI models (e.g., LLMs, GANs)
Personalizing experiences	Recommendation systems (collaborative filtering, content-based filtering)
Identifying unusual patterns	Anomaly detection models (e.g., one-class SVM, isolation forest)
Understanding natural language	Natural Language Processing (NLP) techniques (e.g., sentiment analysis, topic modeling, named entity recognition, question answering)

This table provides a helpful starting point, but the real power often comes from combining these capabilities. A single, sophisticated product feature rarely relies on just one AI technique; instead, it layers multiple approaches to solve a complex user problem. Understanding how these techniques can be woven together is key to envisioning truly innovative solutions.

Let's break down a few common product features to see how this works in practice:

Feature: Search Functionality in a Document Management System

The core user problem is finding relevant documents quickly, especially when users can't remember the exact title or keywords. A truly intelligent search feature addresses this by creating a multi-layered, responsive experience that understands what the user is truly looking for. To achieve this, it combines:

- **NLP:** To understand the *intent* and *meaning* behind a user's query, not just matching keywords.

- **Recommendation:** To proactively suggest other relevant documents based on the user's search history and the content they've previously viewed.

- **Classification:** To work behind the scenes, automatically categorizing documents to power the search filters that help users narrow their results.

Feature: Customer Support Chatbot

Modern chatbots are designed to solve the business problem of high ticket volumes and slow response times by providing immediate, 24/7 assistance. An effective chatbot seamlessly blends several AI techniques to understand and respond to users effectively. These include:

- **NLP:** To understand the nuances of a user's question, even when phrased in different ways.

- **Classification:** To instantly categorize the support ticket (e.g., "technical issue," "billing question") to begin routing it correctly.

- **Generative AI:** To provide an immediate, helpful response for common, well-defined questions.

- **Sentiment Analysis:** To detect if a user is becoming frustrated, allowing the system to adjust its tone or escalate the issue to a human agent more quickly.

Feature: Reporting Dashboard for Marketing Campaigns

Marketers often spend an enormous amount of time manually sifting through data to find insights. An AI-enhanced dashboard transforms this workflow by automating analysis and proactively surfacing key information. This is accomplished by layering several capabilities:

- **Prediction:** To forecast future campaign performance, helping marketers adjust their strategies before a campaign ends.

- **Clustering:** To automatically segment users based on their response to the campaign, revealing valuable target audiences that might have been missed.

- **Anomaly Detection:** To flag unusual patterns, like a sudden drop in click-through rates, which prevents wasted ad spend and alerts marketers to potential problems.

- **Generative AI:** To create natural language summaries of the key findings, turning raw data into actionable, easy-to-understand insights.

By understanding these core AI/ML capabilities and how they map to different types of problems, you can start to think more strategically about how to leverage AI to enhance your product. This "toolkit" approach empowers you to collaborate effectively with your engineering team and build truly innovative AI-powered features. You will be able to have conversations that are way more productive and understand what engineers propose.

Finding AI Opportunities in the User Journey

Understanding your users' journey—every step they take within your product or feature—is fundamental to good product management. Now, we're going to layer on an "AI lens" to that understanding. This means analyzing each step of the user journey, not just from a usability perspective, but also from the perspective of *how AI/ML could potentially improve, automate, or personalize that step.* Think of yourself as a user experience architect, now equipped with AI-powered tools.

Mapping the User Journey: Charting the Course

Before you can analyze the journey through an AI lens, you first need to have a clear and detailed map of that journey. Creating a user journey map is a fundamental product management exercise that involves deconstructing the user's experience into a structured, visual format. This map becomes the canvas upon which we will later identify opportunities for AI-driven enhancements.

The process can be broken down into three initial steps:

1. **Visualize the User's Path:** Start by creating a clear, visual map of the typical user journey for your feature or product. This could be

a simple flowchart, a user journey map, or any other visualization that helps you see the complete process from the user's perspective. Include *every* step, no matter how small.

2. **Identify All Touchpoints:** Mark each point where the user interacts with your product. This includes clicks, taps, form submissions, searches, page views—any action the user takes.

3. **Document User Goals:** For each step, clearly define what the user is trying to *achieve*. What is their goal at that particular point in the journey?

A user journey map doesn't need to be overly complex to be effective. The following table provides a simple but powerful way to break down the user journey for a common scenario: a customer landing on an e-commerce product page.

STEP	USER ACTION	USER GOAL	POTENTIAL PAIN POINTS
1	Arrives on product page.	Learn about the product, decide if to buy it.	Overwhelmed by information, can't find key details.
2	Scrolls through images.	See the product from different angles.	Images are low quality or don't show key features.
3	Reads description.	Understand product features and benefits.	Description is unclear, too technical, or too long.
4	Reads reviews.	See what other customers think.	Reviews are unhelpful, irrelevant, or overwhelming.
5	Selects size/color.	Choose desired product options.	Options are confusing or out of stock.
6	Adds to cart.	Prepare to purchase the product.	Process is slow or complicated.
7	Proceeds to checkout.	Complete the purchase.	Checkout process is lengthy or confusing.

As the table demonstrates, by breaking down a process into these distinct steps, you can clearly identify user goals and potential pain points at each stage. This detailed map is the foundation for our analysis.

For example, consider Step 4: Reads reviews. The user's goal is to quickly gauge product quality from the experience of others, but the pain point is being overwhelmed by hundreds of irrelevant or unhelpful reviews. This specific friction point is a perfect candidate for an AI-powered solution. Could an AI summarize the most common themes? Could it highlight the most helpful positive and negative reviews? This is the type of targeted, problem-oriented thinking that the "AI lens" enables, which we will explore in the next section.

Identifying Pain Points and Opportunities: The AI Detective Work

With your user journey mapped, it's time to put on your AI detective hat. At *each* step, ask yourself these critical questions:

QUESTION	FOCUS AREA	POTENTIAL AI/ML SOLUTIONS
Where are users experiencing friction?	Usability, frustration	Simplify workflows, provide intelligent assistance, offer personalized guidance.
Where are users spending excessive time?	Efficiency, automation	Automate repetitive tasks, provide shortcuts, streamline processes.
Where could AI automate a task?	Automation, efficiency	Use ML for tasks like data entry, categorization, or content generation.
Where could AI provide intelligent assistance?	Guidance, support	Offer proactive help, suggest relevant information, provide personalized recommendations.
Where could AI personalize the experience?	Relevance, engagement	Tailor content, recommendations, or interactions based on user behavior, preferences, or demographics.
Where are users making decisions?	Decision support	Provide data-driven insights, predict outcomes, recommend optimal choices.
Where are users inputting data?	Data entry, accuracy	Use NLP for text input, image recognition for image input, or voice recognition for voice input.

QUESTION	FOCUS AREA	POTENTIAL AI/ML SOLUTIONS
Where are users searching for information?	Information retrieval	Improve search results with NLP, provide contextual information, offer proactive suggestions.

Applying AI/ML to Enhance Touchpoints: The Transformation

Now, let's connect those pain points and opportunities to specific AI/ML capabilities. Here are some examples, building on the idea of enhancing various touchpoints within a user journey:

- **Personalized Onboarding:**

  - **Scenario:** New users often struggle to understand how to use a complex product.

  - **AI/ML Solution:** Analyze user behavior during onboarding (what features they explore, where they get stuck) and dynamically adjust the onboarding process. Offer personalized tutorials, tooltips, or even a guided tour based on their needs and learning style. This uses *supervised learning* to predict what help a user needs.

- **Intelligent Assistance:**

  - **Scenario:** Users are filling out a complex form.

  - **AI/ML Solution:** Provide real-time assistance as the user types, using *NLP* to understand the context and offer suggestions, auto-complete fields, or validate input. This can significantly reduce errors and improve completion rates.

- **Automated Task Completion:**

  - **Scenario:** Users repeatedly perform the same sequence of actions.

  - **AI/ML Solution:** Learn these common workflows and offer to automate them. For example, in a project management tool, if a user always assigns tasks of a certain type to the same team member, the system could learn this pattern and automatically assign those tasks in the future. This uses *reinforcement learning* or *supervised learning*.

- **Personalized Recommendations:**

  - **Scenario:** Users are browsing a large catalog of products or content.

  - **AI/ML Solution:** Use *recommendation systems* (collaborative filtering or content-based filtering) to suggest items that are relevant to the user's interests, based on their past behavior and the behavior of similar users.

- **Predictive Actions:**

  - **Scenario:** Users often forget to perform important actions.

  - **AI/ML Solution:** Use predictive models to anticipate user needs and take proactive actions. For example, if a user typically saves documents to a specific folder, the system could automatically suggest that folder as the default save location. Or, if a user is running low on a regularly purchased item, the system could proactively offer to reorder it.

- **Contextual Information:**

  - **Scenario:** Users are viewing a complex data visualization.

  - **AI/ML Solution:** Use *NLP* and *data analysis* to automatically generate captions or summaries that explain the key insights from the visualization, making it easier for users to understand the data.

- **Error Prevention:**

  - **Scenario:** Users are entering data that needs to conform to specific rules or constraints.

  - **AI/ML Solution:** Use *anomaly detection* or *classification* to identify potential errors in real-time and provide immediate feedback to the user, preventing mistakes before they happen.

To see how these different enhancement types come together, let's revisit our e-commerce product page example. By applying an "AI lens" to each step of the user journey we mapped earlier, we can brainstorm specific AI-powered solutions for each identified pain point. The following table demonstrates this process, connecting each step to potential AI enhancements and the underlying capabilities required.

STEP	USER ACTION	USER GOAL	POTENTIAL PAIN POINTS	AI/ML ENHANCEMENT OPPORTUNITIES	AI/ML CAPABILITY
1	Arrives on product page.	Learn about the product, decide if to buy it.	Overwhelmed by information, can't find key details.	AI-powered product summary highlighting key features and benefits.	Generation (LLM).
2	Scrolls through images.	See the product from different angles.	Images are low quality or don't show key features.	AI-powered image enhancement; automatic generation of 3D models or virtual try-on.	Generation, Computer Vision.
3	Reads description.	Understand product features and benefits.	Description is unclear, too technical, or too long.	AI-powered rewriting of product descriptions for clarity and conciseness; personalized descriptions based on user segment.	Generation (LLM), Personalization.
4	Reads reviews.	See what other customers think.	Reviews are unhelpful, irrelevant, or overwhelming.	AI-powered sentiment analysis of reviews; summarization of key pros and cons; identification of fake reviews.	NLP, Anomaly Detection.
5	Selects size/color.	Choose desired product options.	Options are confusing or out of stock.	AI-powered recommendations for size/color based on past purchases or browsing history; real-time inventory prediction.	Recommendation, Prediction.
6	Adds to cart.	Prepare to purchase the product.	Process is slow or complicated.	Streamlined "add to cart" process with AI-powered suggestions for related products.	Recommendation.
7	Proceeds to checkout.	Complete the purchase.	Checkout process is lengthy or confusing.	AI-powered form filling; fraud detection; personalized payment options.	NLP, Anomaly Detection, Prediction.

As you can see from the table, nearly every step of a user's journey contains an opportunity for an AI-driven enhancement. Let's return to our specific example of Step 4: Reads reviews. We identified the user's pain point: being overwhelmed by too many reviews. The table shows a clear path forward by combining several AI capabilities. We could use NNLP to perform sentiment analysis and then use generative AI to create a concise summary of the most common "pros" and "cons" mentioned in the reviews. We could even layer on anomaly detection to flag and hide potentially fake or unhelpful reviews.

This detailed, step-by-step analysis transforms vague ideas into concrete, actionable AI feature concepts. It's a fundamental process for every AI-Experiences PM.

Feature Enhancement Through AI/ML— Transforming Existing Functionality

Sometimes, the most impactful way to leverage AI isn't to build something entirely new, but to make what you *already have* significantly better. Think of it like upgrading your car's engine—you're not changing the fundamental purpose of the car, but you're dramatically improving its performance and capabilities. This section focuses on how to use AI/ML to *supercharge* your existing features, making them smarter, more efficient, and more user-friendly.

This approach has several advantages:

- **Faster Time to Value:** You're building on existing infrastructure and user familiarity, reducing development time and user adoption barriers.

- **Lower Risk:** You're improving proven features, rather than starting from scratch, which reduces the risk of failure.

- **Targeted Improvements:** You can focus on specific pain points or limitations within existing features, delivering targeted and measurable improvements.

Identifying Enhancement Opportunities: Finding the Weak Spots

The key to successful feature enhancement is to identify where your existing features are falling short or could be significantly improved. Here's a systematic approach:

1. **Analyze User Feedback:** Dive deep into user reviews, support tickets, surveys, and any other feedback channels. Look for recurring complaints, pain points, and areas where users are struggling.

2. **Examine Usage Data:** Analyze how users are interacting with your features. Are they using them as intended? Are there drop-off points, errors, or signs of confusion?

3. **Benchmark Against Competitors:** How do your features compare to similar features in competing products? Are there areas where competitors are offering a better user experience, potentially through AI?

4. **Ask "What If?" Questions:** Imagine you had perfect information and unlimited processing power. How could you improve this feature? This helps you think beyond incremental improvements and identify opportunities for transformative change.

To put these methods into practice, it helps to ask specific, targeted questions about your product. The following table provides a set of starting questions, categorized by common feature areas, to guide your brainstorming and help you uncover hidden opportunities for AI-powered enhancements.

FEATURE AREA	QUESTIONS TO IDENTIFY ENHANCEMENT OPPORTUNITIES
Search	Are users finding what they need quickly and easily? Are search results relevant? Do users struggle with complex queries?
Data Entry	Are users making errors? Is data entry time-consuming or tedious? Is data validation effective?
Navigation	Are users getting lost? Are they struggling to find specific features or information? Are there common navigation paths that could be optimized?

Continues

(continued)

FEATURE AREA	QUESTIONS TO IDENTIFY ENHANCEMENT OPPORTUNITIES
Reporting/ Analytics	Are users able to easily extract insights from data? Are reports clear and actionable? Do users spend excessive time creating reports?
Personalization	Are users receiving relevant content and recommendations? Are there opportunities to tailor the experience to individual needs?
Communication (e.g., email, messaging)	Is communication efficient and effective? Are users struggling to manage large volumes of messages? Are there opportunities for automation?

This question-based approach helps transform general observations into specific, actionable problem statements. For example, instead of just knowing that "reporting is hard," asking "Are users able to easily extract insights from data?" forces you to investigate the specific user struggle. You might discover that users are exporting data to spreadsheets to manually create charts—a clear signal that an AI-powered insight generation or automated summarization feature could provide immense value. Pinpointing these 'weak spots' is the primary goal; the next step is to match them with the right AI capabilities.

Applying AI/ML to Enhance Features: The Transformation Process

With specific areas for improvement identified, you can now consider how different AI/ML capabilities can address those limitations. Here are some common ways AI/ML can enhance existing features:

ENHANCEMENT AREA	DESCRIPTION	AI/ML CAPABILITIES	EXAMPLE (TASK MANAGEMENT TOOL)
Improved Accuracy	Making predictions, classifications, or other data-driven tasks more precise	Supervised learning (classification, regression), computer vision, NLP	Improving the accuracy of task due date prediction based on historical data and task complexity

ENHANCEMENT AREA	DESCRIPTION	AI/ML CAPABILITIES	EXAMPLE (TASK MANAGEMENT TOOL)
Increased Efficiency	Automating repetitive tasks and streamlining workflows, saving users time and effort	Supervised learning (classification), NLP, Robotic Process Automation (RPA) powered by AI	Automatically categorizing tasks based on their description, assigning them to the appropriate team member, or setting priorities
Enhanced Personalization	Tailoring the user experience to individual needs and preferences, making the product more relevant and engaging	Recommendation systems, supervised learning, unsupervised learning (clustering)	Suggesting relevant collaborators for a task based on past collaborations and project context
Proactive Assistance	Anticipating user needs and providing help or guidance before they explicitly ask for it	Supervised learning (prediction), reinforcement learning, NLP	Predicting potential roadblocks in a project and suggesting solutions proactively
Contextual Understanding	Enabling features to better understand the context of user actions and data, leading to more intelligent and relevant responses	NLP, computer vision, deep learning	Understanding the meaning of a user's search query within the task management tool, not just matching keywords
Error Reduction	Detecting and automatically correcting or suggesting corrections	Supervised Learning, Anomaly Detection	Automatically fixing typos on a task description

To illustrate these enhancement areas with concrete examples, let's consider a few common feature types and how AI/ML can transform them:

Feature: Standard Search Functionality

The problem with a traditional keyword-based search is that users often struggle to find relevant information if they don't use the exact terminology present in the documents. AI/ML offers a powerful solution:

- **Enhancement:** Implement semantic search using NLP. The search engine understands the meaning of the user's query and the content of the documents, not just matching keywords.

- **Benefit:** This leads to more relevant results, even if the user's query doesn't contain the exact words used in the documents.

Feature: Data Entry Form

Users frequently encounter frustration and introduce errors when manually filling out lengthy forms. AI/ML can significantly improve this experience by:

- **Auto-Completing Fields:** Predicting what the user is going to type based on previous entries and context.

- **Validating Data in Real-Time:** Identifying potential errors (e.g., incorrect date formats, invalid email addresses) as the user types and providing immediate feedback.

- **Suggesting Values:** Based on the data entered in other fields.

Feature: Reporting Dashboard

Extracting meaningful insights from a dashboard filled with raw data can be time-consuming and challenging. AI/ML can empower users by:

- **Automatically Generating Summaries:** Providing concise text summaries of the key trends and pattern.

By focusing on feature enhancement, you can leverage AI/ML to deliver significant value to your users quickly and efficiently. This approach allows you to build on existing successes, address known pain points, and create a more intelligent and user-friendly product. You can also gather data that may help building other AI-powered features in the future.

Proactive Product Management—Anticipating User Needs with AI

One of the most transformative aspects of AI/ML is its ability to move from *reactive* to *proactive* product management. Instead of just responding to user needs *after* they arise, you can use AI to *anticipate* those needs and provide solutions *before* users even realize they have a problem. This section focuses on identifying opportunities to leverage the predictive and automation power of AI to create truly intelligent and user-friendly products. Think of it as becoming a proactive, rather than reactive, Product Manager.

Understanding the Power of Prediction and Automation

To become a truly proactive Product Manager, you must learn to leverage the two most powerful capabilities AI offers for anticipating user needs. These are the ability to predict future events and the power to automate complex processes. Understanding how each works is the first step toward identifying these transformative opportunities in your own product.

- **Predictive Capabilities:** Imagine your product could "see into the future," not in a magical sense, but in a data-driven way. By analyzing historical data and identifying patterns, AI/ML models can predict future events, user behavior, or potential problems. This allows you to:
    - **Forecast User Actions:** Predict what a user is likely to do next, allowing you to personalize the experience and provide relevant recommendations.
    - **Anticipate Potential Problems:** Identify risks, bottlenecks, or issues *before* they impact the user.
    - **Proactively Offer Solutions:** Provide assistance, guidance, or resources *before* the user even asks for them.

- **Automation Capabilities:** AI/ML can take over repetitive, time-consuming tasks, freeing up users to focus on more strategic and creative work. This is about more than just efficiency; it's about making your product feel *effortless* to use. Automation can:
    - **Streamline Workflows:** Eliminate unnecessary steps and simplify complex processes.

- **Reduce Errors:** Automate tasks that are prone to human error.
- **Increase Efficiency:** Allow users to accomplish more in less time.

Key Areas for Predictive and Automation Opportunities

Now that we understand the concepts of prediction and automation, let's explore how they can be applied to a real product. To make these ideas concrete, we will use a single, familiar example throughout the following table: a modern calendar application. By examining different areas within this app, we can see how various AI capabilities can be layered to create a truly proactive and intelligent user experience.

AREA	DESCRIPTION	AI/ML CAPABILITIES	EXAMPLE (CALENDAR APP)
Proactive Assistance	Providing help or guidance before the user explicitly asks for it.	Prediction, NLP, Classification	Predicts when a user might be double-booking themselves and provides a warning before they confirm the new appointment.
Personalized Recommendations	Suggesting relevant content, features, or actions based on user behavior and preferences.	Recommendation systems, Clustering, Prediction	Recommends optimal meeting times based on the attendees' past scheduling patterns and availability.
Automated Workflows	Automating sequences of tasks that users frequently perform.	Supervised learning (classification), Reinforcement learning	Automatically creates meeting invites based on emails or messages, extracting the date, time, and attendees.

AREA	DESCRIPTION	AI/ML CAPABILITIES	EXAMPLE (CALENDAR APP)
Predictive Maintenance	Anticipating and preventing system failures or performance issues. (More relevant to infrastructure/ hardware, but included for completeness.)	Anomaly detection, Time series analysis, Prediction	N/A (Not directly applicable to a calendar app, but relevant in other contexts, like predicting server load for a cloud-based calendar service.)
Intelligent Scheduling	Optimizing schedules and resource allocation to improve efficiency.	Optimization algorithms, Reinforcement learning, Prediction	Automatically finds the best time for a meeting that accommodates all participants' schedules and preferences (e.g., preferred meeting times, time zones). Can also optimize travel time and suggest meeting locations.
Smart Defaults	Anticipating user preferences and setting default values accordingly.	Prediction, Classification	Automatically sets the default meeting duration based on the user's past meetings or the type of meeting.
Error Prevention	Anticipating and avoiding user errors.	Prediction, Anomaly Detection	If the user is scheduling a meeting on a date that's already booked full, it automatically notifies the user.

As the calendar app example illustrates, a "proactive" product is often the sum of many small, intelligent parts. It's rarely about one single "prediction" feature, but rather about weaving numerous micro-features—like smart defaults, proactive warnings, and automated workflows—into the core user experience. Your goal as a Product Manager is to identify these moments of potential enhancement throughout the entire user journey. The next section provides a practical, step-by-step approach to help you do just that.

Identifying Opportunities: A Practical Approach

Here's a step-by-step approach to identify opportunities for prediction and automation:

1. **Revisit User Journeys:** Go back to your user journey maps (from Section 3, "Mapping the User Journey: Charting the Course"). For each step, ask: "Could we predict what the user will need or do next?" and "Could we automate any part of this step?"

2. **Analyze User Data (Again!):** Look for patterns in user behavior that suggest opportunities for prediction or automation.

   - **Frequent Sequences of Actions:** Are users repeatedly performing the same series of steps? This is a prime candidate for automation.

   - **Common Errors:** Are users frequently making the same mistakes? This could be addressed with proactive assistance or error prevention.

   - **Points of Delay or Frustration:** Where are users getting stuck or spending excessive time? This might indicate a need for intelligent assistance or automation.

3. **Brainstorm "What If" Scenarios:** Imagine your product could anticipate user needs perfectly. What would that look like? What tasks would be automated? What information would be provided proactively?

   - **Prioritize High-Impact Areas:** Focus on opportunities that will have the greatest positive impact on the user experience and your business goals. Consider factors like:

   - **Frequency of the Task:** Automating a frequently performed task will have a greater impact than automating a rare one.

- **Severity of the Pain Point:** Addressing a major pain point will be more valuable than addressing a minor inconvenience.

- **Feasibility of Implementation:** Consider the data requirements and technical complexity of implementing different solutions.

By focusing on prediction and automation, you can transform your product from a reactive tool to a proactive partner, anticipating user needs and providing a more seamless, efficient, and delightful experience. This is where AI/ML can truly shine, creating products that feel intuitive and almost magical. This approach moves the PM from being a feature builder to a strategic partner.

Responsible AI Foundations—Ethical and Feasibility Considerations

Before diving headfirst into implementing AI/ML solutions, it's critical to take a step back and consider the *ethical implications* and *practical feasibility* of your ideas. This isn't just about ticking boxes; it's about building AI responsibly and sustainably. Failing to address these considerations early on can lead to costly mistakes, damage your product's reputation, and even have legal consequences. Think of this as building a strong foundation for your AI project—you wouldn't build a house on shaky ground, would you?

As a Product Manager, you are the advocate for both the user *and* the business. This means you have a responsibility to ensure that AI is used in a way that is both beneficial and ethical.

Ethical Considerations: The "Do No Harm" Principle

AI has the potential to do great good, but it can also cause significant harm, often unintentionally. As a Product Manager, it is your responsibility to proactively identify and mitigate these ethical risks from the very beginning. To make these concepts concrete, we will explore them through the lens of a hypothetical job recommendation system. The following table breaks down key ethical concerns you must address in the initial stages of product discovery.

ETHICAL CONCERN	DESCRIPTION	KEY QUESTIONS FOR PRODUCT MANAGERS	EXAMPLE (JOB RECOMMENDATION SYSTEM)
Bias and Fairness	AI models can perpetuate and amplify existing biases present in the data they are trained on, leading to unfair or discriminatory outcomes.	<ul><li>Could this AI/ML application disadvantage or discriminate against any particular group of users?</li><li>What steps can we take to mitigate potential bias in the data and the model?</li><li>How will we monitor the system for bias after deployment?</li></ul>	The system might recommend fewer high-paying jobs to women or minorities if the training data reflects historical biases in the job market.
Privacy	AI often relies on collecting and analyzing user data, raising concerns about privacy and data security.	<ul><li>What data will we collect, and how will we use it?</li><li>How will we ensure compliance with data privacy regulations (e.g., GDPR, CCPA)?</li><li>How will we be transparent with users about our data practices?</li><li>How can we minimize data collection while still achieving our goals?</li></ul>	The system collects and analyzes users' browsing history, resume data, and application history, raising concerns about the privacy of sensitive personal information.

ETHICAL CONCERN	DESCRIPTION	KEY QUESTIONS FOR PRODUCT MANAGERS	EXAMPLE (JOB RECOMMENDATION SYSTEM)
Transparency and Explainability	Users should understand how AI is being used in your product and why it's making certain decisions, especially if those decisions impact them.	■ How can we explain the AI/ML system's decisions to users in a clear and understandable way? ■ Is a "black box" model acceptable for this application, or do we need a more interpretable model? ■ How will we handle situations where the AI makes an incorrect or unexpected decision?	The system recommends a specific job to a user without explaining why that job was chosen, making it difficult for the user to understand the recommendation.
Potential for Misuse	Consider how your AI-powered feature could be used in ways you didn't intend, potentially causing harm.	■ What are the potential risks of misuse or unintended consequences? ■ How can we mitigate these risks through design, monitoring, or safeguards?	The system could be used by malicious actors to create fake job postings or to discriminate against certain applicants.
Accountability	Who is in charge of making sure that everything is working as it is intended to?.	■ Who will be responsible of creating the AI? ■ Who is responsible if something goes wrong?	The system is built by a third-party. The models used are outdated, causing problems with the data provided by the LLM.

This table demonstrates that ethical AI development is not an abstract goal but a series of practical questions and trade-offs. By asking these questions *before* development begins, you move from a reactive "damage control" mindset to a proactive one of "responsible design." Addressing these ethical concerns is the first half of the equation. Next, we must consider the practical feasibility of building the solution.

Feasibility Considerations: Can We Actually Build This?

Beyond the ethical considerations, you need to assess the practical feasibility of your AI/ML project. This involves evaluating your data, resources, and technical capabilities. To systematically assess whether you can (and should) build a proposed AI solution, it's very important to evaluate a few key areas. The following table provides a framework of critical questions—covering data, resources, and scope—that every Product Manager should consider before an AI project gets the green light.

FEASIBILITY FACTOR	DESCRIPTION	KEY QUESTIONS FOR PRODUCT MANAGERS
Data Availability and Quality	AI models need high-quality data to learn effectively.	▪ Do we have access to the right data to train the model? Is it relevant to the problem? ▪ Is the data clean, accurate, and representative? Or will we need to invest significant time and effort in data cleaning and preparation? ▪ How much data do we have, and is it enough to train a robust model?
Data Accessibility	Even if the data exists, it needs to be in a format that can be used for training.	▪ Is the data stored in a way that we can easily access and use? ▪ Do we have the necessary tools and infrastructure to process the data? ▪ Are there any technical limitations that might prevent us from using the data?
Data Usage Rights	You need to ensure you have the legal right to use the data for AI/ML purposes.	▪ Do we have the necessary permissions and consents to use this data for AI/ML training and deployment? ▪ Are there any privacy regulations or contractual obligations that we need to consider?

FEASIBILITY FACTOR	DESCRIPTION	KEY QUESTIONS FOR PRODUCT MANAGERS
Technical Resources	AI/ML development requires specialized skills and infrastructure.	▪ Do we have the in-house expertise (data scientists, Machine Learning engineers) to build and deploy this solution? Or will we need to hire or outsource? ▪ Do we have the necessary computational resources (e.g., GPUs, cloud computing) to train and run the model?
Project Scope	Start small and iterate. Avoid trying to build an overly ambitious AI solution from the outset.	▪ Can we break down this project into smaller, more manageable phases? ▪ What is the Minimum Viable Product (MVP) for this AI/ML feature? What is the core functionality we can deliver first?

By proactively addressing these ethical and feasibility considerations *early* in the ideation process, you can significantly increase the likelihood of building a successful and responsible AI-powered product. This upfront investment in due diligence will save you time, resources, and potential headaches down the road. It also sets a strong foundation for building trust with your users and creating a positive impact with your AI initiatives. You are preparing the ground so that every action your team does is aligned.

Practical Ideation Techniques for AI/ML Use Cases—Thinking Like an AI-First Product Manager

You've now got a solid understanding of AI/ML capabilities, user journey analysis, feature enhancement, and the importance of ethical and feasibility considerations. It's time to put it all together and start brainstorming *specific* AI/ML use cases for your product. This section provides a set of practical ideation techniques designed to help you think like a Product Manager with an "AI-first" mindset—someone who proactively looks for opportunities to leverage AI to solve user problems and create innovative solutions.

This isn't about forcing AI into your product; it's about *thoughtfully exploring* how AI can enhance the user experience and achieve your product goals.

Ideation Techniques: Unleashing Your AI Creativity

Here are several structured approaches to brainstorming AI/ML use cases.

"AI Feature Storming": The Brain Dump

The goal of this technique is to generate a large quantity of AI/ML feature ideas, focusing on breadth rather than depth. Don't worry about feasibility at this stage; just let the ideas flow!

To start, choose a specific focus area, such as a user problem or a particular feature, and set a time limit (e.g., 15–30 minutes). Then, individually or as a team, brainstorm as many AI/ML feature ideas as possible using prompts like "How could AI/ML automate this task?" or "How could AI/ML personalize this experience?" The key is to document every idea without judgment.

For instance, if you were brainstorming for a customer support feature, your team might generate ideas across different categories, as shown in the following table:

PROMPT	POTENTIAL AI FEATURE IDEAS
How could AI/ML automate this task?	Auto-categorize tickets, auto-generate responses to FAQs, auto-assign tickets to agents.
How could AI/ML personalize this?	Tailor responses to user sentiment, personalize knowledge base recommendations based on user history.
How could AI/ML predict user needs?	Predict ticket volume, predict customer churn, predict the likelihood of a ticket requiring escalation.
How could it improve accuracy?	Use an LLM to improve the accuracy of the chatbot's responses.
How could it bring new insights?	Analyze text from interactions to understand what customers are looking for the most.

"AI Scenario Planning": Walking in the User's Shoes

This technique helps you explore how AI/ML could enhance specific user scenarios. Start by identifying 2–3 key scenarios within your product and then, for each one, document the "before" (current experience) and "after" (AI-enhanced experience).

To illustrate this, let's consider a file sharing feature and explore how different user scenarios could be improved with AI, as shown in the table below:

SCENARIO	BEFORE AI (CURRENT EXPERIENCE)	AFTER AI (IMPROVED EXPERIENCE)
Sharing a large file with a colleague	User manually selects the file, chooses sharing options (permissions, expiry), enters recipient email addresses, and sends the file.	AI suggests relevant recipients based on past collaborations and the content of the file. AI automatically sets appropriate sharing permissions based on organizational policies and the sensitivity of the file. AI suggests expiry time.
Collaborating on a document with a team	Users manually track changes, manage versions, and resolve conflicts.	AI automatically tracks changes, highlights potential conflicts, and suggests resolutions. AI provides a summary of changes made by each collaborator.
Searching for a specific file	User manually searches for the file using keywords, often with limited success.	AI-powered semantic search understands the meaning of the user's query and the content of the files, providing more relevant results. AI suggests related files based on the user's current task.

"Data Opportunity Mapping": Leveraging Your Data Assets

This approach involves identifying AI/ML opportunities based on the data you have available. Start by inventorying all the types of data your product collects, and then for each data type, brainstorm how AI/ML could be used to extract insights, make predictions, generate recommendations, or automate tasks. Finally, connect these potential applications to user value.

The following table provides an example of how this mapping might look:

DATA TYPE	POTENTIAL AI APPLICATIONS	USER VALUE EXAMPLE
User activity logs	Identify user segments, predict churn, personalize recommendations, detect anomalies (e.g., fraudulent activity)	Improved user experience
Customer support tickets	Categorize tickets, generate automated responses, identify common issues, analyze sentiment	Faster support resolution
Product usage data	Identify popular features, understand user workflows, personalize onboarding, predict future usage patterns	Increased feature adoption
Text content (e.g., articles, reviews)	Summarize content, extract key themes, translate languages, generate related content	Better understanding of the available information

"AI Capability Alignment": The Matching Game

This technique helps you directly match specific AI/ML capabilities to the problems and opportunities you've identified. Start by reviewing your list of problems, and then for each one, identify the AI/ML capabilities (from Section 2, "Matching Capabilities to Problems: A Practical Approach") that could be applied.

The following table provides an example of how you might align problems with potential AI capabilities:

PROBLEM/OPPORTUNITY	POTENTIAL AI/ML CAPABILITIES
Improve search results in a knowledge base	NLP (semantic search), recommendation systems (suggesting related articles), classification (categorizing articles)
Reduce customer support response times	NLP (understanding user queries), generation (automated responses), classification (ticket routing), sentiment analysis (prioritizing urgent/angry customers)

PROBLEM/OPPORTUNITY	POTENTIAL AI/ML CAPABILITIES
Personalize product recommendations	Recommendation systems (collaborative filtering, content-based filtering), clustering (identifying user segments)
Automate data entry in a form	NLP (predictive text, auto-completion), computer vision (extracting data from images)

"AI-Powered Feature Reverse Engineering": Learning from Others

This final technique involves getting inspiration from successful AI/ML features in other products. Start by identifying AI-powered features you admire, analyze how they work at a high level, and then consider how you could adapt or apply those concepts to your own product.

The following table provides an example of how you might reverse engineer features from well-known products:

PRODUCT	AI-POWERED FEATURE	LIKELY AI/ML CAPABILITY	POTENTIAL APPLICATION TO YOUR PRODUCT (E.G., PROJECT MANAGEMENT TOOL)
Gmail	Smart Compose	NLP (text generation)	Suggesting task descriptions, comments, or project updates as the user types
Netflix	Personalized Recommendations	Recommendation systems	Recommending relevant collaborators, tasks, or resources based on the user's current project
Grammarly	Grammar and Spell Check	NLP (error detection, correction)	Providing real-time grammar and spell checking within task descriptions and comments

Cultivating an AI-First Mindset

Beyond these specific techniques, it is important to cultivate an "AI-first" mindset. This means:

- **Challenge Assumptions:** Constantly question why things are done a certain way and whether AI/ML could offer a better approach.

- **Embrace Experimentation:** Don't be afraid to try new things and test AI/ML ideas, even if they seem unconventional. Start with small, low-risk experiments.

- **Focus on User Value:** Always prioritize AI/ML applications that provide clear and measurable value to your users. Avoid using AI just for the sake of it.

- **Stay Informed:** The field of AI/ML is rapidly evolving. Make an effort to stay up-to-date on the latest advancements and trends.

- **Collaborate:** Work closely with engineers, designers, and other stakeholders.

By combining these practical ideation techniques with an AI-first mindset, you'll be well-equipped to identify and explore a wide range of AI/ML opportunities, transforming your product and delivering exceptional user experiences. You will be able to see AI opportunities in every product and in every task, no matter how simple it is.

Chapter Summary and Key Takeaways

You are now equipped with a comprehensive set of frameworks for discovering and evaluating AI opportunities within any product. This chapter walked you through the process of putting on your "AI lens," starting with the AI Opportunity Discovery Framework to find data-rich problems. You learned how to analyze the user journey, enhance existing features, and use structured ideation techniques to move from vague ideas to concrete AI use cases. The goal was to provide you with a repeatable process for finding high-impact problems where AI can be a truly transformative solution.

Key Takeaways

- You always start with the user or business problem, not the AI technology. Your role is to be a disciplined problem-finder first.

- You analyze the entire user journey to find specific moments of friction or opportunity that AI can enhance, making the experience more seamless and intelligent.

- You recognize that creating value can come from enhancing existing features with AI, not just from building entirely new AI products from scratch.

- You use structured ideation techniques (like AI Feature Storming or Data Opportunity Mapping) to systematically uncover and articulate potential AI-powered solutions.

Onward: Measuring the Value of Your Ideas

Once you have identified a promising opportunity, the next critical step is to justify its value and define how you will measure its success. The next chapter will focus on ROI Calculation for AI Projects, providing you with the tools to measure and demonstrate the potential impact of your AI initiatives.

ROI Calculation for AI Projects: Measuring the Impact and Demonstrating Value

You've identified potential AI opportunities; now comes a very important step: figuring out how to measure the *value* of your AI investments. This is where we talk about Return on Investment (ROI) for AI projects. Calculating ROI for AI can be more complex than for traditional software projects, but it's essential for justifying investments, securing resources, and demonstrating the impact of your work. As a Product Manager, you play a key role in defining how success will be measured.

This chapter isn't about complex financial modeling. It's about establishing a clear framework for understanding and quantifying the *impact* of your AI initiatives. We'll focus on defining the right metrics and establishing baselines to measure progress.

From Model Performance to Business Impact: A PM's Guide to AI Metrics

Calculating the ROI for an AI feature isn't a single formula; it's a process of connecting the model's technical performance to tangible business results. This requires understanding two layers of measurement. First, we need to evaluate the model itself—is it accurate? Is it fast? These are the *model performance metrics*. Second, we need to measure how that performance impacts our goals—did it reduce churn? Did it increase revenue? These are the *business outcome metrics*.

As a Product Manager, your very important role is to build the bridge between these two layers, demonstrating how improvements in model performance drive real business value. In this section, we will walk through the essential components of this measurement framework. We'll start by defining the specific metrics used to evaluate AI models, then discuss the importance of baselines, and finally explore how to select the right metrics for your unique product context.

Defining AI/ML-Specific Metrics: The Foundation for Measuring ROI

To accurately measure the ROI of AI, you need to go beyond traditional business metrics (like revenue and cost savings) and incorporate *AI/ML-specific metrics*. These metrics provide objective measures of your AI model's *performance*, which is the foundation for understanding its broader business impact. Think of it like this: you can't assess the overall health of a car (business impact) without checking the engine's performance (AI/ML metrics).

These metrics fall into several categories. We will examine the specific formulas and use cases for these metrics—like accuracy, precision, and recall—in the upcoming section, "Key Performance Metrics for AI/ML Models." For now, the key takeaway is that they are the core of measuring a model's performance.

The Importance of Baselines: Knowing Where You Started

Before you implement any AI/ML solution, it's very important to establish *baseline metrics*. This is like taking a "before" picture. You need to know how your product or feature is performing *without* AI to be able to measure the *improvement* (or lack thereof) after AI is implemented.

- **What to Measure:** The specific baseline metrics you choose will depend on the problem you're trying to solve. They should be directly related to the user problem and the goals of your AI project.

  - **Example:** If you're building an AI-powered spam filter, your baseline metrics might include the current false positive rate (legitimate emails incorrectly flagged as spam) and the false negative rate (spam emails that get through to the inbox).

  - **Example:** If you're using AI to improve search relevance, your baseline metrics might include the average time users spend searching, the click-through rate on search results, and user satisfaction scores.

  - **Example:** If you're automating a customer support task, your baseline metrics might include the average time it takes agents to resolve tickets of that type, the cost per resolution, and customer satisfaction ratings.

- **How to Measure:** You might need to gather data through:

  - Analyzing existing logs and databases.

  - Conducting user surveys.

  - Running A/B tests (without the AI component yet).

  - Manually tracking key performance indicators (KPIs).

The key is to get a clear, quantitative picture of the *current state* before you introduce AI. This baseline will be your benchmark for measuring success.

Understanding the Confusion Matrix: Decoding Classification Performance

One of the most fundamental tools for evaluating the performance of classification models is the **confusion matrix**. Don't let the name intimidate you—it's a simple and powerful concept for understanding the nuances of your model's performance beyond a single accuracy score.

The confusion matrix is essentially a table that visualizes how well your model's predictions align with the actual outcomes (the ground truth). It provides a clear breakdown of where the model succeeded and where it was "confused," as shown in Figure 9-1.

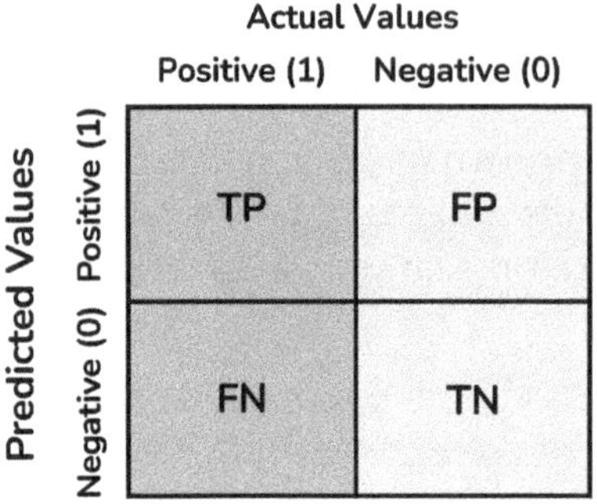

Figure 9-1: The confusion matrix visually breaks down a classification model's performance by comparing predictions against actual outcomes. It is the foundation for calculating key metrics like precision and recall.

To interpret the matrix, let's break down its four quadrants using a spam filter as our running example:

- **True Positive (TP):** The model correctly predicted a positive outcome.
  Example: An email was actually spam, and the filter correctly identified it as spam. *(This is a correct prediction.)*

- **False Negative (FN):** The model incorrectly predicted a negative outcome when the actual outcome was positive. This is a "miss."
  Example: An email was actually spam, but the filter failed to identify it and let it through to the user's inbox. *(This is a dangerous error.)*

- **False Positive (FP):** The model incorrectly predicted a positive outcome when the actual outcome was negative. This is a "false alarm."
  Example: An email was an important, legitimate message, but the filter incorrectly flagged it as spam. *(This is a frustrating error.)*

- **True Negative (TN):** The model correctly predicted a negative outcome.
  Example: An email was not spam, and the filter correctly identified it as not spam, leaving it in the inbox. *(This is a correct prediction.)*

Why this matters to a PM: The value of the confusion matrix is that it moves the conversation beyond a single accuracy score and forces you to consider the **cost of different types of errors**. A simple accuracy metric can be dangerously misleading, and here is a classic example of why.

Imagine a spam filter where 99% of all incoming emails are legitimate ("not spam") and only 1% are actual spam. A lazy model could be built to *always* predict "not spam." On the surface, this model would be **99% accurate**, which sounds fantastic.

However, this model is completely useless because it lets **100% of the spam** into the user's inbox.

The confusion matrix would immediately expose this flaw. It would show that the model has zero **True Positives** (it never correctly identifies spam) and a high number of **False Negatives** (it misses every single piece of spam).

This forces you to ask the essential product question: what type of error is more harmful to our user? Is it a **False Negative** (letting a spam email into the inbox) or a **False Positive** (sending an important, legitimate email to the spam folder)? Answering this question is the foundation for selecting the right evaluation metrics, like precision and recall, which we will cover next.

Key Performance Metrics for AI/ML Models: Beyond the Confusion Matrix

The confusion matrix gives us the raw ingredients, but we need to combine those ingredients into meaningful metrics. These metrics are like the key performance indicators (KPIs) for your AI model. They tell you how well it's performing its specific task. As a Product Manager, you don't need to be able to *calculate* these metrics yourself (your data science team will handle that), but you *do* need to understand what they mean and which ones are most relevant to your product.

The following table shows a breakdown of some of the most important AI/ML performance metrics:

METRIC	DEFINITION	FORMULA	WHEN TO USE	PM'S PERSPECTIVE (WHY IT MATTERS)
Accuracy	The overall proportion of correctly predicted outcomes (both positive and negative).	$\dfrac{(TP + TN)}{(TP + TN + FP + FN)}$	Generally useful as a high-level overview, but can be misleading with imbalanced datasets (where one class is much more frequent than the others).	Easy to understand, but be cautious! High accuracy doesn't always mean a good model, especially if you have imbalanced data (e.g., very few fraudulent transactions in a large dataset).
Precision	The proportion of correctly predicted positive outcomes out of all predicted positive outcomes.	$\dfrac{TP}{(TP + FP)}$	When the cost of false positives is high. You want to be very sure that when the model predicts "positive," it's actually positive.	*Think*: spam filter. High precision means fewer legitimate emails are wrongly classified as spam (fewer false positives). You'd rather miss some spam (false negatives) than lose important emails.
Recall (Sensitivity)	The proportion of correctly predicted positive outcomes out of all actual positive outcomes.	$\dfrac{TP}{(TP + FN)}$	When the cost of false negatives is high. You want to make sure you're catching all the actual positive cases, even if it means having a few false alarms.	*Think*: medical diagnosis. High recall means fewer cases of a disease are missed (fewer false negatives). You'd rather have some false alarms (false positives) than miss a diagnosis.

METRIC	DEFINITION	FORMULA	WHEN TO USE	PM'S PERSPECTIVE (WHY IT MATTERS)
F1-Score	The harmonic mean of precision and recall, providing a balanced measure of performance.	$\dfrac{2 * (Precision * Recall)}{(Precision + Recall)}$	When you need a good balance between precision and recall. Useful when you care about both minimizing false positives and minimizing false negatives.	A good overall measure when you don't have a strong preference for minimizing either false positives or false negatives specifically.
Latency	The time it takes for the AI/ML model to generate a prediction or response.	Measured in milliseconds (ms) or seconds (s)	Critical for real-time applications, like self-driving cars, chatbots, or fraud detection systems, where speed is essential.	Directly impacts user experience. A slow model, even if accurate, can be unusable.
Throughput	The number of predictions the model can perform in a given time period.	Predictions per second/minute/etc.	Important for high-volume applications, where the model needs to handle a large number of requests.	Affects scalability. Can your model handle the expected load?
Model Drift	A measure of how much a deployed models performance changes over time.	Calculated by comparing current model performance to the performance baseline.	Important to monitor the model after deployment and make sure that it remains useful and doesn't degrade.	

Continues

(continued)

METRIC	DEFINITION	FORMULA	WHEN TO USE	PM'S PERSPECTIVE (WHY IT MATTERS)
Mean Squared Error (MSE)	The average squared difference between the predicted and actual values. (For regression problems only).	(Sum of squared errors) / (Number of data points) $$MSE = \frac{1}{n}\sum_{i=1}^{n}(Y_i - \hat{Y}_i)^2$$	Used when you're predicting a continuous value (e.g., predicting house prices, forecasting sales). Penalizes larger errors more heavily.	Lower MSE is better. Gives you a sense of the magnitude of the errors.
Root Mean Squared Error (RMSE)	The square root of the MSE. (For regression problems only).	$\sqrt{MSE}$ $$RMSE = \sqrt{\frac{\sum_{i=1}^{N}\left\|Y_i - \hat{Y}_i\right\|^2}{N}},$$	Same use case as MSE, but the result is in the same units as the target variable, making it more interpretable.	Easier to understand than MSE because it's in the same units as the thing you're predicting (e.g., dollars, inches, etc.).
Mean Absolute Error (MAE)	The average absolute difference between the predicted and actual values. (For regression problems only).	(Sum of squared errors) / (Number of data points) $$MAE = \frac{1}{n}\sum_{i=1}^{n}\left\|Y_i - \hat{Y}_i\right\|$$	Used when you're predicting a continuous value, and you want a metric that's less sensitive to outliers than MSE/RMSE.	Less sensitive to extreme errors than MSE/RMSE. Gives you the average size of the error.

(Note: TP = True Positive, TN = True Negative, FP = False Positive, FN = False Negative)

It's important to remember these are tools. And as a PM you should decide which tools are more important for your product. As an example:

- **High Precision:** Important if the cost of a false positive is high (e.g., flagging a legitimate transaction as fraudulent).

- **High Recall:** Important if the cost of a false negative is high (e.g., failing to detect a disease in a medical diagnosis).

- **Low Latency:** Critical for real-time applications (e.g., self-driving cars, chatbots).

- **High Throughput:** Needed if you are going to process a lot of requests.

This table provides a starting point. The specific metrics you choose will depend on the nature of your AI/ML application and your overall business goals. The next section will delve deeper into selecting the *right* metrics for your specific context. The key is to be able to have data-driven conversations with your team.

Context Matters: Selecting the Right Metrics for Your AI/ML Application

Choosing the right metrics for your AI/ML project is like choosing the right instruments for a scientific experiment. You need to select the tools that will accurately measure the specific phenomena you're interested in. There's no one-size-fits-all answer; the *best* metrics depend heavily on the specific application, your business goals, and the potential costs of different types of errors. This is where your product judgment comes in.

This isn't just a technical exercise for the data science team. As a Product Manager, you need to be actively involved in selecting metrics because they define *success*. They determine how your AI-powered feature will be evaluated, and ultimately, whether it's considered a win or a loss.

Here's a step-by-step guide to help you navigate this critical process:

1. Define Your Business Goals (and Connect Them to User Needs):

Start with the "why": Before you even think about metrics, clearly articulate the *business goals* of your AI/ML project. What problem are you trying to solve? What user need are you trying to address? How will this AI feature contribute to the overall product strategy?

- **Be specific:** Avoid vague goals like "improve user engagement." Instead, be specific: "Increase click-through rates on recommended articles by 15 percent," or "Reduce customer support ticket resolution time by 20 percent."

- **Connect to user needs:** Always link your business goals back to user needs. For example, "Reduce customer support ticket resolution time" (business goal) translates to "Help users get their problems solved faster" (user need).

Mapping your business goals to specific user needs and potential AI applications is a critical first step. The following table provides a simple framework for this thought process.

BUSINESS GOAL	USER NEED	POTENTIAL AI/ML APPLICATION
Increase customer retention.	Get problems solved quickly and efficiently.	AI-powered chatbot for faster support.
Reduce operational costs.	Reduce manual effort.	Automate data entry with AI.
Improve product recommendations.	Discover relevant and interesting products.	AI-powered recommendation system.
Detect and prevent fraud.	Keep accounts and transactions secure.	AI-powered fraud detection system.

This initial alignment provides the clarity needed for the rest of the process. Without a well-defined business goal and a clear understanding of the user need, you cannot select meaningful metrics, and you won't be able to measure the true impact or ROI of your AI feature. Once you have this clear objective, the next step is to consider the specific type of AI application you are building.

2. Consider the Type of AI/ML Application (and Its Inherent Trade-Offs)

Once you have a clear business objective, the next step is to consider the *type* of AI/ML problem you are solving. Different types of problems require different evaluation metrics because they measure success in fundamentally different ways.

For **Classification** problems, where the goal is to categorize data (like spam detection), you'll focus on the metrics derived from the confusion matrix. The central product question here is understanding the **trade-off between precision and recall**. For a medical diagnosis tool, you would prioritize **Recall** to minimize false negatives (missed diseases). Conversely, for a spam filter where incorrectly flagging an important email (a false positive) is highly undesirable, you might prioritize **Precision**. A balanced approach often uses the **F1-Score**.

When dealing with **Regression** problems, where you predict a continuous value like a house price, your metrics shift to measuring the *magnitude of the error*. You'll use metrics like **Mean Absolute Error (MAE)** or **Root Mean Squared Error (RMSE)**. The key question for a PM is: "Are large errors disproportionately costly?" If so, RMSE, which penalizes large errors more heavily, might be the better choice.

For **Recommendation Systems**, the goal is to present a useful, ordered list of items. Metrics here focus on the quality of that list, such as **Precision@k** (how many of the top k recommendations are relevant) or **NDCG** (which also accounts for the position of relevant items). Your main consideration is whether you're optimizing for showing *only* relevant items or for making sure you show *all* relevant items within that top list.

Finally, for specialized tasks like **Natural Language Processing (NLP)** or **Anomaly Detection**, you'll use specific metrics. For NLP tasks like translation or summarization, you might see scores like **BLEU** or **ROUGE**. For Anomaly Detection, you'll often come back to **Precision and Recall**, but focused specifically on how well the model catches the rare "anomaly" class.

3. Evaluate the Cost of Errors: The Risk Assessment

Perhaps the most critical part of selecting metrics is a clear-eyed assessment of the **cost of errors**. As a PM, you must think like a risk manager and determine the real-world consequences of your model being wrong. The central trade-off often comes down to this: what is worse for your user and your business—a False Positive or a False Negative?

- **Example: Credit Card Fraud Detection**
  A **False Positive** occurs when a legitimate transaction is flagged as fraudulent. This inconveniences the customer, may cause embarrassment, and can damage their trust in your service. A **False Negative** is when a fraudulent transaction is missed, leading to direct financial loss. In this high-stakes scenario, most businesses prioritize **high Recall** to catch as many fraudulent cases as possible, even if it means occasionally inconveniencing a customer with a false alarm.

- **Example: Content Moderation**
  A **False Positive** occurs when safe, legitimate content is flagged and removed. This can lead to user frustration and accusations of censorship, damaging community trust. A **False Negative** is when harmful or inappropriate content is missed and remains visible. This can create an unsafe environment for other users. Here, the costs are balanced and complex, making a balanced metric like the **F1-Score** a more appropriate choice.

4. Translate Technical Metrics into Business Impact

Finally, to truly demonstrate the value of your AI initiative, you must connect the technical model metrics to tangible business outcomes. Stakeholders and leadership may not understand what "an F1-Score of 0.85" means, but they will understand its impact on revenue, costs, or customer satisfaction.

This means translating your findings into clear value statements. Instead of just reporting on model performance, you should aim to say things like:

- "By automating this task, we **reduced operational costs by X percent.**"

- "Our new recommendation engine increased user click-through rates by Y percent, leading to a **direct increase in sales.**"

- "The improved fraud detection model reduced false positives by Z percent, which in turn **decreased customer support calls and saved the company money.**"

- "By predicting user churn with 85 percent recall, our interventions **retained an additional X customers this quarter**, resulting in a **revenue impact of Y dollars.**"

Important Considerations

Finally, beyond the specific steps, it's helpful to keep a few high-level principles in mind. These considerations will guide you as you navigate the inevitable trade-offs and complexities of measuring AI performance and value.

- **Context is king:** The "best" metrics are always context-dependent.

- **Balance is key:** Often, you'll need to find a balance between competing metrics (e.g., precision and recall).

- **Trade-offs exist:** There will almost always be trade-offs between different metrics (e.g., accuracy vs. latency). Be prepared to make informed decisions about these trade-offs.

- **Iterate and refine:** Your choice of metrics might evolve as you learn more about your model's performance and its impact on the user experience. Don't be afraid to adjust your metrics as needed.

- **Business impact is very important:** Always be able to explain what your metrics mean for the product and for the overall goals.

By carefully considering these factors and following this step-by-step guide, you can select the right AI/ML metrics to accurately measure the ROI of your AI projects and demonstrate their value to stakeholders. This process transforms you from a passive observer of technical metrics to an active participant in defining and measuring the success of your AI initiatives.

End-to-End Example—Predicting Churn in a Subscription Service

Let's walk through a complete example to illustrate how the concepts we've discussed can be applied to a real-world product scenario: predicting customer churn in a subscription-based online learning platform. This example will demonstrate the entire process, from defining the business goal to calculating ROI and ongoing monitoring.

1. Identify the Business Goal: Defining the "Why"

The first step in any AI project is to clearly define the business goal. For this project, our primary objective is to reduce customer churn. This is a critical goal for any subscription-based business, as high churn directly impacts revenue and growth, and retaining existing customers is often more cost-effective than acquiring new ones.

To effectively reduce churn, we must first understand the underlying user needs and pain points that cause it. Churn isn't random; it's often driven by specific, addressable issues. For example, as Figure 9-2 highlights, industry data shows that over half of customer churn in subscription services can be attributed to just a few leading causes, like ineffective onboarding, weak relationship building with customers, and subpar customer service. By addressing these core user needs, we can create a more effective retention strategy.

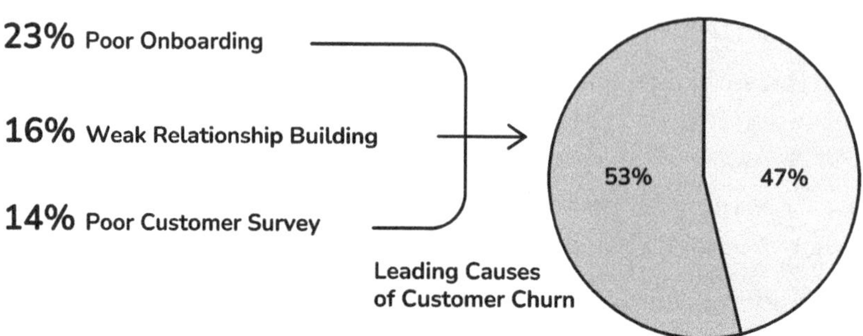

Figure 9-2: The leading causes of customer churn in subscription services. A significant portion of churn can be attributed to a small number of core issues, such as poor customer service and weak relationship building with customers. (*Source:* Relently).

2. Define the AI/ML Application and Solution

With the business goal and user need clearly defined, the next step is to outline the specific AI-powered solution. Our proposed application is to develop a machine learning model that predicts which users are at high risk of churning before they actually cancel their subscriptions.

Figure 9-3 illustrates this concept. An AI/ML approach is particularly suitable here because this is a classic prediction problem (specifically, a classification task of "churn" vs. "not churn"). We can leverage the wealth of historical user data available, as behavioral patterns often precede a customer's decision to cancel.

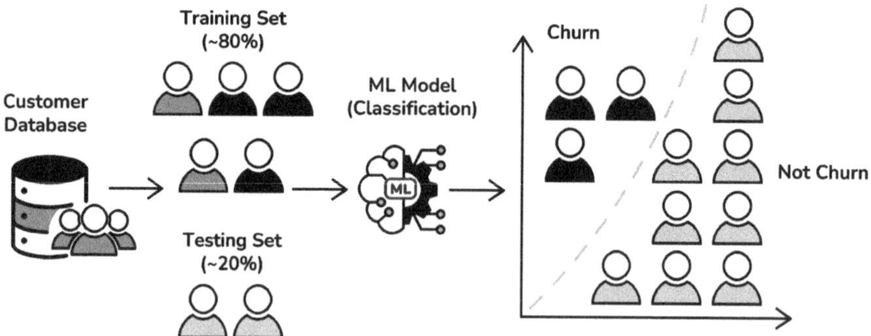

Figure 9-3: A conceptual model for churn prediction. The AI system analyzes various user data points to generate a churn risk score, classifying users into groups like "(likely to) Churn" and "(likely to) Not Churn" to enable targeted interventions

3. Identify Data Sources and Engineer Features: The Raw Materials

Once the AI application is defined, the focus shifts to its most critical component: data. This stage is a two-part process. First, we must identify and gather all the potential "raw materials"—the available data sources that might contain predictive signals. Then, through a process of creative analysis called *feature engineering*, we refine those raw materials into the high-quality ingredients our model will actually use to learn.

Available Data

We need to identify the data sources that might contain information relevant to churn. This typically includes:

CATEGORY	DATA POINTS
User Demographic	Age, location, subscription tier, profession, interests (if available)
User Activity	■ Course completion rates ■ Login frequency and recency ■ Time spent on the platform ■ Forum participation (posts, comments, replies) ■ Engagement with learning materials (downloads, views, quizzes taken) ■ Customer support interactions ■ Use of specific features
Subscription History	Start date, plan type, payment frequency, billing history, discounts used
Feedback Data	Survey responses, reviews, ratings

Feature Engineering

Having access to this raw data is the first step. However, data points like a raw "login date" aren't always in the most useful format for a model. The next very important step is feature engineering, where we transform this raw data into more meaningful signals that boost the model's performance. It's like a chef turning basic ingredients into a flavorful sauce. Examples of engineered features include:

FEATURE NAME	EXAMPLE VALUE	EXPLANATION
Days Since Last Login	15	The user last accessed the platform fifteen days ago.
Average Courses Completed per Month	1.5	On average, the user completes 1.5 courses each month.
Number of Support Tickets in Last Thirty Days	0	The user has not opened any support tickets in the past month.
Forum Posts per Week	0.2	The user posts infrequently on the forum (e.g., about once every five weeks).
Subscription Length (in Months)	24	The user has been subscribed for two years (24 months).
Discount Usage Rate	0.10	The user has applied a discount code on 10% of their subscription payments.
Has User Given Feedback? (Boolean)	Yes	The user has submitted feedback through surveys or ratings.

The Product Manager's Role in This Stage

While data identification and feature engineering are highly technical, the Product Manager plays a vital collaborative role:

- **Provide domain expertise:** You understand the user and the product better than anyone. Your insights are very important for brainstorming meaningful features. For example, you might hypothesize that "users who complete the onboarding checklist are less likely to churn"—a suggestion that directly leads to a valuable feature for the model.

- **Champion data quality and ethics:** You are responsible for ensuring the data used is ethically sourced and that potential biases are considered. You'll advocate for high-quality data, as it's the foundation of your feature's performance.

- **Help prioritize:** Given that countless features can be engineered, you can help the data science team prioritize which ones to build and test first, based on your hypotheses about user behavior and their potential impact on the model.

4. Select the Metrics: Defining Success

With the data sources identified and potential features engineered, the next step is to define exactly how we will measure the model's success. This requires translating our business goal (reducing churn) into specific, quantifiable model performance metrics.

The Cost of Errors: Prioritizing What Matters

For our churn prediction model, not all errors are equal. We must first consider the relative cost of a *false positive* versus a *false negative*.

- A **false positive** would be incorrectly flagging a happy user as "high risk." The cost is the resources spent on an unnecessary intervention (like sending them a discount they didn't need).

- A **false negative** would be failing to identify a user who is actually about to churn. The cost is lost subscription revenue, which is significantly higher.

Given this, our primary goal is to minimize false negatives—we want to catch as many potential churners as possible. This directly informs our choice of metrics.

The relationship between these metrics—especially Precision and Recall—is derived from the four outcomes of the confusion matrix. Figure 9-4 provides a visual reference for these key formulas.

Our Chosen Metrics

Based on our analysis of the cost of errors, we will use the following metrics to evaluate our model:

- **Primary Metric—Recall (Sensitivity):** We will prioritize Recall to maximize the proportion of actual churners that our model correctly identifies, thereby minimizing costly false negatives.

- **Secondary Metrics:**

  - **Precision:** While less critical than Recall for this problem, we still need to be reasonably precise to avoid wasting too many resources on unnecessary interventions.

  - **F1-Score:** The F1-Score will be monitored to provide a balanced measure of performance by calculating the harmonic mean of Precision and Recall, giving us a single number to track the model's overall health.

  - **Model Drift:** Model Drift will be monitored to track how the model's performance changes or degrades over time as it encounters new, real-world data.

- **Business Metric:** Ultimately, the model's success will be measured by its impact on the key business metric: the overall Churn Rate.

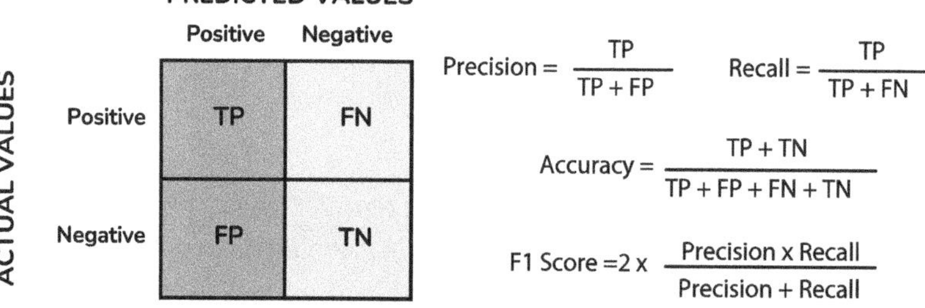

$$Precision = \frac{TP}{TP + FP} \qquad Recall = \frac{TP}{TP + FN}$$

$$Accuracy = \frac{TP + TN}{TP + FP + FN + TN}$$

$$F1\ Score = 2 \times \frac{Precision \times Recall}{Precision + Recall}$$

Figure 9-4: The foundational metrics for classification models. The confusion matrix (left) provides the core counts of True Positives (TP), False Negatives (FN), False Positives (FP), and True Negatives (TN). These counts are then used in the formulas for key performance indicators like Precision, Recall, and F1-Score (right).

5. Establish Baseline Metrics: Setting the Starting Point

Before we can measure the improvement from our new AI model, we must first establish a baseline. This is our "before" picture, showing how the product currently performs. A clear baseline is essential to prove the ROI of the AI initiative.

For our churn prediction project, we have two key benchmarks. First, the overall business metric: our platform currently has a monthly churn rate of 20 percent. Second, we'll measure against the existing manual process. Let's say our customer success team uses simple rules (like "user hasn't logged in for thirty days") to flag at-risk users, and this method only correctly identifies 30 percent of users who eventually churn. These two numbers are the benchmarks our new model must beat.

6. Conduct Model Training and Evaluation: Building and Testing the AI

With our data and metrics defined, the data science team begins the core technical work. This process starts with **data splitting**, where the historical data is divided into separate training, validation, and testing sets to ensure the model is evaluated on data it has never seen before. Next is **model selection**. Data scientists often experiment with several algorithms to find the best fit for the problem. For a classification task like this, they might test various models, each with different levels of complexity, as illustrated in Figure 9-5.

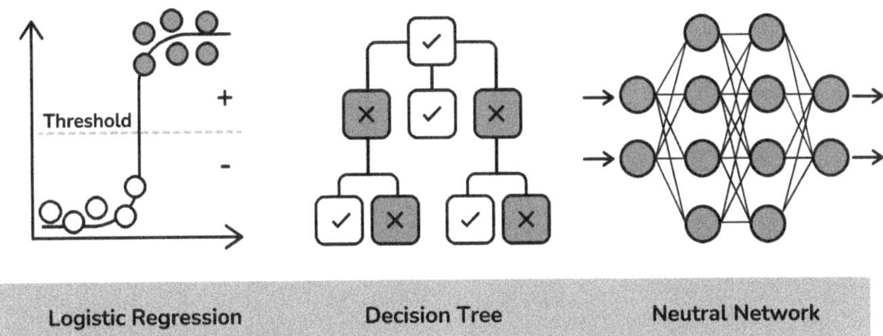

Figure 9-5: A visual representation of different classification algorithms. Data scientists often test multiple model types, such as the relatively simple logistic regression, the rule-based decision tree, or the more complex neural network, to find the best performer for a given problem.

After training and tuning various models, the best-performing one is selected and its performance is measured on the final, held-out test set. For our churn model, let's say the initial results are:

- **Recall: 85 Percent** (The model correctly identifies 85 percent of the users who actually churned.)

- **Precision: 60 Percent** (Of the users flagged as high-risk by the model, 60 **percent** actually churned.)
- **F1-Score: 70 Percent** (A balanced measure of performance.)

7. Conduct A/B Testing: Measuring Real-World Impact

With a promising model built, the next very important step is to rigorously evaluate its real-world impact by conducting an **A/B test**. This allows us to compare the outcomes for users who experience the AI-powered interventions against those who don't. The test is structured as follows:

- **Group A (Control Group):** A randomly selected group of users who continue to receive the standard product experience without any new AI-driven interventions. This group serves as our baseline for comparison.

- **Group B (Treatment Group):** A second group of users where the AI model is active. Users that the model identifies as "high-risk" in this group receive targeted interventions, which could include:
  - Personalized emails with course recommendations.
  - Special offers or discounts.
  - Proactive outreach from the customer success team.
  - In-app messages highlighting relevant features or content.

After running the test for a defined period, for example one month, we compare the churn rates. The results show the control group's churn rate held steady at our 20 percent baseline, while the treatment group's churn rate dropped to just 15 percent—a statistically significant reduction.

8. Calculate the Results and ROI: Quantifying the Value

The successful A/B test confirmed that the AI-powered model and interventions resulted in a five percentage point reduction in churn (from 20 percent to 15 percent). To understand what this means for the business, we can translate this percentage into a direct impact on user retention and revenue. The following table breaks down this calculation based on a hypothetical platform of 10,000 subscribers, and the average monthly subscription fee is $50.

METRIC	CONTROL GROUP (BASELINE)	TREATMENT GROUP (AI + INTERVENTION)
Inputs:		
User Base	10,000	10,000
Avg. Monthly Revenue/User	$50	$50
Monthly Churn:		
Churn Rate	20%	15%
Churned Users (#)	2,000	1,500

Translating Results into Business Impact

The table's results show a clear positive impact. By translating the five percentage point drop in churn into financial terms, we can demonstrate the value of the initiative:

- **Users Retained:** 500 users per month.
- **Monthly Revenue Saved:** $25,000.
- **Annualized Revenue Saved:** $300,000.

This demonstrates a significant potential ROI, though a complete calculation must also account for the project's development, deployment, and intervention costs.

Monitoring for Long-Term Success

While financial impact is the ultimate business outcome, a Product Manager must also track the model's technical performance to ensure its long-term health and efficiency. These model-specific metrics act as early warning systems for future problems. Therefore, we will also continuously monitor:

- **Model Drift:** To make sure our model's predictions remain accurate as real-world user behavior evolves over time.

- **Precision:** To ensure we are not wasting too many resources on interventions for users who would not have churned anyway.

- **F1 Score:** To check that we are maintaining a healthy balance between catching potential churners (recall) and not over-flagging happy customers (precision).

9. Monitor and Maintain the Model for Long-Term Success

The launch of the AI feature is not the end of the project; it is the beginning of its ongoing lifecycle. Ensuring long-term success requires a commitment to a continuous loop of observing, learning, and improving. This process involves several key, ongoing activities:

- **Continuous Monitoring:** The model's performance metrics (Recall, Precision, F1-Score) and the core business metric (Churn Rate) are tracked on production dashboards. Alerts are configured to detect any significant performance degradation or model drift.

- **Model Retraining:** Based on monitoring results or a set schedule, the model is periodically retrained with new, real-world user data to adapt to changing behaviors and maintain its predictive accuracy.

- **Intervention Refinement:** Beyond just maintaining the model, the product strategy itself must evolve. This involves continuously A/B testing the different interventions (e.g., trying a new discount offer or a different email copy) to optimize their effectiveness.

- **Establishing a Feedback Loop:** All of these activities feed into a continuous feedback loop. Insights from model performance, A/B tests, and direct user feedback are used to holistically improve the model, the data, and the overall churn reduction program.

This end-to-end example demonstrates how a Product Manager can use AI/ML to address a critical business problem (churn), measure the impact of the solution, and ensure its long-term success. It highlights the importance of a data-driven approach, careful metric selection, and ongoing monitoring and maintenance.

A/B Testing for AI and ML Projects: Validating Impact and Optimizing Performance

We've seen how A/B testing played a very important role in our churn prediction example, allowing us to *quantify* the impact of the AI-powered interventions. But A/B testing isn't just a step in that specific example; it's a *fundamental methodology* for validating and optimizing any AI/ML-powered feature. Think of it as the scientific method applied to product development.

What Is A/B Testing (in a Nutshell)?

At its core, A/B testing is a controlled experiment. As shown in Figure 9-6, you divide your users into two (or more) groups:

- **Group A (Control Group):** This group experiences the *existing* version of your product or feature (the "status quo").

- **Group B (Treatment Group):** This group experiences the *new* version of your product or feature, with the AI/ML enhancement.

  You then compare the performance of these groups on your key metrics (e.g., churn rate, click-through rate, conversion rate, etc.). If Group B (with the AI) performs significantly better than Group A, you have evidence that your AI/ML feature is having a positive impact.

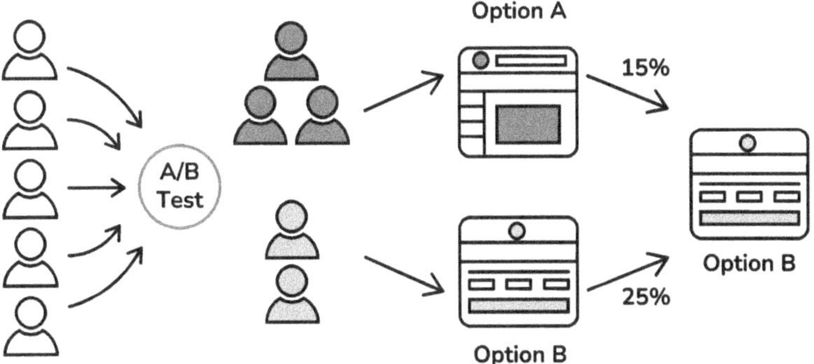

Figure 9-6: A/B testing can help determine if a new feature or change in your product will affect a specific metric.

Why Is A/B Testing *Especially* Important for AI/ML?

A/B testing is always important for product development, but it's *particularly* important for AI/ML projects for several reasons:

- **AI models are probabilistic, not deterministic:** Unlike traditional software, which follows explicit rules, AI/ML models make *predictions* based on probabilities. There's always a chance of error (false positives, false negatives). A/B testing helps you quantify the *real-world impact* of these errors.

- **Unintended Consequences:** AI models can sometimes behave in unexpected ways, especially when exposed to real-world data that differs from the training data. A/B testing helps you identify and mitigate any unintended negative consequences *before* they affect your entire user base.

- **Model performance ≠ user experience:** A model might perform well on a test dataset (e.g., high precision and recall), but that doesn't guarantee it will improve the *user experience*. A/B testing measures the impact on actual user behavior and business outcomes.

- **Continuous Optimization:** AI/ML is rarely a "set it and forget it" technology. A/B testing allows for *continuous optimization*. You can test different model versions, different parameter settings, or different ways of integrating the AI into the user experience.

- **Data-driven Decisions:** A/B testing provides *objective, quantitative evidence* to support your product decisions. It removes the guesswork and helps you build confidence in your AI investments.

In essence, A/B testing is your safety net and your optimization engine for AI/ML. It allows you to:

- **Validate:** Prove that your AI/ML feature is actually having the desired impact.

- **Optimize:** Fine-tune your model and its integration to maximize its effectiveness.

- **Mitigate risk:** Identify and address any negative consequences before they cause widespread problems.

- **Learn:** Gain valuable insights into how users interact with your AI-powered features.

How to Conduct A/B Testing for AI and ML: A Step-by-Step Guide

Now that you understand *why* A/B testing is essential for AI/ML, let's dive into the *how*. Here's a step-by-step guide to conducting effective A/B tests for your AI-powered features:

1. **Define a clear hypothesis: What do you expect to happen?**

   - **Start with a specific question:** Don't just test "Does the AI feature work?" Formulate a precise, testable hypothesis about *how* the AI/ML feature will impact user behavior and your key metrics. For example:

POOR HYPOTHESIS	GOOD HYPOTHESIS
"The AI-powered chatbot will improve customer satisfaction."	"The AI-powered chatbot will reduce the average time to resolution for customer support tickets by at least 15%." (This is specific, measurable, and directly tied to a business outcome).

   - **Be measurable:** Your hypothesis should include a *quantifiable* expected change.

2. **Select a target metric (or metrics): How will you measure success?**
   Once you have a clear hypothesis, you must select the right metrics to measure success. It's very important to choose a primary metric that directly measures the outcome stated in your hypothesis—this should be the same metric you used for your baseline. However, to get a complete picture, it is best practice to also track secondary metrics to monitor for unintended consequences (e.g., did speed hurt satisfaction?) or additional benefits.
   For instance, if your hypothesis is that an AI chatbot will reduce resolution times, your metrics might be:

   - **Primary Metric:** Average time to resolution.

   - **Secondary Metrics:** Customer satisfaction (CSAT) scores, ticket escalation rate, chatbot usage rate.

Ultimately, your chosen metrics must connect back to tangible business outcomes like cost savings or customer retention. The goal of the A/B test is to see a statistically significant improvement in your primary metric between the two groups. Figure 9-7 illustrates a successful outcome for our chatbot example, where the AI-powered variant dramatically reduced the resolution time.

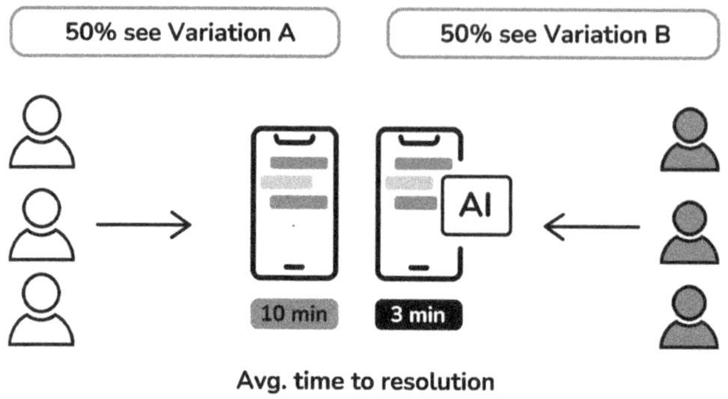

Figure 9-7: An example of A/B test results for an AI-powered chatbot. The treatment group (Variant B), which used the AI, showed a significant improvement in the primary metric—Average Time to Resolution—compared to the control group (Variant A).

3. **Determine a sample size: How many users do you need?**

   - **Statistical Significance:** You need a large enough sample size to ensure that any observed difference between the control and treatment groups is statistically significant—meaning it's unlikely to have occurred by chance. Figure 9-8 illustrates the concept of drawing a representative sample from a larger target population.

   - **Factors Affecting Sample Size:**

     - **Baseline Metric Value:** The current performance of your control group.

     - **Minimum Detectable Effect (MDE):** The *smallest* change in the target metric that you want to be able to detect reliably. A smaller MDE (detecting a smaller change) requires a larger sample size.

     - **Statistical Power (Typically 80 Percent):** The probability of detecting a statistically significant difference *if one actually exists*. Higher power (more certainty) requires a larger sample size.

     - **Significance Level (Alpha, Typically 5 Percent):** The probability of *incorrectly* concluding there's a difference when there isn't one (a "false positive"). A lower alpha (less chance of a false positive) requires a larger sample size.

- **Tools:** Use online sample size calculators (many are available for free) or statistical software (like R or Python) to determine the appropriate sample size.

- **PM's Role:** You don't need to do the calculations yourself, but you *do* need to understand the inputs (especially the MDE) and work with your data science team to determine an appropriate sample size. The sample size has direct implications for how long the A/B test will need to run.

- **Small Number of Users:** Having a small number of users may cause problems, as the variability will be too high.

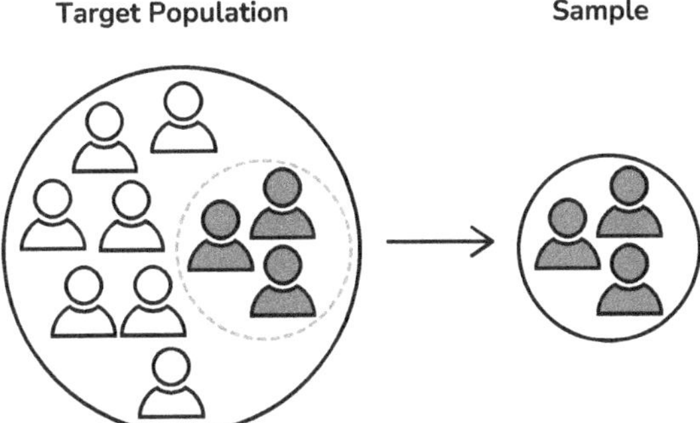

Figure 9-8: A visual representation of sampling. A smaller, representative Sample is selected from the larger Target Population to conduct the A/B test. The results from this sample are then used to infer the impact on the entire population.

4. **Randomly assign users: Ensuring a fair comparison**

- **Randomization is key:** The foundation of a valid A/B test is *random assignment*. You must ensure that users are randomly assigned to either the control group (A) or the treatment group (B). This helps to eliminate bias and ensure that the groups are comparable.

- **Consistent Randomization:** Use a consistent randomization method throughout the experiment. Don't change the assignment rules mid-test!

- **Tools:** Most A/B testing platforms provide built-in randomization functionality.

5. **Implement and deploy: Launching the experiment**

   - **Control Group (A):** This group continues to experience the existing version of your product or feature (no AI enhancement).

   - **Treatment Group (B):** This group experiences the new version with the AI/ML feature.

   - **Isolate the Variable:** Ensure that the *only* difference between the two groups is the AI/ML feature you're testing. Avoid making any other changes to the user experience during the experiment.

6. **Run the experiment: Patience is a virtue**

   - **Sufficient Duration:** Allow the experiment to run for a long enough period to collect enough data to reach statistical significance. The required duration will depend on your sample size and the variability of your target metric.

   - **Consider external factors:** Be aware of any external factors that might influence your results (e.g., holidays, marketing campaigns, seasonality).

   - **Don't peek (too much!):** Resist the temptation to constantly check the results and make premature conclusions. While it is important to keep track of the main metrics, looking too often might cause you to see a false positive.

7. **Analyze the results: Interpreting the data**

   - **Statistical Significance:** Use statistical methods (typically a t-test or chi-squared test) to determine whether the difference in your target metric between the control and treatment groups is statistically significant. This involves calculating a *p-value*.

   - **P-Value:** The probability of observing the results you obtained (or more extreme results) *if there were actually no difference* between the groups.

   - **Significance Level (Alpha):** A predetermined threshold (usually 0.05). If the p-value is *less* than alpha, the result is considered statistically significant.

   - **Confidence Intervals:** Calculate confidence intervals to estimate the *range* of the likely true effect size. This gives you a sense of the uncertainty around your results.

- **Beyond Statistical Significance:** Even if a result is statistically significant, consider its *practical significance*. Is the observed difference large enough to be meaningful in terms of user experience or business impact?

8. **Draw conclusions and take action: Learning and iterating**
   The outcome of your analysis will determine your next course of action. The following table provides a clear decision-making framework for how to proceed based on whether the result was positive, negative, or not statistically significant.

A/B TEST OUTCOME	INTERPRETATION	RECOMMENDED NEXT STEPS
Significant Positive Result	Strong evidence the AI feature *improved* the target metric.	1. Evaluate practical significance (is the improvement meaningful?). 2. If yes, roll out the feature (potentially phased). 3. Monitor performance closely. 4. Document and share.

No Significant Result	No conclusive evidence of an effect (positive or negative). Could be due to various factors.	1. **Investigate:**
		  - Was the hypothesis correct?
		  - Does the AI model need refinement?
		  - Was the implementation flawed?
		  - Was the sample size too small (underpowered test)?
		  - Were there confounding external factors?
		2. Iterate **on the** feature/model *or* conclude the experiment.
		3. Document and share.

Significant Negative Result	Strong evidence the AI feature *harmed* the target metric.	1. Halt any planned rollout. 2. Investigate the root cause thoroughly. 3. Revert changes if necessary. 4. Iterate based on findings or **abandon** the feature. 5. Document and share.

- **No Statistically Significant Result:** If there's no statistically significant difference, it doesn't necessarily mean the AI feature is useless. It might mean:

    - The hypothesis was incorrect.

    - The AI model needs further refinement.

    - The implementation needs adjustment.

    - The sample size was too small.

    - There were external factors influencing the results.

- **Iterate:** A/B testing is an iterative process. Use the insights from each experiment to refine your hypotheses, improve your AI models, and optimize the user experience.

Key Considerations for AI/ML A/B Testing

While the previous steps outline a solid framework for any A/B test, testing AI-powered features introduces unique complexities. Unlike testing a simple button color change, evaluating a probabilistic model requires additional rigor. As a Product Manager, being aware of the following considerations will help you design more robust experiments and have more insightful conversations with your technical team.

- **Model Versioning:** If you're testing different versions of an AI/ML model, you *must* have a robust versioning system in place. You need to be able to track which users saw which version of the model and compare the results accurately.

- **Data Drift:** AI/ML models are trained on data, and data can change over time. This is called *data drift*. Monitor for data drift during the experiment, as it can affect model performance and invalidate your results. If you detect significant drift, you might need to retrain your model.

- **User Experience Consistency:** Ensure that the overall user experience is consistent across the control and treatment groups, *except* for the AI/ML feature being tested. Avoid introducing any confounding variables.

- **Ethical Considerations:** Reiterate the ethical considerations discussed earlier. A/B testing should never be used to manipulate or deceive users.

- **Monitoring:** Continuously monitor the performance of your AI/ML feature *after* the A/B test, both in terms of technical metrics and user feedback.

- **Segmentation:** Consider segmenting your users and running separate A/B tests for different segments. The AI feature might have different effects on different groups of users.

- **Cold Starts:** The **"cold start" problem** is a common challenge for personalization and recommendation systems. It occurs when a new user or a new item enters the system, and the AI model has no historical data to make an informed prediction. In this situation, the model cannot provide a personalized experience and must revert to a default, non-personalized state (e.g., showing globally popular items instead of personalized recommendations). Your A/B testing plan must account for how to handle these new users and what their initial experience will be.

A/B testing is a powerful tool for validating and optimizing AI/ML features. By following these steps and keeping these considerations in mind, you can ensure that your AI investments are delivering real value to your users and your business. As a Product Manager you will be able to have more meaningful conversations with engineers and data scientists, and understand the nuances of A/B testing for AI/ML.

Chapter Summary and Key Takeaways

This chapter provided you with the essential tools for measuring the impact and demonstrating the value of your AI initiatives. You learned how to define both model-level metrics (like precision and recall) and connect them to business-level metrics (like revenue or churn). We broke down the confusion matrix, established the importance of baselines, and walked through a detailed end-to-end example to see how these concepts come together. You now have a clear framework for quantifying the success of an AI feature.

Key Takeaways

- You understand that measuring an AI product requires two layers: technical model performance and tangible business impact, and your job is to connect them.

- You can articulate the very important trade-off between Precision and Recall by analyzing the cost of errors for your specific product.

- You know that A/B testing is the gold standard for validating the real-world impact of an AI feature against a control group.

- You must establish a clear baseline before launching an AI feature to effectively prove its value and calculate ROI.

Onward: From the Lab to a Live Product

After identifying an opportunity and defining how you'll measure its success, the final step is to understand how it gets built and managed at scale. The next chapter will introduce you to the world of Building and Deploying AI Solutions, focusing on the critical operational practices known as MLOps.

Building and Deploying AI Solutions: From Lab to Live

You've identified a promising AI opportunity, defined your metrics, and even validated your approach with A/B testing. Now comes the critical stage: bringing your AI-powered feature to life. This isn't just about handing a model off to the engineering team; it's about understanding the entire process of building, deploying, and maintaining AI solutions in a real-world production environment. This is where *MLOps* comes in.

MLOps: The Key to Reliable and Scalable AI

MLOps, or Machine Learning Operations, is a set of practices that aims to bridge the gap between *developing* AI models (the work of data scientists) and *deploying and operating* them reliably in a production setting (the work of engineers and operations teams). Figure 10-1 illustrates the MLOps lifecycle. Think of it as DevOps, but specifically tailored for the unique challenges of machine learning. You can also imagine it as the difference between a chef perfecting a recipe in their test kitchen (model development) versus running a busy restaurant kitchen that serves hundreds of meals a night (MLOps). Both require culinary skill, but the restaurant kitchen needs a whole system for efficiency, consistency, and handling the unexpected.

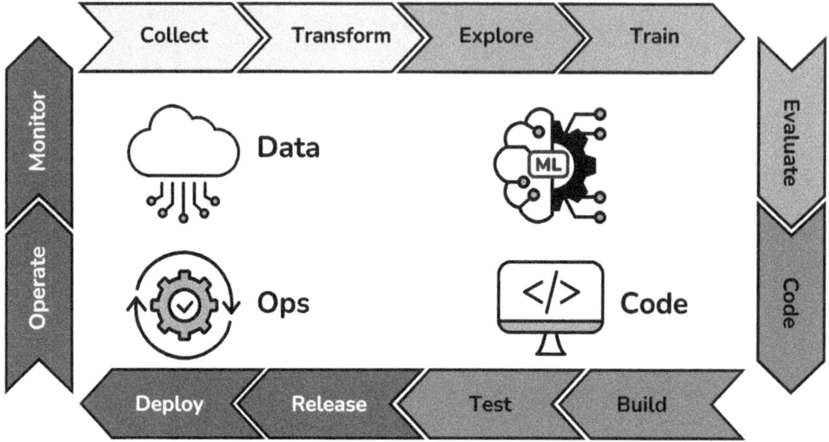

Figure 10-1: The cycle of MLOps in a nutshell

Building a great AI model in a research environment is only half the battle. Getting that model to work consistently, reliably, and at scale in a real-world product is a different challenge altogether. Unlike traditional software, which tends to be more static once deployed, AI models are *dynamic*. Their performance depends on the data they're fed, and that data can change over time (data drift). This is a key difference that makes MLOps essential. MLOps addresses this challenge by:

- **Automating the ML Lifecycle:** MLOps automates key stages of the machine learning pipeline, from data preparation to model deployment and monitoring. This speeds up development, reduces errors, and allows for faster iteration.

- **Ensuring Reproducibility:** MLOps emphasizes version control for both code, *data*, and *models*. This is more complex than just code versioning. This ensures that models can be consistently reproduced and tested. This is critical for debugging, auditing, and maintaining model quality.

- **Enabling Continuous Improvement:** MLOps facilitates *continuous integration and continuous delivery (CI/CD)* for machine learning. This means that models can be continuously updated, tested, and deployed, allowing your product to adapt to changing data and user needs.

- **Scaling AI Solutions:** MLOps provides the infrastructure and processes needed to scale AI models to handle large volumes of data and user requests.

- **Improving Collaboration:** MLOps fosters collaboration between data scientists, engineers, and product managers, ensuring that everyone is aligned on goals and processes.

- **Reducing Risk:** By automating testing, deployment, and monitoring, MLOps reduces the risk of errors and inconsistencies in production.

As a Product Manager, you don't need to be an MLOps expert, but you *do* need to understand the principles and appreciate its importance. This allows you to:

- **Ask the Right Questions:** Understand the deployment plan, the monitoring strategy, the rollback plan, and the process for updating the model.

- **Plan for the Long Term:** Recognize that deploying an AI model is not a one-time event; it's an ongoing process that requires continuous monitoring and maintenance.

- **Collaborate Effectively:** Work effectively with your data science and engineering teams to ensure a smooth and successful deployment.

- **Set Realistic Expectations:** Understand the timelines and the processes.

While you don't need to know the specifics, it's helpful to be aware that there are tools and platforms designed to support MLOps. These might include:

- **Model Registries:** (e.g., MLflow, Amazon SageMaker Model Registry).

- **Data Versioning Tools:** (e.g., DVC, Pachyderm).

- **CI/CD Platforms:** (e.g., Jenkins, GitLab CI, CircleCI).

- **Monitoring Tools:** (e.g., Prometheus, Grafana, cloud-specific monitoring services).

- **Feature Stores** (e.g., Feast, Vertex AI Feature Store).

Key Components of MLOps—The AI Production Line

In the previous section, we visualized MLOps as a continuous, cyclical process to emphasize its ongoing nature. Now, we will break that cycle down into its key components or stages.

Think of MLOps as an assembly line for AI models. Just like a factory has a well-defined process for manufacturing products, MLOps provides a structured, step-by-step process for building, deploying, and maintaining AI models (see Figure 10-2). Each stage in this assembly line has a specific purpose, and they all work together to ensure the final product is of high quality and meets the needs of the user.

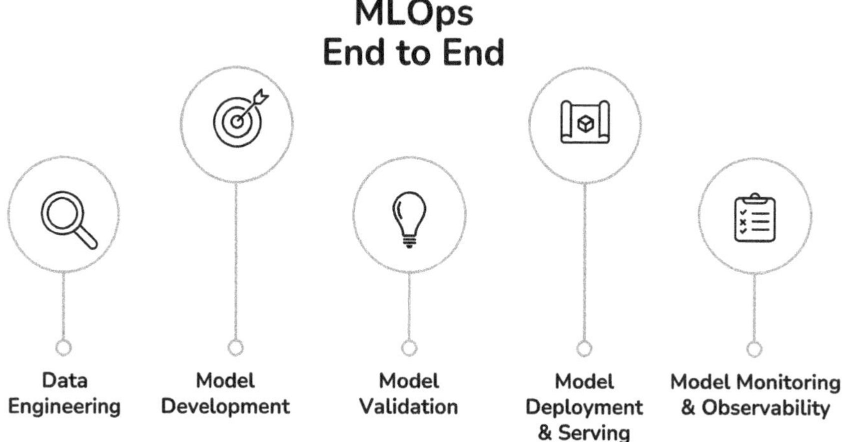

Figure 10-2: The stages of MLOps

The following tables break down these key stages with a focus on the Product Manager's perspective:

Data Engineering: Sourcing and Preparing the Raw Materials   This foundational stage focuses on gathering, cleaning, and preparing the data that fuels your AI model. Think of it as sourcing high-quality raw materials for your assembly line—the quality of the input data directly impacts the quality of the final AI product ("Garbage in, garbage out!").

DATA ENGINEERING ACTIVITY	PRODUCT MANAGER'S ROLE AND FOCUS
Data Collection Gathering raw data from various internal and external systems (databases, logs, APIs, etc.).	**Ensure Relevance and Compliance** Work with the data team to confirm collected data is relevant to the defined problem. Ensure collection methods comply with privacy regulations (GDPR, CCPA, etc.) and ethical guidelines.
Data Cleaning and Transformation Handling errors, missing values, inconsistencies, and converting data into a usable format for ML models.	**Advocate for Quality and Understand Impact** Champion efforts for high-quality, accurate data. Understand how data cleaning decisions (e.g., handling missing values, removing outliers) and potential data biases can impact the model and the user experience.
Data Versioning and Data Pipelines Tracking changes to datasets (versioning) and building automated workflows (pipelines) for efficient data processing.	**Understand Process and Ensure Reproducibility** Have a high-level understanding of how data flows and is versioned. Ensure processes are in place for reproducibility (very important for debugging, audits, and retraining).
Data Availability and Access Ensuring that the necessary data exists and that technical teams have the required permissions and tools to use it.	**Facilitate Access and Identify Gaps** Help the technical team gain access to necessary data sources. Identify any data gaps early and work with relevant stakeholders to acquire needed data if feasible.

Model Development: Designing the Prototype   This is where the core AI model is built and refined by data scientists. Think of it as designing and creating the functional prototype in our factory, involving experimentation and iteration to find the best approach.

MODEL DEVELOPMENT ACTIVITY	PRODUCT MANAGER'S ROLE AND FOCUS
Feature Engineering Creating, selecting, and transforming input variables (features) from raw data to optimize model performance.	**Provide Domain Context and Prioritize Insights:** Share your deep understanding of the user and business context to guide the creation of relevant features. Help prioritize which data insights or potential features are most likely to impact the desired outcome.
Algorithm Selection Choosing the most appropriate machine learning algorithm (e.g., decision tree, neural network) based on the problem type, data characteristics, and goals.	**Understand Trade-Offs and Align with Goals:** Discuss the pros and cons (e.g., accuracy vs. interpretability, speed, data needs) of different algorithm options with the data science team. Ensure the selected algorithm aligns with the product's goals and constraints.
Hyperparameter Tuning Optimizing the internal settings (hyperparameters) of the chosen algorithm to achieve the best performance on evaluation metrics.	**Define Success Metrics and Evaluation Criteria:** Clearly articulate the key performance indicators (KPIs) and evaluation metrics (e.g., prioritize Recall over Precision) that the tuning process should aim to optimize. Ensure these metrics align with the product's success definition.
Model Versioning Tracking and managing different versions of the model as it's developed, including changes in code, data, and parameters.	**Understand Progress and Iteration:** Keep track of different model versions and their performance improvements. Use this understanding to communicate progress and manage expectations during the iterative development process.

Model Validation and Testing: Quality Control   Before releasing an AI model to users, it must undergo rigorous testing to ensure it meets performance standards, functions reliably, and aligns with ethical guidelines. This is the critical quality control checkpoint in our AI assembly line.

MODEL VALIDATION AND TESTING ACTIVITY	PRODUCT MANAGER'S ROLE AND FOCUS
Performance Evaluation (Cross-Validation and Held-Out Test Set) Assessing the model's predictive accuracy and generalization ability using data not seen during training.	**Define Acceptance Criteria and Interpret Results:** Work with the team to set clear, measurable performance thresholds (e.g., minimum Recall of 85%, maximum latency of 500ms) based on product goals. Understand and interpret the evaluation results to make the go/no-go decision for deployment.
Bias and Fairness Testing Evaluating model performance across different user segments (e.g., based on demographics) to detect and mitigate unfair biases.	**Champion Fairness and Ensure Ethical Alignment:** Ensure that fairness testing is conducted thoroughly using appropriate metrics. Review results to confirm the model performs equitably and aligns with responsible AI principles and legal requirements. Advocate for necessary adjustments if bias is detected.
Security Testing Assessing the model and its deployment infrastructure for vulnerabilities to potential attacks or manipulation.	**Understand Risks and Ensure Robustness:** Understand the potential security risks associated with the AI feature's specific use case. Ensure appropriate security testing is performed to protect user data and prevent model misuse.
A/B Testing Setup Preparing the framework to compare the new AI model's performance against a baseline or control version in a live environment.	**Define Hypothesis and Success Metrics:** Define the specific hypothesis for the A/B test (e.g., "New model will reduce churn by 5%") and the key metrics that will determine success. Ensure the test setup aligns with the validation goals.

Model Deployment: Rolling Off the Assembly Line   This is the very important step where the validated AI model is integrated into your product and made available to users, either fully or as part of an experiment. It's like the finished product rolling off the assembly line and heading to the customer.

MODEL DEPLOYMENT ACTIVITY	PRODUCT MANAGER'S ROLE AND FOCUS
Choosing a Deployment Environment Deciding where the model will run (e.g., cloud server, on-premises, edge device) based on factors like cost, latency, and scalability needs.	**Align Environment with Product Needs:** Understand the implications of the deployment environment choice on user experience (latency), cost, and scalability. Ensure the chosen environment meets the product's requirements and constraints.
Creating an API (Application Programming Interface) Building the interface that allows your product or other applications to send data to the model and receive predictions.	**Define API Requirements for Product Integration:** Define *how* the product will interact with the model via the API. Ensure the API design supports the planned user experience and integration points within the existing product features.
Packaging the Model Preparing the model and its necessary software dependencies into a deployable unit (e.g., a container).	**Understand Implications for Updates and Rollout:** While primarily technical, understand how the packaging impacts the ability to update the model and support the planned rollout strategy (e.g., enabling phased rollouts or A/B testing). Ensure smooth transitions between model versions.
Implementing Rollout Strategy Executing the planned rollout (e.g., canary release, phased rollout, full launch, A/B test deployment).	**Oversee Rollout and Communication:** Own the overall rollout plan. Monitor the deployment closely, coordinate with engineering and marketing, and manage communication with users and internal stakeholders about the new AI feature.

Model Monitoring: Tracking Performance in the Real World   Launching the model isn't the end; it's the beginning of its life in production. Continuous monitoring is essential to ensure the AI model performs as expected, delivers ongoing value, and doesn't degrade over time. Think of it as conducting regular health checks and tracking customer satisfaction for your AI feature after launch.

MODEL MONITORING ACTIVITY	PRODUCT MANAGER'S ROLE AND FOCUS
Tracking Key Performance Metrics Continuously measuring the model's performance in production using the same metrics defined during evaluation (e.g., accuracy, precision, recall, latency, F1-score, business KPIs).	**Define Monitoring KPIs and Thresholds:** Specify *which* metrics are critical to track post-deployment and define the acceptable performance thresholds. Work with engineering to ensure dashboards reflect these KPIs clearly. Regularly review performance against goals.
Detecting Model Drift Identifying when the model's performance degrades over time due to changes in real-world data patterns or shifts in the underlying concepts the model learned.	**Understand Impact and Trigger Action:** Understand the potential user experience and business impact if model drift occurs. Ensure mechanisms are in place to detect drift and work with the technical team to determine when drift necessitates model retraining or other interventions.
Setting Up Alerts Configuring automated notifications that trigger when key performance metrics drop below predefined thresholds or when significant data drift is detected.	**Define Alert Criteria and Response Plan:** Define the specific conditions that should trigger alerts (e.g., "Alert if Recall drops below 80% for 24 hours"). Establish a clear process and escalation path for responding to alerts, involving the appropriate technical teams.
Monitoring User Feedback Actively tracking user feedback channels (reviews, support tickets, forums) for qualitative insights into the AI feature's real-world performance and user satisfaction.	**Be the Voice of the User:** Complement quantitative monitoring by constantly monitoring user feedback. Identify issues, usability problems, or unexpected model behaviors reported by users that might not be captured by automated metrics alone.

Model Retraining and Updating: Continuous Improvement   AI models aren't static; their performance can degrade as the real world changes. This stage involves periodically retraining the model with new data to ensure it remains accurate, relevant, and adapts to evolving conditions. Think of it as regularly updating your product's engine based on new performance data and changing road conditions.

MODEL RETRAINING AND UPDATING ACTIVITY	PRODUCT MANAGER'S ROLE AND FOCUS
Triggering Retraining Deciding when to initiate the retraining process, based on monitoring data (e.g., performance degradation, detected drift), a set schedule, or availability of significant new data.	**Prioritize Retraining and Define Triggers:** Use performance monitoring data, model drift alerts, and business context to determine *when* retraining is necessary. Prioritize retraining efforts against other product initiatives based on potential impact.
Automated Retraining Pipelines Utilizing MLOps tools and workflows to automatically handle the process of retraining the model with new data, ensuring consistency and efficiency.	**Understand Pipeline and Ensure Alignment:** Have a high-level understanding of the automated retraining process. Ensure the frequency and scope of automated retraining align with product needs and data availability.
Model Versioning Maintaining a clear record of different trained model versions, including the data used, parameters, and performance metrics.	**Track Performance and Manage Releases:** Keep track of different model versions and their performance metrics. Use this information to compare models, understand improvements or regressions, and manage the release process for updated models.
A/B Testing Updated Models Comparing the performance of a newly retrained model against the currently deployed version in a live environment before a full rollout.	**Define Success Criteria and Approve Deployment:** Define the criteria for the A/B test (e.g., "New model must show X% improvement in Recall without decreasing Precision"). Review A/B test results and make the final decision on whether to deploy the updated model to all users.
Rollback Strategy Having a defined plan and mechanism to quickly revert to a previous, stable model version if a newly deployed update causes unexpected issues or performs poorly.	**Ensure Risk Mitigation:** Confirm that a reliable rollback plan exists for model updates. Understand the process for initiating a rollback if necessary to minimize negative user impact.

CI/CD, IaC, and Collaboration: The Foundational Pillars of MLOps

These three concepts, borrowed and adapted from modern software development, are fundamental to making the entire MLOps lifecycle efficient, reliable, and scalable. They are the pillars supporting the AI production line:

- **CI/CD (Continuous Integration/Continuous Delivery): Automating the Flow**

  CI/CD involves automating the building, testing, and deployment pipeline, from code/data changes through to production release.

  It enables rapid iteration on models, reduces manual errors in deployment, ensures consistent testing, and allows for faster delivery of updated AI capabilities into the product. It's the engine that drives the continuous improvement cycles of monitoring and retraining.

- **IaC (Infrastructure as Code): Building Reliable Environments**

  IaC involves managing and provisioning the underlying infrastructure (servers, databases, networks) using code and automation, rather than manual configuration.

  It guarantees consistent and reproducible environments for training, testing, and deploying models. This is very important for reliable model performance, scalability, and simplifying disaster recovery or environment replication.

- **Collaboration: The Human Element**

  Collaboration involves the close, continuous teamwork and communication between all involved teams—Data Science, ML Engineering, Software Engineering, DevOps, Product Management, and potentially others (Legal, Security).

  AI projects are inherently cross-functional. Effective collaboration is essential to bridge the gap between different areas of expertise, ensure alignment on goals, troubleshoot issues quickly, and successfully navigate the entire lifecycle from data preparation to ongoing model maintenance.

Understanding these pillars is key for Product Managers. They represent the operational foundation that allows AI features to be developed, deployed, and maintained effectively. Recognizing their importance helps you ask the right questions about automation, reliability, scalability, and team alignment when discussing AI initiatives.

Glossary of Key MLOps Terms

This glossary provides concise definitions of key MLOps terms, grouped by their role in the machine learning lifecycle. It focuses on providing context and relevance for Product Managers, rather than being a comprehensive technical dictionary. Terms that have been thoroughly explained in previous sections are referenced here rather than redefined.

- **Core Concepts:**
  - **MLOps (Machine Learning Operations):** The overarching set of practices for building, deploying, and maintaining AI solutions.
- **Data Management:**
  - **Data Pipeline:** An automated process for collecting, cleaning, transforming, and preparing data for use in machine learning models. Think of it as the supply chain for your data.
  - **Data Versioning:** The practice of tracking and managing changes to datasets, ensuring reproducibility. Essential for understanding *which* data was used to train a specific model version.
  - **Feature Engineering:** The process of creating new, informative features from raw data to improve model performance. This is where domain expertise is critical.
  - **Feature Store**: A centralized repository for storing and managing features used in machine learning models. Facilitates feature reuse and consistency across different models and teams.
- **Model Building:**
  - **Model Development:** The overall process of creating a machine learning model.
  - **Algorithm Selection:** Choosing the right type of machine learning algorithm (e.g., linear regression, decision tree, neural network) for a given problem and dataset. Different algorithms have different strengths and weaknesses.
  - **Hyperparameter Tuning:** Optimizing the settings (hyperparameters) of a chosen algorithm to achieve the best performance. This is like fine-tuning a car's engine for optimal performance.

- **Model Evaluation and Validation:**
  - **Model Validation:** The process of assessing a trained model's performance on unseen data.
  - **Cross-Validation:** A technique for evaluating model performance by splitting the data into multiple folds and training/testing on different combinations.
  - **Bias Testing:** Evaluating a model for systematic errors that could unfairly discriminate against certain groups. Essential for building responsible and ethical AI.
  - **Fairness Testing:** Evaluating a model to ensure it treats different groups equitably. Closely related to bias testing, but with a broader focus on societal impact.
  - **Security Vulnerability Testing:** Assessing a model for potential security weaknesses that could be exploited by attackers.
- **Model Deployment and Serving:**
  - **Model Deployment:** The process of making a trained model available for use in a production environment.
  - **API (Application Programming Interface):** A set of rules and specifications that allow different software applications to communicate with each other. For AI, this often means creating an API that allows other applications to send data to the model and receive predictions.
  - **Cloud-Based Deployment:** Deploying a model on cloud computing platforms (e.g., AWS, Google Cloud Platform, Microsoft Azure). Offers scalability and flexibility.
  - **On-Premises Deployment:** Deploying a model on local servers or hardware within an organization's own infrastructure. May be required for security or compliance reasons.
  - **Edge Deployment:** Deploying a model on devices at the "edge" of a network (e.g., smartphones, IoT devices). Enables local processing and reduces latency.
- **Model Monitoring and Maintenance:**
  - **Model Monitoring:** The continuous tracking of a deployed model's performance.

- ▪ **Model Drift:** The degradation of a model's performance over time due to changes in the input data or environment.

- ▪ **Model Retraining:** The process of updating a deployed model with new data to maintain its accuracy.

- ▪ **Latency:** The delay.

- ▪ **Throughput:** The amount of work done.

- ▪ **Supporting Practices:**

  - ▪ **CI/CD (Continuous Integration/Continuous Delivery):** Automating the software development and deployment process. In MLOps, this extends to automating the entire machine learning pipeline.

  - ▪ **Infrastructure as Code (IaC):** Managing and provisioning infrastructure using code. Enables consistent and reproducible deployments.

  - ▪ **A/B Testing:** A method of comparing two versions (A and B) of a product or feature to determine which performs better. Essential for validating the impact of AI features.

MLOps End-to-End Example: Churn Prediction in a Subscription Service (Product Manager's Perspective)

Let's revisit our churn prediction example from Chapter 9, but now we'll walk through it from an MLOps perspective, focusing on the Product Manager's role and the key decisions involved in taking this AI feature from concept to production.

1. **Prepare the data foundation**

   - ▪ **What Happens (Technical):** The data engineering team pulls data from various sources (user databases, activity logs, payment systems), cleans it (handles missing values, outliers), transforms it into a usable format (e.g., one-hot encoding), and creates automated data pipelines to keep the data fresh. They also implement data versioning to track changes. They might use tools such as Apache Airflow.

- **PM's Role and Key Questions:**
  - **Data Relevance:** Is the data being collected actually relevant to predicting churn? Work with the data team to ensure the data aligns with the identified user behaviors and pain points that contribute to churn (from our user journey analysis).

  - **Data Privacy:** Are we collecting and using data ethically and in compliance with privacy regulations? This is a critical responsibility.

  - **Data Quality:** Is the data reliable and accurate? Garbage in, garbage out! Understand the limitations of the data.

  - **Data Availability:** Is all the necessary data available? If not, work with the relevant teams to get access.

  - **"Why This Matters":** The quality and relevance of the data are *the* foundation of the entire project. A flawed foundation will lead to a flawed model.

2. **Develop and train the model**
   - **What Happens (Technical):** Data scientists experiment with different machine learning algorithms (e.g., LightGBM, as mentioned before), engineer features, and tune hyperparameters to create a model that accurately predicts churn. They use tools like MLflow to track their experiments.

   - **PM's Role and Key Questions:**
     - **Feature Prioritization:** Which features are most important to include in the model, based on our understanding of user behavior and churn drivers? Provide product context to guide feature engineering.

     - **Algorithm Choice Justification:** Why was this particular algorithm chosen? What are its strengths and weaknesses in this context? Understand the trade-offs.

     - **Model Interpretability:** To what extent can we understand why the model is making its predictions? This is critical for trust and debugging. It may also help improve the product, as it may reveal reasons why users churn.

     - **"Why This Matters":** You need to understand the model's capabilities and limitations to set realistic expectations and guide product decisions.

3. **Validate and test the model**

- **What Happens (Technical):** The model is rigorously tested using various techniques (cross-validation, held-out test set) to evaluate its performance. critically, this includes A/B testing (as discussed in Chapter 9) and testing for bias and fairness.

  - **PM's Role and Key Questions:**

    - **Define Acceptance Criteria:** What level of performance (recall, precision, F1-score) is acceptable for this feature? This should be based on the business goals and the cost of errors.

    - **Interpret Test Results:** Do the test results (including A/B test results) support deploying the model? Understand the trade-offs between different metrics.

    - **Bias and Fairness:** Is the model performing fairly across different user groups (e.g., different demographics)? This is an ethical and legal imperative.

    - **"Why This Matters":** This stage ensures that the model is accurate, reliable, fair, and ready for real-world use. It's your last chance to catch major problems before they impact users.

4. **Deploy the model into the product**

- **What Happens (Technical):** The model is packaged and deployed to a production environment (e.g., a cloud server), and an API is created so that other applications (like your product's backend) can interact with it.

- **PM's Role and Key Questions:**

  - **User Experience:** How will the model's predictions be presented to the user (or used internally)? Design the user interface and interactions.

  - **Integration with Existing Features:** How will this AI feature integrate with existing product features and workflows?

  - **Rollout Strategy:** How will we roll out the feature to users (e.g., A/B test, phased rollout)?

  - **"Why This Matters":** A great model is useless if it's not integrated into the product in a way that's useful and intuitive for users.

5. **Monitor performance and detect drift**

   - **What Happens (Technical):** The deployed model's performance is continuously monitored, tracking key metrics (recall, precision, latency, etc.). Alerts are set up to notify the team of any issues. Data drift is also monitored.

   - **PM's Role and Key Questions:**

     - **Define Monitoring Requirements:** Which metrics are most important to track? What are acceptable performance thresholds?

     - **Monitor User Feedback:** Are users reporting any issues with the AI-powered feature?

     - **Understand Alerts:** What do the alerts mean? What actions should be taken in response to different alerts?

     - **"Why This Matters":** Continuous monitoring ensures that the model continues to perform well and deliver value over time. It's like regular checkups for your AI.

6. **Retrain and update the model**

   - **What Happens (Technical):** The model is periodically retrained with new data to maintain its accuracy and adapt to changing conditions. New models are A/B tested against the current production model.

   - **PM's Role and Key Questions:**

     - **Prioritize Retraining:** When is retraining necessary? This is based on monitoring data and business needs.

     - **Approve Updates:** Review A/B testing results for new model versions and approve deployments.

     - **"Why This Matters":** Regular retraining ensures that the model remains accurate and relevant, providing continued value to users.

7. **CI/CD, IaC, and Collaboration (A Quick Recap)**

   These are the supporting pillars:

   - **CI/CD:** Automates the entire process, making it faster and more reliable.

- **IaC:** Ensures consistent and reproducible deployments.

- **Collaboration:** Close teamwork between data scientists, engineers, and product managers is *essential* throughout the entire MLOps lifecycle.

This end-to-end example, viewed through the lens of MLOps and the Product Manager's role, demonstrates the practical steps involved in bringing an AI-powered feature to life. It highlights the importance of a structured process, continuous monitoring, and close collaboration between different teams. It's not just about building a model; it's about building a *system* that delivers ongoing value to your users and your business. The PM is the key element that brings all these teams together.

Chapter Summary and Key Takeaways

This chapter explored the critical discipline of MLOps (Machine Learning Operations)—the engine that takes an AI model from a data scientist's notebook to a live, production environment. We walked through the entire "AI Production Line," from data engineering and model development to the very important post-launch stages of deployment, monitoring, and retraining. You now understand the key components and practices required to build and maintain reliable, scalable, and impactful AI solutions.

Key Takeaways

- You recognize that MLOps is the very important bridge between data science (research and development) and engineering (operations and scale), ensuring AI models can be deployed reliably.

- You understand that launching an AI model is the beginning of its lifecycle, which requires continuous monitoring for issues like model drift and performance degradation.

- You can identify the PM's role at each stage of the MLOps lifecycle, from providing context during data engineering to defining monitoring requirements post-deployment.

- You appreciate the importance of automation (CI/CD) and collaboration for the long-term success and maintainability of any AI product.

Onward: Building with Integrity

Now that you understand the entire process of identifying, measuring, and deploying AI solutions, we will revisit one of the most important topics in full detail. The next chapter will provide a deep dive into Responsible AI and Ethical Considerations, ensuring the products you build are not only effective but also fair and safe.

Responsible AI and Ethical Considerations: Building AI with Integrity

We've explored the technical capabilities of AI, how to identify opportunities, and how to deploy and manage AI solutions. Now, we arrive at a critically important topic: *responsible AI*. Building AI-powered products isn't just about maximizing efficiency or accuracy; it's about building products that are *ethical*, *fair*, and *beneficial* to all users. As a Product Manager, you are on the front lines of this effort. You are responsible for ensuring that the AI features you build are not just innovative, but also responsible.

This chapter is about understanding the potential pitfalls of AI, particularly regarding bias and fairness, and taking proactive steps to mitigate those risks. It's about building AI with *integrity*.

Understanding AI Bias and Fairness: The Foundation of Responsible AI

AI systems learn from data. This is their power, but it's also their potential weakness. If the data used to train an AI model reflects existing societal biases (e.g., gender bias, racial bias, age bias), the model will likely learn and perpetuate those biases. This is known as AI bias, and it can lead to unfair or discriminatory outcomes.

For Product Managers, addressing AI bias isn't just an abstract ethical ideal; it's a core business imperative with tangible consequences. Prioritizing fairness in your AI systems is critical for several key reasons:

- **Moral Obligation:** As creators of technology that impacts people's lives, there is a fundamental duty to ensure that these systems treat all individuals equitably and do not cause discriminatory harm.

- **Legal and Regulatory Risk:** Ignoring fairness can have serious legal consequences. Jurisdictions globally, such as Europe with its GDPR, are establishing legal frameworks that mandate non-discrimination in automated systems, with steep penalties for non-compliance.

- **Business Performance:** Beyond legal risks, biased products directly harm the business. They can erode user trust, leading to customer attrition and significant damage to the company's brand reputation.

- **Societal Scale:** AI systems operate at a massive scale, giving them the power to affect society broadly. If a system is biased, it can reinforce and even amplify existing societal inequalities, causing tangible harm to marginalized groups.

Identifying Potential Biases: Where Bias Can Creep In

Bias in an AI system is rarely intentional; it often creeps in subtly at different stages of the development process, from how data is collected to how the model itself is designed. Understanding these different sources of bias is the first step toward mitigating them. Figure 11-1 illustrates several common types of bias that a Product Manager should be aware of.

Let's break down these types:

- **Sample Bias**

  This occurs when the data used to train a model is not representative of the user base or the real-world environment where the model will be used. If your training sample is skewed, your model's performance will be skewed too.

  Example (Image Recognition): A facial recognition system trained primarily on images of light-skinned individuals will have a higher error rate when identifying people with darker skin tones because the training sample was not sufficiently diverse.

- **Prejudice Bias**

  This happens when the training data reflects existing societal stereotypes, prejudices, or historical inequalities. The model, in its effort to find patterns, learns and then replicates these harmful human biases.

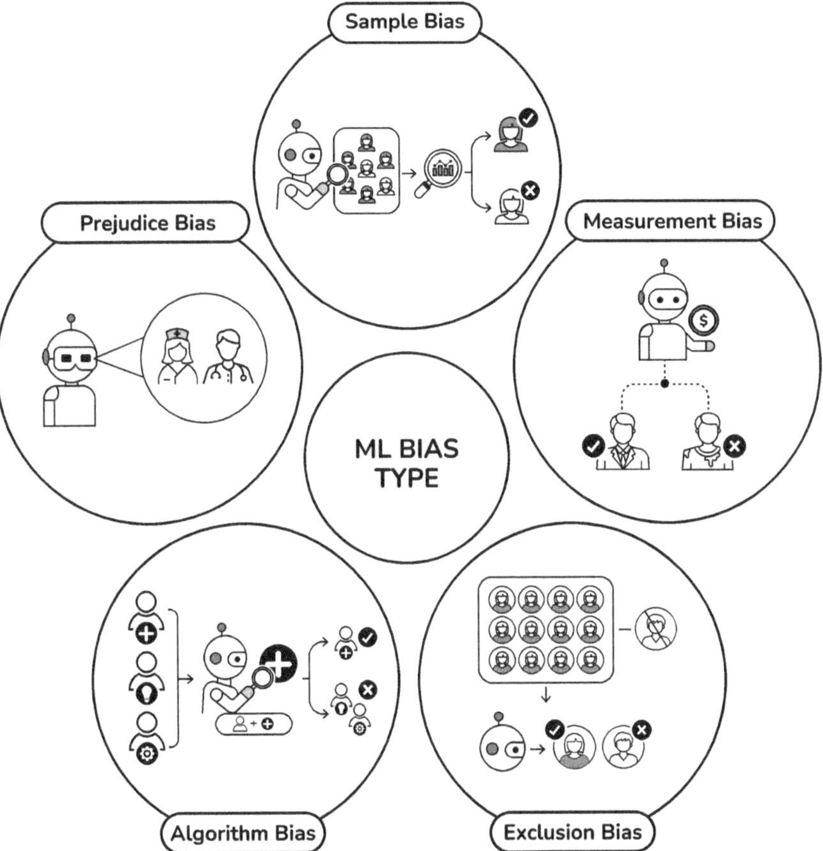

Figure 11-1: Common sources of bias in AI systems. Bias can be introduced at various stages, from collecting a non-representative *Sample* to embedding historical *Prejudice* in the data or designing a flawed *Algorithm*.

Example (Hiring Tool): A model trained on a company's historical hiring data from the last 20 years might learn to associate male candidates with senior technical roles, perpetuating past discriminatory practices.

Example (Loan Application): If historical loan data shows lower approval rates for applicants from certain neighborhoods (due to systemic bias), a model trained on this data will learn to penalize new applicants from those same neighborhoods.

- **Measurement Bias**

This type of bias is introduced when the tool or method used to collect or measure data is flawed or inconsistent across different groups. The data itself is a distorted reflection of reality.

Example: Imagine training a quality control model using images from two different factory cameras. If one camera has a faulty sensor that gives images a slight yellow tint, the model might incorrectly learn to associate "defective product" with the color yellow, rather than the actual defect.

- **Exclusion Bias**

This often happens during data cleaning or feature selection, where important data points or entire groups are left out, frequently by accident.

Example: When building a credit approval model, a team might decide to drop all records for users who have no prior credit history. This systematically excludes and penalizes entire groups like young people, recent immigrants, or others who have not had the opportunity to build credit.

- **Algorithmic Bias**

Even with perfect data, bias can be introduced by the model's objective or design. This happens when the algorithm itself, through its optimization goals, produces unfair outcomes.

Example: A content recommendation algorithm optimized solely to maximize user engagement might learn to push increasingly extreme or sensationalized content, as that type of content often generates strong reactions. This creates a negative user experience, even if it's "successful" based on its narrow metric.

Mitigating Potential Biases: A Proactive Approach

Identifying sources of bias is the first step; actively mitigating it is the critical next one. This isn't a one-time fix but a continuous effort that involves the entire product team. As a Product Manager, you play a key role in championing these mitigation strategies throughout the AI lifecycle. The following table breaks down several proactive approaches and details your specific responsibilities within each.

STRATEGY	DESCRIPTION	PM'S ROLE
Data collection and preparation	Ensure that your training data is as diverse, representative, and unbiased as possible.	Advocate for diverse data collection. Question the data sources. Understand the limitations of the data.
Data augmentation and synthetic data	Use techniques to artificially increase the size and diversity of your training data, particularly for underrepresented groups.	Discuss these options with the data science team. Understand the trade-offs.
Algorithm selection and design	Choose algorithms that are less prone to bias, or that have built-in fairness mechanisms. Prioritize transparency and explainability.	Ask about algorithm choices and their potential for bias. Advocate for interpretable models whenever possible.
Evaluation and testing	Rigorously evaluate your AI system for bias using fairness metrics (we'll discuss these later). Test on diverse datasets and user groups.	Define fairness metrics before development begins. Ensure that testing includes diverse user groups. Interpret test results with a critical eye.
Human oversight	Incorporate human review into the decision-making process, especially for high-stakes applications. Don't rely solely on the AI's output.	Design workflows that include human review where appropriate. Establish clear guidelines for human intervention.

Continues

(continued)

STRATEGY	DESCRIPTION	PM'S ROLE
Continuous monitoring	Continuously monitor your AI system for bias after deployment. Bias can emerge over time as data changes.	Establish monitoring processes and dashboards. Respond promptly to any signs of emerging bias.
Transparency and explainability	Be transparent about the use of AI.	Communicate with users, providing clear explanations on how the model works.

While the strategies in the table provide a tactical framework, they all stem from a core set of principles that every Product Manager should internalize. To effectively lead in this domain, it's very important to focus on these key takeaways:

- **Bias Awareness:** Understand that AI bias is a *real* and *serious* problem. It's not just a technical issue; it's a product issue, a business issue, and an ethical issue.

- **Prioritize Fairness:** Make fairness a *core requirement* for your AI-powered features, not an afterthought.

- **Collaborate with Experts:** Work closely with data scientists, ethicists, legal experts, and your engineering team to identify and mitigate potential biases. You are the bridge between these teams.

- **Communicate Transparently:** Be open and honest with your users about how your AI system works, what data it uses, and how you are addressing bias.

- **Continuous Monitoring:** Bias detection and mitigation is not a one-time task; it's an ongoing process.

The next sections will delve deeper into specific fairness metrics, legal and ethical frameworks, and how to align your AI development with societal values. But the foundation is this: building responsible AI starts with *awareness* and a *commitment* to fairness.

Protected Classes and AI Fairness—Designing for Inclusion

We've established that AI bias is a serious concern, regardless of bias type. Now, let's focus on a particularly important aspect of fairness: ensuring that AI systems don't discriminate against *protected classes*. These are groups of people who are legally protected from discrimination based on specific characteristics. This isn't just about avoiding legal trouble; it's about building AI that is truly inclusive and equitable.

What are Protected Classes?

Protected classes vary depending on the specific laws and regulations of a country or region. However, they typically include characteristics like:

- **Race and Ethnicity:** Ensuring AI systems don't discriminate based on racial or ethnic background.

- **Sex/Gender:** Preventing AI from favoring or disfavoring individuals based on their gender identity (including male, female, non-binary, etc.).

- **Age:** Safeguarding against age-based discrimination, particularly for older individuals, but also potentially for younger individuals in certain contexts.

- **Religion:** Protecting individuals from discrimination based on their religious beliefs or lack thereof.

- **National Origin:** Ensuring AI systems don't discriminate based on a person's country of origin or ancestry.

- **Disability:** Preventing AI from discriminating against individuals with physical or mental disabilities.

- **Other Characteristics:** Depending on the jurisdiction, this might also include sexual orientation, marital status, genetic information, veteran status, or other characteristics.

Why Focus on Protected Classes? (The Legal and Ethical Imperative)

As a Product Manager, paying special attention to protected classes is not an optional ethical exercise; it is a fundamental requirement for building safe, legal, and trustworthy products. The consequences of deploying a system that discriminates against these groups are severe and can impact your product across legal, business, and societal dimensions. Here are the key reasons why this focus is non-negotiable:

- **Legal Compliance:** Anti-discrimination laws (like the Civil Rights Act in the US, GDPR in Europe, and many others) often *directly* apply to AI systems, especially in areas like:

  - **Hiring and Employment:** AI used for resume screening, candidate selection, or performance evaluation.

  - **Lending and Credit:** AI used for loan applications, credit scoring, or insurance pricing.

  - **Housing:** AI used for tenant screening or property valuation.

  - **Education:** AI used for admissions, grading, or personalized learning.

  - **Criminal Justice:** AI used for risk assessment or predictive policing (this area is particularly fraught with ethical concerns).

- **Ethical Responsibility:** Even *without* explicit legal requirements, it's a fundamental ethical principle that AI systems should treat all individuals fairly, regardless of their protected class status.

- **Reputational Risk:** Biased AI can severely damage your company's reputation and erode user trust.

- **Societal Impact:** AI has the power to shape society. We have a responsibility to ensure it does so in a way that promotes fairness and equality, not one that exacerbates existing inequalities.

How Protected Classes Relate to AI Bias: The Mechanisms of Discrimination

AI bias related to protected classes often arises from the following subtle, but powerful, mechanisms:

- **Data Imbalance**

  This is the most common source of bias. If the training data over-represents or under-represents certain protected classes, the model will likely learn biased patterns.

Example: A facial recognition system trained primarily on images of white faces will likely perform poorly on faces of people from other racial groups. This is a direct result of data imbalance. There have been documented cases of this, with real-world consequences.

Example: An algorithm to approve loans is trained mostly on data that historically approved more men than women, it will likely continue that pattern, even if no gender data is explicitly given.

- **Proxy Features**

  Even if you remove protected class information (like race or gender) from your dataset, other features might act as proxies for those protected characteristics, leading to indirect discrimination.

  Example: Using zip code as a feature in a loan application model might indirectly discriminate against certain racial groups, as residential segregation is often correlated with race. The zip code acts as a proxy for race.

  Example: In a resume screening system, using information on attended schools might lead to discriminate some groups, if those groups historically don't have access to the top schools.

- **Algorithmic Bias (Revisited)**

  As mentioned before, the algorithm's design itself can introduce bias, even with balanced data.

Mitigating Bias Related to Protected Classes: Actionable Steps for PMs

The following table describes what you, as a Product Manager, can do to mitigate bias related to protected classes:

ACTION	DESCRIPTION	PM'S ROLE
1. Data Auditing	Carefully examine your training data for potential biases related to protected classes. Look for imbalances in representation, missing data, or features that might act as proxies for protected characteristics.	Advocate for thorough data audits. Ask critical questions about the data sources and potential biases.

Continues

(*continued*)

ACTION	DESCRIPTION	PM'S ROLE
2. Fairness Metrics	Use specific fairness metrics to evaluate your model's performance across different protected groups. These metrics go beyond overall accuracy to measure disparities in outcomes.	Work with your data science team to define and implement appropriate fairness metrics. Understand the trade-offs between different metrics.
3. Bias Mitigation Techniques	Explore various techniques to actively reduce bias in your model, such as:	Discuss these techniques with your data science team and understand their implications.
a. Re-Sampling	Adjusting the proportions of different groups in the training data (e.g., oversampling underrepresented groups or undersampling overrepresented groups).	
b. Re-Weighting	Assigning different weights to different data points during training to counteract imbalances.	
c. Adversarial Debiasing	Using more advanced techniques (often involving neural networks) to explicitly train the model to be fair.	
4. Transparency and Explainability	Strive for transparency in how your AI system makes decisions. This makes it easier to identify and address potential biases.	Advocate for interpretable models whenever possible. Ensure that users understand how the AI is being used and how decisions are being made.
5. Continuous Monitoring (Post-Deployment)	Bias detection is not a one-time task. Continuously monitor your AI system for bias after deployment, as data and user behavior can change over time.	Establish monitoring processes and dashboards. Set up alerts for significant disparities in performance across different groups.

ACTION	DESCRIPTION	PM'S ROLE
6. Human-in-the-Loop	Incorporate human review into the decision-making process, especially for high-stakes applications (e.g., loan applications, hiring decisions). Human oversight can help catch and correct biased AI decisions.	Design workflows that include human review where appropriate. Provide clear guidelines for human reviewers on how to identify and address potential bias.
7. Diverse Teams	Building diverse teams can reduce bias, bringing in more perspectives.	Advocate for diversity in hiring for all teams working on your product.

By proactively addressing bias related to protected classes, you can build AI systems that are not only more accurate and effective but also more ethical and equitable. This is a critical responsibility for Product Managers in the age of AI. It's about building trust with your users and ensuring that your AI-powered products contribute to a fairer and more inclusive society.

AI Ethics and Legal Compliance—From Principles to Practice

Building responsible AI isn't just about avoiding bias; it's about operating within a broader framework of ethical principles and legal regulations. This section moves from the *what* (the principles) to the *how* (the practical steps you can take as a Product Manager). Think of it as your roadmap for navigating the ethical and legal landscape of AI.

Understanding the Ethical Landscape: Core Principles

AI ethics is a rapidly evolving field, but some core principles are consistently emphasized:

- **Fairness:** (Covered in detail in previous sections)—Ensuring equitable outcomes and avoiding discrimination.

- **Transparency:** Being open and honest about how your AI system works, what data it uses, and how it makes decisions. This builds trust with users.

- **Accountability:** Establishing clear lines of responsibility for the AI system's actions and decisions. Who is accountable if the system makes a mistake or causes harm?

- **Privacy:** Protecting user data and respecting individual privacy rights. This is both an ethical and a legal imperative.

- **Beneficence:** Striving to use AI for good—to benefit users, society, and the world.

- **Non-Maleficence:** Avoiding harm—actively working to prevent your AI system from causing unintended negative consequences.

Understanding the Legal Landscape: Key Regulations

The legal landscape surrounding AI is also evolving rapidly. While there isn't yet a single, comprehensive "AI law" in most jurisdictions, existing laws and emerging regulations are increasingly relevant:

- **Data Privacy Laws:**

  - **GDPR (General Data Protection Regulation):** A comprehensive data privacy law in the European Union that has global impact. It sets strict requirements for collecting, processing, and storing personal data, including data used for AI.

  - **CCPA/CPRA (California Consumer Privacy Act/California Privacy Rights Act):** California's data privacy laws, which give consumers more control over their personal data.

  - **Other Privacy Laws:** Many other countries and regions have their own data privacy laws, which may apply to your AI system.

- **Anti-Discrimination Laws:** Existing anti-discrimination laws (e.g., in employment, housing, lending) often apply to AI systems, even if the law doesn't explicitly mention AI.

- **Product Liability:** If your AI-powered product causes harm, your company could be held liable.

- **Sector-Specific Regulations:** Certain industries (e.g., healthcare, finance) have specific regulations that govern the use of AI. For example, HIPAA in the US regulates the use of patient health information.

- **Emerging AI-Specific Legislation:** Governments around the world are actively developing new laws and regulations specifically designed to address AI. The EU AI Act is a prominent example.

Actionable Steps for Product Managers: Building Ethically and Legally Compliant AI

Here's a practical checklist of actions you can take as a Product Manager to ensure your AI projects are both ethical and legally compliant:

1. **Conduct a Pre-Development Ethics and Legal Checklist**
   Before starting any AI project, create a checklist and *document* the answers. This is your first line of defense.

   - **Key Questions:**
   - **Data Sensitivity:** "Will this AI system collect, process, or store sensitive personal data (e.g., health information, financial information, race, religion, sexual orientation)?"
   - **Potential for Bias:** "Could this system perpetuate or amplify existing societal biases? Which protected classes are most at risk?"
   - **High-Stakes Decisions:** "Will this AI system automate decisions that significantly impact people's lives (e.g., loan applications, hiring decisions, medical diagnoses)?" If so, extra caution is required.
   - **Transparency:** "How can we explain the AI's decisions to users in a clear and understandable way?"
   - **User Control:** "How can we give users control over their data and how it's used by the AI?"
   - **Potential for Misuse:** "How could this technology be misused, and how can we prevent that?"
   - **Legal Review:** "Have we consulted with legal counsel to ensure compliance with all relevant regulations?"

   If any of these questions raise concerns, conduct a more in-depth *ethical impact assessment*.

2. **Implement a Data Governance Framework**

   - **Establish Clear Policies:** Create clear, written policies for data collection, usage, storage, and retention. These policies should address privacy, security, and ethical considerations.

   - **Purpose Limitation:** Only collect and use data for the specific, legitimate purpose for which it was collected. Be transparent with users about this purpose.

   - **Data Minimization:** Collect only the minimum amount of data necessary to achieve your goals.

   - **Anonymization/Pseudonymization:** Where possible, anonymize or pseudonymize data to protect user privacy.

   - **Data Security:** Implement robust security measures to protect data from unauthorized access, use, or disclosure.

   - **Data Retention Policy:** Establish a clear policy for how long data will be retained and when it will be deleted.

   - **Data Protection Officer (DPO):** Consider appointing a DPO (required under GDPR for some organizations) to oversee data governance.

3. **Build Explainability into AI Systems (Whenever Possible)**

   - **Prioritize Interpretable Models:** When possible, choose AI models that are inherently more interpretable (e.g., decision trees, linear regression) over "black box" models (like deep neural networks).

   - **Use Explainability Techniques:** If you *must* use a complex model, explore techniques like:

     - **Feature Importance Analysis:** Identifying which input features are most influential in the model's predictions.

     - **LIME (Local Interpretable Model-Agnostic Explanations):** Explaining individual predictions by approximating the complex model with a simpler, interpretable model locally.

     - **SHAP (SHapley Additive ExPlanations):** A game-theoretic approach to explaining the output of any machine learning model.

   - **Provide User-Friendly Explanations:** Don't just provide technical explanations; provide clear, concise, and user-friendly explanations of *why* the AI made a particular decision or recommendation.

4. **Establish a Feedback and Redress Mechanism**

   ▪ **Make it Easy for Users to Report Concerns:** Provide a clear and accessible channel for users to report concerns about AI bias, fairness, or errors.

   ▪ **Investigate Complaints Thoroughly:** Establish a process for promptly and thoroughly investigating user complaints.

   ▪ **Provide Redress:** If an AI system makes an incorrect or unfair decision, provide a mechanism for users to appeal the decision and seek redress. This might involve human review.

   ▪ **Document and Report:** Keep track and document the concerns raised and share information with stakeholders.

5. **Stay Abreast of Evolving Regulations**

   ▪ **Assign Responsibility:** Designate someone on your product team (or work with your legal team) to monitor AI-related regulations and guidelines. This is a rapidly changing area.

   ▪ **Subscribe to Updates:** Subscribe to newsletters and alerts from relevant regulatory bodies and industry organizations.

   ▪ **Consult with Legal Counsel:** Regularly consult with legal counsel specializing in AI and data privacy to ensure compliance.

6. **Implement a Human-in-the-Loop System (for High-Stakes Applications)**

   ▪ **Human Oversight:** For AI systems that make decisions with significant consequences (e.g., loan applications, medical diagnoses, hiring decisions), incorporate human review into the process.

   ▪ **Clear Guidelines:** Provide clear guidelines for human reviewers on how to identify and address potential bias or errors.

   ▪ **Escalation Paths:** Establish clear escalation paths for handling complex or ambiguous cases.

   ▪ **Auditability:** Human intervention should be documented and auditable.

7. **Document AI Development and Deployment**

   ▪ **Comprehensive Documentation:** Maintain detailed records of the entire AI development and deployment process. This is critical for accountability, debugging, and auditing.

- **Key information to document:**
  - Data sources and preprocessing steps.
  - Model training procedures and parameters.
  - Model evaluation results (including fairness metrics).
  - Versioning information for models and data.
  - Deployment details.
  - Monitoring data.
  - Any incidents or issues encountered.

8. **Create an AI Ethics Board or Review Process (for Larger Organizations)**

   - **Formal Review:** Consider establishing a formal process for reviewing AI projects for ethical concerns, similar to an Institutional Review Board (IRB) in research.

   - **Diverse Membership:** Include individuals with diverse backgrounds and expertise (e.g., product, engineering, legal, ethics, user representatives).

   - **Regular Reviews:** Conduct regular reviews of both new AI projects and existing AI systems.

9. **Provide Ongoing Training and Education**

   - **What To Do:** Implement regular training programs for your product, engineering, and data science teams on AI ethics, bias mitigation, and relevant legal regulations.

   - **PM's Role:** Advocate for and support these training initiatives. Ensure that training is incorporated into onboarding processes and ongoing professional development.

   - **Resources:** Encourage teams to stay up-to-date, reading blogs and articles, and following experts and organizations in the field.

10. **Conduct Impact Assessments**

    - **What To Do:** Before launching a significant AI-powered feature, conduct a formal impact assessment. This should consider:
      - Potential benefits to users and the business.
      - Potential risks and harms (bias, privacy violations, etc.).

- ▪ Impact on different user groups.

- ▪ Long-term societal consequences.

▪ **PM's Role:** Lead or participate in the impact assessment process. Ensure that the assessment's findings are incorporated into product decisions.

Engaging with the Community and External Stakeholders

Building responsible AI is not just an internal exercise limited to your development team. To truly understand the impact of your product and build lasting trust, you must look outward and engage directly with the users and communities your AI will affect. This outward-facing engagement is essential for identifying blind spots, fostering transparency, and ensuring your product aligns with broader societal values. The following strategies outline how you can foster this very important dialogue:

▪ **Transparency and Communication**

Be transparent with your users about how your AI system works, what data it uses, and how it makes decisions. This builds trust and allows for informed consent.

Example: Publish a clear and accessible "AI Principles" document outlining your commitment to responsible AI.

Example: Provide in-app explanations of how AI-powered features work.

▪ **User feedback Mechanisms**

Create easy-to-use feedback mechanisms for users to report concerns about bias, fairness, or other ethical issues.

Example: Include a "Report a Problem" button on AI-generated recommendations or decisions.

▪ **Community Forums**

Consider creating a community forum or other platform for users to discuss their experiences with your AI-powered features and provide feedback.

▪ **Expert Consultation**

Consult with external experts in AI ethics, law, and relevant domains (e.g., healthcare, finance) to get feedback on your AI system and your responsible AI practices.

- **Industry Collaboration**

  Participate in industry initiatives and collaborations focused on responsible AI. Share best practices and learn from others.

- **Public Documentation**

  Be transparent, consider having public documentation with how your model has been built.

By implementing these actionable steps, Product Managers can play a vital role in ensuring that AI is developed and deployed responsibly, ethically, and in compliance with legal requirements. This is not just about avoiding negative consequences; it's about building trust with users, creating a positive societal impact, and unlocking the full potential of AI for good. It also helps mitigate risks, ensuring the long-term success of your product.

Chapter Summary and Key Takeaways

This chapter established that building AI with integrity is not an optional extra—it is a core responsibility of every Product Manager. You've moved beyond a surface-level understanding of ethics to a deep dive into the specific sources of AI bias, the legal and moral importance of protecting vulnerable classes, and the overarching landscape of ethical principles and legal compliance. We didn't just discuss problems; this chapter provided a practical toolkit of actionable steps, from pre-development checklists to post-deployment engagement, to help you lead with responsibility.

Key Takeaways

- **Responsible AI is Proactive, Not Reactive:** You must integrate ethical considerations, fairness, and privacy into the product development lifecycle from the very beginning, not as an afterthought.

- **Bias is a Systemic Risk:** You now understand that bias can enter a system from many sources—including data, algorithms, and human choices—and your job is to be vigilant at every stage.

- **You are the Ethical Champion:** As the Product Manager, you are the primary advocate for the user and for responsible innovation, tasked with asking the hard questions and ensuring the team builds with integrity.

- **Transparency Builds Trust:** The foundation of a successful, long-term AI product is user trust, which is built through clear communication, explainability, and providing mechanisms for user feedback and redress.

Onward: Paving Your Path

You now have the complete picture: the foundational concepts, the different PM roles, and the frameworks for identifying, building, deploying, and ethically guiding AI products. With this comprehensive knowledge, you are ready for the final step. The concluding chapter will help you synthesize everything you've learned to pave your own path to success in AI Product Management.

Conclusion: Paving Your Own Path to AI PM

You've explored the core AI/ML concepts, deep-dived into different AI PM specializations, and examined how to integrate ethical, user-centric, and business-focused practices into your product development. Now comes the part that matters most: charting your own personal course to becoming (and thriving as) an AI Product Manager. Think of this as your personal roadmap, bridging all the knowledge and awareness you've gained in this workbook with the tangible actions needed to carve out your unique path in the AI PM realm.

Figure 12-1 illustrates the practical steps and guiding principles that can help you turn what you've learned into forward momentum. Whether you're currently a PM eager to pivot toward AI, or a newcomer drawn to the fusion of AI and product management, these strategies will equip you to confidently step into the next phase of your career.

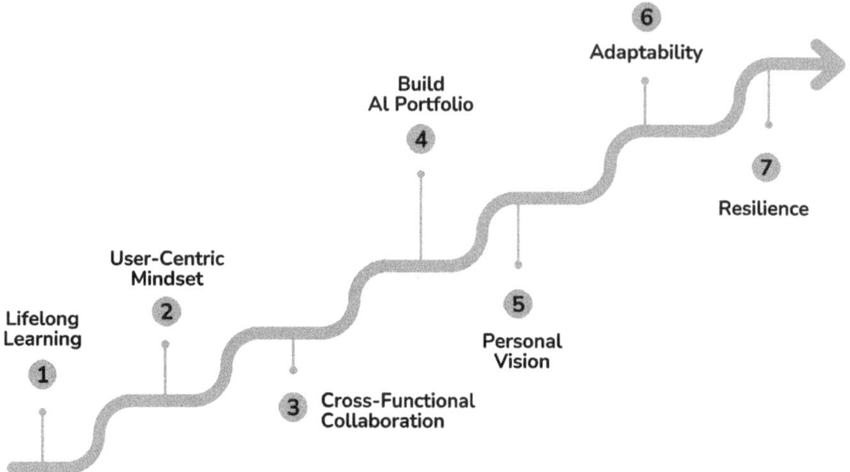

Figure 12-1: 7 practical steps towards your AI PM career

Embrace Lifelong Learning: Stay Curious and Iterative

AI—and particularly AI product management—is not a static field. The technologies, best practices, and regulatory landscapes are constantly evolving. The PM who thrives in AI is the one who's always learning and never assumes they're "finished."

- **Continuously track AI trends:** Subscribe to leading AI research repositories and communities; skim through the latest at least once a week. Even if you don't have time for a deep read, knowing the titles and summaries of new breakthroughs will keep you connected to the larger pulse of innovation.

- **Tinker and experiment:** Dedicate small blocks of time—maybe an hour every other week—to explore new frameworks, tools, or open-source models. Try applying them to a side project. Getting hands-on with simple prototypes, even if they're experimental, will deepen your intuition around AI's possibilities and limitations.

- **Seek structured education:** Whether it's an online course, a certificate program, or targeted workshops, formal learning can offer a quick boost in specialized topics (like NLP, prompt engineering, or advanced data ethics).

Think of yourself as your own R&D department. By staying curious, you'll maintain a sense of forward momentum and position yourself to seize unexpected opportunities.

Cultivate a User-Centric AI Mindset

No matter the sophistication of the underlying model, an AI feature is ultimately judged by the user experience it delivers. Keeping your user's needs, goals, and context at the center is what separates an effective AI solution from a flashy gadget.

- **Conduct ongoing user research:** Make sure your user research methods (interviews, surveys, prototype testing) don't stop when you launch an AI-powered feature. AI systems learn and adapt over time, which can change the user's experience in unexpected ways. Schedule periodic "checkpoints" to see how user behavior and feedback evolve.

- **Balance simplicity with transparency:** Particularly with AI, the "behind-the-scenes" can be complex. Design front-end experiences that feel simple, while still giving power users or curious minds enough transparency to understand what the AI is doing. For instance, using brief tooltips or "How this feature works" modals can help build trust.

- **Solicit and act on feedback loops:** Build in ways for users to correct or override AI. This is especially critical for generative tools, predictive features, or recommendation engines. When users can easily say, "Hey, that's not accurate," they feel more in control, and your model gets direct signals to improve.

A relentless user focus helps you craft experiences that resonate, ensuring your AI features don't just "work" but also delight, empower, and earn user trust.

Deepen Cross-Functional Collaboration Skills

As you move into (or deepen in) AI PM work, your cross-functional partnerships become even more critical. While standard PM roles already require you to collaborate, AI adds extra layers of complexity—both technically and ethically.

- **Speak the language of data scientists:** You don't need to be a data scientist yourself, but you do need to understand concepts like data labeling, overfitting, validation sets, and interpretability. Ask your data science peers to walk you through model outputs. Instead of memorizing definitions, try to "see" how data flows from ingestion to final predictions.

- **Partner with UX on explainability:** Work with designers to transform complicated AI outputs into intuitive experiences. Brainstorm how to convey model confidence or uncertainty. Consider using guardrails, disclaimers, or layered UI to accommodate a diverse range of user comfort with AI-driven decisions.

- **Align with legal and compliance early:** AI is increasingly under scrutiny. Proactively involve legal and compliance teams whenever you design features around user data, personalization, or generative content. Early alignment preserves your team's agility and helps you navigate regulatory changes with minimal disruption.

Great AI product leaders are the hub of communication—translating user insights and business goals into data needs, bridging technical constraints with design aspirations, and orchestrating it all under the umbrella of ethical AI practices.

Build a Distinct AI Portfolio (Show, Don't Just Tell)

Whether you're transitioning from a non-AI PM role or you're just starting out, building a tangible portfolio is critical. Concrete artifacts demonstrate your skills better than a resume line could.

- **Launch a side project or hackathon idea:** Nothing beats learning by doing. Pick a realistic scope—maybe a small chatbot for a volunteer organization, or a data-driven recommendation engine for an online community you're part of. Document your product decisions, challenges, and outcomes. Even if it's not an official work project, the experience is invaluable.

- **Create case studies:** Don't just share the final outcomes. Show your approach—how you defined the problem, set metrics, collaborated with data scientists, addressed ethical risks, iterated based on user feedback, and measured success. Highlight the user stories, the "why" behind every decision, and the lessons you gleaned.

- **Contribute to open-source or local data projects:** Check if there are open-source AI communities or local data science groups you can volunteer with. By contributing features, documentation, or user-focused improvements, you prove your capacity to drive AI initiatives across diverse teams.

In the world of AI, outcomes speak volumes. Showing that you can effectively ideate, build, deploy, and iterate on AI products—even at small scale—instills confidence in future employers, teams, and stakeholders.

Develop a Personal Vision for Your AI Career

Working in AI means you'll be a part of shaping tomorrow's world. Defining your personal "north star" can keep you motivated and guide your choices in projects, roles, or even companies.

- **Identify your unique strengths:** Maybe you have a knack for simplifying complex concepts for any audience, or you excel at running rigorous A/B tests for iterative improvement. Embrace those strengths; they'll set you apart in a competitive field.

- **Map out milestones:** Consider short- and long-term goals. Maybe your next step is to become the in-house AI champion for your current product team, or perhaps it's moving into a more specialized AI PM role at a larger tech company with robust ML infrastructure.

- **Reflect on ethical impact:** AI can do immense good, but it can also amplify biases or intrude on privacy if misused. Ask yourself how you want to contribute. Perhaps you prioritize roles that emphasize transparent data practices, responsible AI guidelines, or bridging AI with social good initiatives.

A clear personal vision will keep you centered when facing the complexities and ethical dilemmas that often come with pushing boundaries in AI.

Keep Resilience and Adaptability at the Core

AI projects can be unpredictable. A model that worked brilliantly during testing might underperform in production because of user behavior you didn't anticipate. New regulations might disrupt your data strategy. Big leaps in generative AI can shift user expectations overnight. The best AI PMs see these twists as opportunities to learn and adapt.

- **Embrace fast iterations:** Don't fall into the trap of big-bang AI releases that are difficult to pivot if user reception or performance isn't as expected. Break down your AI initiatives into smaller bets: test, learn, and iterate quickly.

- **Build contingencies:** Develop fallback plans for when the AI doesn't meet performance thresholds or hits unexpected hurdles. This might mean having a simpler rule-based system that takes over if the ML model's confidence is too low.

- **Celebrate incremental wins:** AI progress can come in bursts. Celebrate each step forward—a small improvement in user satisfaction or a modest increase in model accuracy. These milestones keep the team motivated and sharpen your sense of what truly matters to users.

Resilience makes you a steady influence on your team; adaptability makes you a visionary who seizes fresh angles when they appear.

Final Thoughts

You are now standing at the intersection of product leadership and cutting-edge AI. This blend of skills—technical awareness of AI's capabilities, the empathy to weave user-focused experiences, the strategic mindset to align business goals, and the ethical backbone to do it responsibly—positions you to craft solutions that are both innovative and genuinely meaningful.

Remember, there's no single "right" path or specialization for you. Your journey may involve small steps on one specialization or a big leap on another, lateral moves or advanced specializations, personal projects or formal certifications. What remains constant is the imperative to keep learning, stay user-centric, collaborate deeply, and remain resilient in the face of constant change.

What we want to leave you with is to enable you to apply the insights you've gained throughout this playbook—integrating AI/ML knowledge with solid PM craft—you are already on your way to making an impact as an AI Product Manager. Now, reimagine what's possible in your industry, and join the AI PM world.

Index